D0887724

Reconstructing 'Drop-out'

A Critical Ethnography of the Dynamics of Black Students' Disengagement from School

As many as one million untrained youths will enter the Canadian labour market by the year 2000. And yet, 60 per cent of jobs being created in Canada require at least a high-school education. The drop-out rate is one of the most crucial issues that Canadian educators face.

Traditionally, we have attributed dropping out to individual failure or associated it with specific situations such as pregnancy, substance abuse, and family troubles. The authors of this book suggest that the problem is more complex. Race, class, gender, and other forms of social difference can affect how education is delivered. For Black students, whose drop-out rate is disproportionately high, race is a key element in disengagement. The authors turn to the experiences of Black and non-Black students, teachers, parents, and community workers to try to reconstruct the social, structural, and institutional practices that lead Black youth to lose interest in and to leave school.

Based on a three-year study in the greater Toronto area, *Reconstructing 'Drop-out'* establishes a new frame of reference for understanding the drop-out dilemma. It is a call for social action and transformation that should not be ignored by researchers, teachers, administrators, and the Black community at large.

GEORGE J. SEFA DEI is Associate Professor in the Department of Sociology in Education, Ontario Institute for Studies in Education/ University of Toronto.
JOSEPHINE MAZZUCA and JASMIN ZINE are both doctoral candidates in the Department of Sociology in Education at OISE/UT.
ELIZABETH MCISAAC currently teaches at Centennial College in Toronto.

Reconstructing 'Drop-out'

A Critical Ethnography
of the Dynamics of
Black Students'
Disengagement from School

George J. Sefu Dei,
Josephine Mazzuca,
Elizabeth McIsaac,
Jasmin Zine

UNIVERSITY OF TORONTO PRESS
Toronto Buffalo London

© University of Toronto Press Incorporated 1997
Toronto Buffalo London
Printed in Canada

Reprinted 2007

ISBN 0-8020-4199-X (cloth)
ISBN 0-8020-8060-X (paper)

Printed on acid-free paper

Canadian Cataloguing in Publication Data

Main entry under title:

Reconstructing 'drop-out': a critical ethnography of the
dynamics of Black students' disengagement from
school

Includes bibliographical references and index.
ISBN 0-8020-4199-X (bound)   ISBN 0-8020-8060-X (pbk.)

1. Dropouts – Ontario. 2. Students, Black – Ontario.
3. Blacks – Education – Ontario. I. Dei, George Jerry Sefa,
1954–   .

LC145.C3R42 1997   371.2'913'089960713   C97-930939-5

University of Toronto Press acknowledges the financial assistance to its
publishing program of the Canada Council and the Ontario Arts Council.

This book has been published with the help of a grant from the Humanities
and Social Sciences Federation of Canada, using funds provided by the Social
Sciences and Humanities Research Council of Canada.

Contents

vi Contents

Foreword

It is common knowledge, supported by a large body of research, that in Canada and the United States, Black students constitute a disproportionate number of those who leave school prematurely. This book is an important study of the problem in the Ontario public school system in Canada.

The work examines how institutionalized structures and processes of schooling lead to premature school-leaving of Blacks, from the perspectives of Black school drop-outs, Black students, Black parents, non-Black students, and school personnel. For Dr Dei and his team of researchers, a major problem in conventional study of school drop-outs is methodology. The field has traditionally been dominated by quantitative research. Although informative in regard to the magnitude of the problem and its correlation with school, family, and personal variables, the quantitative approach tells us very little about the mechanism of dropping out or the subjective experiences of the drop-outs. There are, of course, observational studies of what goes on inside the school and the classroom, in the family, or in peer culture leading to students' dropping out. But these studies also leave many questions unanswered, especially in the context of race. For example, they do not tell us how Black school drop-outs themselves feel, what makes them decide to leave school, or what is their understanding of the school system in a racially stratified society.

To overcome these difficulties, the authors of this book chose the critical ethnographic method. This enabled them to address issues ignored in previous studies. It is evident throughout that this method gave their subjects a stronger voice in expressing their collective struggle and in making meaningful the interaction of many complex issues. One is impressed with the authors' analysis and presentation of their findings. They successfully bring their subjects into real partnership in the interpretation of their findings. They achieved this by letting their subjects tell their own story and by using the narratives to guide their analysis. The work is a major contribution to methodology.

Among the main findings of the study is that dropping out is a developmental process influenced by a series of school and off-school experiences. Students drop out finally when they see no other viable course of action. The emphasis of the study is definitely on school factors that lead to students' disengagement with the school culture: low teacher expectations, differential treatment of Black students, conflict with school authorities because they do not respect Black students, and academic labelling and streaming that significantly narrow students' options and chances for the future. A major issue in the alienation of Black students which eventually results in dropping out of school is that of racial identity. This issue occupies a large part of students' complaints about the content of the curriculum, which they say has no relevance to their lives. The authors tell us that students who see a lack of curriculum content devoted to their history and experience are likely to drop out. One related interesting finding is that, contrary to conventional wisdom, Black students do not drop out of school because of lack of self-esteem; rather, they are forced out because they have a strong sense of cultural pride and self-esteem, which schools ignore or seek to contain. This and other findings suggest that Black students face an educational dilemma. On the one hand, Black students and their parents recognize the importance of finishing school for employment and social mobility; on the other hand, their interpretation of the curriculum content and treatment in terms of racial identity causes them to disengage from the system.

While the authors do not fully explore the Black students' dilemma noted above, the work does make an important theoretical contribution to the study of the Black school drop-out problem.

There are many explanations of why and how Black students drop out of school. But as the authors convincingly argue, even such widely accepted explanations as the 'resistance school' err in defining the Black school drop-out problem in terms of social class. It has been more or less the practice since 1977, when Paul Willis published his important study of White working-class students in England, *Learning to Labour: How Working-Class Kids Get Working-Class Jobs*, for resistance theorists to generalize the opposition behaviour emanating from the White lower-class students' culture to school authority to that of racial minorities. They fail to understand that being White and lower-class is clearly different from being Black and lower-class. For example, Willis's 'lads' can drop out of school and confidently expect to get a job they consider fit for a man; by choice, they wanted a 'working-class job,' not a 'middle-class job.' Such is not the case with Black school drop-outs. The latter know full well that there are no 'working-class jobs' out there waiting for them. Resistance theorists also fail to understand something else: the fact that Blacks are over-represented among the lower class should not be interpreted that lower-class Blacks and lower-class Whites share the same culture or experience schooling the same way. The authors of this book show this in the different responses of Black and non-Black students to questions about school experiences and opportunity structures. Furthermore, the primacy of race is evident in various chapters where the authors discuss race relations in Canada and the treatment of 'visible minorities,' especially Blacks in the labour market today, and in narratives of Black parents and students about their personal and collective experiences. The work is a welcome and important contribution to the theory of the Black school drop-out problem in terms of race.

Dr Dei and his team conducted the study believing that effective change can come about through knowledge and understanding based on research into how the structural processes of delivering education affect Black students. Their findings should be of interest to educators, anthropologists, sociologists, and policy-makers, as well as community activists. The authors' findings, especially with respect to race and identity, lead them to emphasize changes that would reinforce students' racial identity and self-respect. It is worth noting that, while this reflects the perspectives of Black students, and of their families and communities, only a minority of the teachers would see the needed change that way. Teachers and other school authorities still have to be convinced. Black parents and the Black community are expected to become stronger advocates for their children's education, but they also have to become more involved. Finally, Black students themselves have an important responsibility in effecting changes that will enhance their engagement in school learning, but recognition of such responsibility is not obvious in either their narratives or the analysis of their narratives.

John U. Ogbu
Department of Anthropology
University of California, Berkeley

Preface

As co-authors of this book, we would like to begin with a brief note about our personal locations and how we individually and collectively came to see the complex issue of Black youth education and the dilemma of students' disengagement from school. We believe it is important that every social researcher, and particularly the educational researcher, identifies her or his personal and subjective location; for example, how race, ethnicity, gender, social class, culture, and history provide a specific vantage point for the understanding and interpretation of research data. Such personal location provides readers with a context within which to critically examine and make sense of the study. Knowledge, after all, can only be understood in relation to one's subject location and interest.

George Dei

I am an African-Canadian educator who has had the privilege of being educated in Africa and Canada and am now employed as a tenured professor in an internationally renowned Canadian university. I share, with many other racial minorities, common historical experiences of colonialism and the subjugation, particularly in conventional Euro-American texts, of the rich cultural knowledge, scholarship, and social achievements of all colonized peoples. I know very well how the colonial education that I received in my birthplace, Ghana, and my postgraduate studies in Canada deprivileged the ancestral histories and cultural heritage of African peoples. I am also aware how the issues of race identity, representation, and social difference continue to play significant roles in the processes of delivering education in Euro-American contexts. In engaging this study, I do not claim an 'authority of experience.' My claim to some knowledge and understanding of the dynamics of Black students' disengagement is based neither on birth nor on common cultural or historical experiences with the students. I do believe, however, that my personal and historical journeys have come to reflect and influence how I read and interpret the stories of the students.

Josephine Mazzuca
Currently I am a doctoral student at the Ontario Institute for Studies in Education of the University of Toronto, in the Department of Sociology and Equity Studies in Education. My concern with ethnicity and culture in the Canadian context stems, in part, from my personal background as a child of immigrant parents. My research interests include minorities' educational experiences, a topic which relates directly to this project on Black students. In my role as researcher, I do not claim a connection with the participants of this study based on a shared culture or background. I attempted to remain consciously aware of my personal and social location as I made sense of the narratives. The participants' words were the path to our understanding their experiences. I feel strongly that qualitative research is a sound and effective manner in which to take up issues of culture, race, and education as it allows us to capture the 'stories' of various stakeholders.

Elizabeth McIsaac
I am currently teaching at an Ontario community college. My work with this project examining the experiences of Black high-school drop-outs began while I completed my own thesis work in indigenous knowledge at the Ontario Institute for Studies in Education. I began with transcribing the interviews of students, drop-outs, parents, and teachers. While I was not actually able to participate in the interviews, listening to the voices of the informants and the emotion with which they spoke helped me to begin to hear their experiences from their vantage points. This preliminary work with

the 'data' was very instructive for me when we came to analyse and synthesize these voices. As a White woman, I feel that I have been privileged to participate in the project and engage in the process of hearing the students' voices and learning from the students themselves. In this way, I am grateful to George for the opportunity to join in this work, and I am equally grateful to the students who have provided important and insightful lessons for me.

Jasmin Zine
I am a doctoral candidate at the Ontario Institute for Studies in Education of the University of Toronto. Originally from Pakistan, I have lived nearly all of my life in Canada. Growing up as a minority student in the Canadian school system, I understand all too well how the pressures of race and social difference can force students out of school. I am a former high-school drop-out who was unable to cope with these pressures and the alienation experienced as a minority student in a Eurocentric school system. It is with this knowledge and understanding that I approach the issues in this book.

As sociologists, our personal and cultural histories as well as our politics guide our understanding of the issues we choose to study. Knowing firsthand the unfounded perceptions of failure imposed on drop-outs, we hope that this study will serve as a vehicle for understanding their lived realities and for apprehending the true nature of their disengagement from school.

Acknowledgments

We would like to acknowledge the assistance of the many graduate students at the Ontario Institute for Studies in Education of the Univeristy of Toronto (OISE/UT) who worked on various aspects of this longitudinal study. We would like especially to thank Leilani Holmes for her contribution to the analysis and to earlier drafts. Also, we would like to thank Lianne Carley and Rachel Campbell for their contributions. We would like to mention in particular Deborah Elva, Gabrielle Hezekiah, Thato Bereng, Bobby Blanford, Farah Shroff, Les Tager, Anita Sheth, Nigel Moses, Jennifer Pierce, Handel Wright, Rinaldo Walcott, Sandra Anthony, Camille Logan, and Marcia James. We also recognize the invaluable services provided by Bethlehem Kidane and Shae Sanderson. We sincerely thank Irwin Elman of the Pape Adolescent Resource Centre for arranging for Bethlehem, Rachel, and Shae to assist on the project. Special thanks to Olga Williams of the Department of Sociology, OISE/UT, and Adrienne Churchill for transcribing some of the taped interviews. Many Canadian educators and researchers have been helpful throughout various phases of this project. There are so many names, but we should be permitted to mention a few here: Sonja Forstner, Paulette Plummer, Harold Wright, Lynn Tidd, Oscar Brathwaite, Charis Newton, Bill Dolly, Bernard Moitt, Suzanne Ziegler, Robert Brown, Maisy Cheng, Christopher Beserve, Patricia Hayes, Madge Logan, Christopher Spence, Muriel Clarke, Keren Brathwaite, and Agnes Calliste. We are also very grateful for the support we have received from Angela Hidyard, Associate Dean of the Ontario Institute for Studies in Education of the University of Toronto. We are especially grateful to the Ontario Ministry of Education and Training, and the Social Sciences and Humanities Research Council of Canada (SSHRC) for the funds provided for various aspects of this study. We would finally like to thank John Ogbu for taking the time to write the Foreword.

Reconstructing 'Drop-out'

Chapter One

Introduction

In the 1990s North American society is facing the challenge of providing education for an increasingly diverse population. This challenge is neither new nor insurmountable. However, the challenge is compounded by the fact that we live in an epoch which is radically different in its celebration of subjectivity, cultural diversity, and social difference. In our classrooms today are students who increasingly reflect the diverse mix of racial, ethnic, religious, class, gender, and sexual differences and interests in society. This is a healthy sign. Such diversity must be viewed as a source of strength rather than as social and cultural baggage with which schools must contend. Consequently, educators are being called upon to provide far more appropriate and effective ways for educating a citizenry. The call is for an education that respects individual differences, as well as collective and historical experiences, and that equips all youth to deal with the proliferating social, political, economic, cultural, and spiritual interests, and consequent tensions, in the global community.

The issues of race, ethnicity, class, gender, and sexuality present significant challenges and lessons for Euro-Canadian/American schools. There is an increasing and healthy realization that the structures of schooling and education impact differentially on diverse student bodies. Many educators and educational researchers are boldly articulating the necessity and importance of understanding how youth from diverse racial, ethnic, class, and gender backgrounds are responding to the institutionalized processes and structures of schooling in Euro-American contexts. For example, understanding the resistance cultures of some youths of racial minority and working-class backgrounds to the assimilation tendencies of mainstream schools can go a long way in the creation of genuinely inclusive schooling environments for all youth.

In order for schools to carry out any exemplary educational practices to establish a genuine inclusion of all students, it is crucial that there is an initial comprehension of the nature and contexts of the specific problems and experiences that lead some students to leave school prematurely. We believe that schools can respond effectively to the diversity within and among all social groups if there is a clear and *a priori* understanding of how the structural processes of delivering education impact differently on various groups. We need to know how it is that schools engage some students while at the same time disengage others. A good deal of previous educational research has explored how students' home cultures, cultural values and beliefs, as well as personal attitudes sometimes conflict with the norms and values of the conventional school system. Such research has contributed to the development of liberal-democratic theories of education that privilege effective family-school relations by conceptualizing families and homes as important sites and sources of student educational problems and pathologies. In related specific works, it has been argued that cultural disjunctures and disarticulations are factors relevant to understanding why some minority youth are disengaged from school (see Ogbu 1982a; Gibson 1987).

For racial minority youth living on the margins of a White-dominated society, the concern over home cultural values and schooling outcomes, while important, does not present the complete picture of the challenges and difficulties of going to school. Relatively recent research is focusing on a critical examination of the structures for delivering education in order to unravel how schools themselves contribute fundamentally to the problem of students' disengagement and fading out from school. Different and more critical questions are being asked to provide a broader understanding of how learning happens or does not happen for some youth. Of particular interest is the examination of how the institutional processes of schooling (e.g., curriculum administration and delivery as well as classroom pedagogical practices) create unequal outcomes, particularly for racial minority students, as well as those from working-class backgrounds. An important aspect of critical educational research is the demonstration of how the structural processes of schooling are mediated by students' individual and collective forms of resistance and oppositional cultures (see Willis 1977, 1983; Giroux 1983a, 1983b; McCarthy 1990; Apple 1986).

In this book, we discuss the findings of a study that sought to ask different questions about how schooling and education happen for African-Canadian youth, particularly, in the Ontario public school system. We present our work realizing full well, as already alluded to in our preface, that our varied personal locations and social positions have a significant bearing on how we have come to see and understand the complex issue of Black youth education and the dilemma of students' disengagement from school. For every social researcher, and particularly the educational researcher, the issues of race, ethnicity, gender, social class, culture, and history provide a specific vantage point for the understanding and interpretation of research data. Knowledge, after all, can only be understood in relation to one's subject location, politics, desires, and interests. Our personal and collective journeys reflect and influence how we read and interpret the world around us.

In the course of this study, we witnessed the laughter, joy, and emotional satisfaction, as well as the pain, suffering, anger, and anguish, of many Canadian students, parents, guardians, community workers, teachers, and school administrators in the struggle to secure education for themselves or to provide it to others. Having listened to many young people, we could hardly miss the deep sense of frustration and alienation which some of them feel in society and school. This is not to say that all youth are having overwhelming difficulties at school. We simply believe that 'a few' is, in fact, too many and that the process of receiving education must be able to equip every student with the tools to think critically and creatively and to solve daily problems. If the education received is seen as irrelevant to students' daily lived experiences, then such education cannot be considered part of a social and political project to transform society.

We cannot look at the 'crisis' plaguing Black/African-Canadian youth today, with respect to education and achievement, and un-problematically accept the status quo. Therefore, it is important that this book is read as a call to link research knowledge, social commitment, and political action for educational transformation and social change. While there are many people in the Euro-Canadian/American educational system who are doing their utmost, in various capacities, for the cause of youth education, the learning objective of our study is to provide a space for reciprocal dialogue and for critical self- and group reflection about the school system and what we can do collectively to address the dilemma of some students disengaging and fading out from school. We speak about 'fading out' in the sense of students who appear to be in school in body but who are absent in mind and soul. The problem of truancy, for example, should be seen in such a light.

Where criticism is offered about the nature and functioning of schools, it must be seen as directed for the most part at the educational system and societal practices and not at the purposeful intent of specific individuals. Our objective in this book is, therefore, neither to blame nor preach, but rather to achieve a holistic understanding of the 'drop-out' dilemma from the perspectives of those who participated in the study. It is with this more informed understanding that we must convey our discomfort with using the term 'drop-out,' insomuch as it embodies socially constructed notions of individual failure. Our study clearly demonstrated that we can no longer base our understanding of drop-outs on such ill-conceived notions and that we must be prepared to reconceptualize the process of student disengagement based on lived realities rather than social stigma.

Discussions in this book are based on the findings of a three-year study, using the narratives of Black students and school drop-outs in which they discuss their experiences in the Ontario public school system and, in some cases, their reasons for leaving school. The main research objective was the investigation of what students' narratives of their lived experiences could tell us about the drop-

out problem, and particularly about the influence of race/ethnici-
ty, class, gender, power, and social structures on dropping out from
school. The study, therefore, sought to examine all of the possible
factors related to student disengagement, with the focus on what
can be done to solve these problems and make schools work for all
youth.

The study also included in-depth interviews with school teachers,
administrators, and a sample of non-Black students to cross-reference Black youth narratives about their school experiences and
the issue of dropping out. An additional research objective was to
conduct in-depth interviews with Black/African-Canadian parents,
guardians, caregivers, and community groups, again to cross-reference student narratives but also to gain the adults' views and
perspectives on public schooling in Ontario. The overall objective
of the research project was to develop an approach to understanding minority student concerns through the study of their individual lived experiences, these being the basis upon which to build
strategies of action. It was hoped that the study would be useful
to relevant branches of the Ministry of Education and Training
(e.g., Curriculum and Policy Development, Community and Education Outreach, Anti-Racism) and school boards in Ontario. It
was also felt that the study would provide schools and boards of
education with alternative ways of reaching students who have
fallen through the cracks and providing them with appropriate
incentives to remain in school.

In recent years, North Americans have increasingly voiced their
concerns about the public school system, and, in particular, about
the ability of schools to educate and prepare youth to assume the
responsibilities of national and global citizenship. It is generally
acknowledged that one of the most crucial issues facing Euro-
Canadian/American education is the problem of school drop-outs
(see Conference Board of Canada 1991; Cadieux 1991; Employment
and Immigration Canada 1990). Currently, in Canada, it is estimated that between 20 and 30 percent of students do not finish
school, and that at the present drop-out level, as many as one million undereducated and untrained youths will have entered the
Canadian labour market by the year 2000 (Association of Univer-

sities and Colleges 1991, 5; Statistics Canada 1991; Youth Affairs Branch of Employment and Immigration 1990; Stay in School Supplement 1991). This is at a time when more than 60 per cent of new jobs being created in Canada need at least a high-school education (Cadieux 1991, 1). Therefore, school drop-outs exact a huge social and economic cost on Canadians.

In fact, an article in the *Toronto Star* quotes a Conference Board of Canada study which estimates a $4-billion lifetime loss in earning power for the 137,000 students who failed to graduate with the class of 1979 (see Crawford 1993). The same news publication also mentions a January 1993 report of the Liberal party's Senate and House of Commons Committee on Youth which points out that school drop-outs are a great cost to Canadian taxpayers in terms of their weak earning power, the lower taxes these individuals pay, and the additional costs of unemployment insurance, welfare, health, and policing. The Province of Ontario has a $14-billion public school system, comprising $10 billion in provincial spending and another $4 billion collected in local property taxes for the running of schools. The nation, as a whole, has a $55-billion education system. Given such figures, many Canadians are understandably concerned that they are not getting their money's worth in their educational spending.

Many works dealing with the practices of public schooling offer only disconcerting generalizations concerning minority youth in the school system and have failed to deal with the specific social, cultural, and economic contexts which connect the difficulties faced by these students to broader social issues. As such, student and parent concerns about the nature and process of schooling in multi-ethnic communities are usually presented outside the very context in which these concerns arise. In order to better understand the disjunctures between social reality and school policy, it is therefore necessary to focus on the daily experiences and actual lived realities of those who find themselves on the margins of mainstream society and academic discourse. In this way, we can better understand the dynamics of social difference as they operate on an interpersonal as well as institutional level.

The specific context of the problem of student disengagement and fading out from school has been a subject of intense interest and discussion within both academic and public circles. While it definitely has not been only a recent concern, it appears that the 1980s and 1990s have seen a resurgence of local communities' dissatisfaction with the low academic placement and performance of their students. In the 1990s Black/African-Canadian parents, guardians, caregivers, community workers, students, and educators continue to ask fundamental questions about the ability of public schools to equip Black youth with the requisite tools and skills to take advantage of the opportunities available to youth. Therefore, local community fears, anxieties, and frustrations with the school system are predicated on the inefficacy of the current educational system to address the problems of Black youth (see Brathwaite and James 1996; D'Oyley 1994).

The Racialized Context of Canada

It may now be a cliché to speak of Canada as a diverse, multi-ethnic, and multiracial society. The facts behind the rhetoric of Canada's multicultural policies bear out that Canada is one of the most ethnically diverse countries in the world. In 1991 the population of 'visible minorities' in Canada was estimated by Statistics Canada to be 2,488,100 (including non-permanent residents). Within the 'visible minorities' group are the arbitrary classifications of Blacks, Indo-Pakistanis, Chinese, West Asians and Arabs, other Asians, Filipinos and other Pacific Islanders, and Latin Americans (see Michalowski 1991, cited in Kalbach et al. 1993). This 'group' is growing much faster than Canada's total population, which increased at a rate of 9 per cent from 1986 to 1991 in comparison to the 'visible minorities' group, which grew by 58 per cent during the same time period.

Perhaps nowhere is Canadian diversity so prominent as in the province of Ontario. Ontario, with a population of over 10 million people, contains 37 per cent of Canada's total population and slightly over 49 per cent of Canada's 'visible minorities' group. When consideration of ethnicity/nationality is included, nearly half of all people in Canada who reported origins other than British or French resided in Ontario (Statistics Canada 1993). In fact, 'over half of all persons in Canada reporting West Asian, South Asian, African, Caribbean and Black single ethnic origins lived in Ontario' (Statistics Canada 1993, 1). For example, in 1991, 66 per cent of the total of 345,445 people of African descent (African, Black, Caribbean) in Canada were living in Ontario. Similarly, 49 per cent of the total of 1,463,180 people of Asian descent (South Asia, West Asia, East and Southeast Asia) in Canada also resided in Ontario (see Statistics Canada 1993, 1). Kalbach et al. (1993, 33) projected Canada's total Black population could reach 1,381,500 by the year 2016.

All of the above statistics, while of demographic interest, must still be translated into the corresponding provision of social and economic rights and services to adults and children that the numbers represent – two of the most important of these rights being elementary and secondary education. The diversity of society means diversity in the classroom (see Cheng, Yau, and Ziegler 1993). The challenge to family, community, teachers, administration, and other educational stakeholders is to address questions of educational equity, social difference, identity, and knowledge production in the school system, and beyond (see Dei 1997).

The *saliency and centrality of race* in understanding the schooling experiences, as well as social and political actions and interpretative practices, of African-Canadian youth cannot be underestimated. Arguably there are distinctions in Canadian youth and their schooling experiences which demonstrate some urgency in dealing with the challenges, particularly of Black/African Canadians. Academic research has repeatedly demonstrated educational disadvantage for Black youths. Research also shows that race plays a significant mediating force in schooling. For example, in a 1991 high-school survey by one board of education in Toronto, it was revealed that Black/African-Canadian youth were not achieving as well as other students in terms of credit accumulation. It was shown that 36 per cent of Black students were 'at risk' of dropping out because of failure to accumulate sufficient credits to graduate within six years. This compared with 26 per cent for Whites and 18 per cent for Asians (see Yau, Cheng, and Ziegler 1993; Cheng 1995). This survey also confirmed that '45% of Black high-school students were enrolled in the Basic and General levels, as compared to 28% of the entire student body placed in those two lower streams' (Cheng 1995, 2; see also Cheng, Yau, and Ziegler 1993, 15; Brown et al. 1992, 13). In the most revealing statistics, the board of education's study of high-school students who enrolled in 1987 showed that by 1991, 42 per cent of Black students (compared to 33 per cent of the overall student population) dropped out of school (see Brown 1993, 5). Given the fact that this particular board of education had been in the forefront of addressing educational equity issues in the province, it is not inconceivable to suggest that the situation may in fact be worse in other boards of education.

Other research has demonstrated the severity of the issues concerning Black youth education in Canada. A study commissioned by the Canadian Alliance of Black Educators (CABE; see Daenzer 1995) also revealed the alarming extent and consequences of Black youth dropping out of school. Indeed, the 1994 report of the Ontario Royal Commission on Learning highlighted the alarming drop-out rate in its discussions about 'a crisis among Black youth' with respect to 'education and achievement' (RCOL 1994). Reading the commission's report should give all Ontarians, and Black/African Canadians in particular, a reason to reflect critically on the provincial educational system. Among many important messages for Ontario education, there is one that cannot easily be ignored: stakeholders in the provincial education system who take credit for student success should also find it incumbent upon themselves to accept responsibility for any failures.

In order to properly articulate the issues and concerns about student disengagement, it is important to examine the problem of dropping out from school as it is discussed in the literature on schooling and education for minority youth in Euro-Canadian/American contexts.

Review of Literature on Minority Education

The literature on minority education is vast. A number of studies on minorities in the educational system in various countries in the

Organization for Economic Co-operation and Development (OECD) discuss variables which affect the educational progress of racial and ethno-cultural minority youths. Migration stress, cultural differences, family disorganization, domestic responsibilities, dialect interference, low self-esteem, culturally biased tests, low teacher expectations, unsuitable curricula, low socio-economic class status, and racial hostility are among the variables mentioned (see Cummins 1984, 1986, 1989a; Appel 1988; CERI 1987a, 1987b; Ogbu 1978; Ogbu and Matute-Bianchi 1986; Verma 1987, 1989).

Cummins (1986) argued that early explanations of academic underachievement of some minorities were presented in terms of 'bicultural ambivalence,' that is, the lack of cultural identification of students to both home and school cultures. Other explanations refer to the 'caste' status of involuntary minorities (Ogbu 1978). It has been argued that given the economic and social discrimination and marginalization faced by minorities, they themselves have internalized the inferior status ascribed to them by the dominant culture. Feuerstein (1979) refers to the 'disruption of intergenerational transmission processes' caused by the 'alienation of a group from its own culture' (Cummins 1986, 22). While many of these early ideas have since been refined by their proponents, it is important to note that they continue to bear some degree of relevance in confronting the challenges of minority education in Euro-American contexts. Current discourses about culturally contextualized education recognize the importance of critically interrogating students' home and school cultures for the sources of empowering minority youth to succeed in school.

Unfortunately, in the public arena, critical debates along these lines have been sidetracked by other powerful political interests and agendas. Dehli (1994, 8) argues that the 1980s and 1990s have seen public debates about schooling in North America and Europe shift from 'concerns about equality in educational opportunity to arguments about quality, performance, standards, efficiency, accountability and parental choice.' She refers readers to the critical works of Calvert and Kuehn (1993), Claudfield (1993), Apple (1993), Cookson (1992), Woods (1992), Vincent (1992a, 1992b), and Seddon (1990) in pointing out how in public debates about education, the language of the 'market' has replaced concerns about educational equity and social justice. In some social circles there has been a lack of understanding of how issues of equity are inextricably linked to academic excellence and quality education.

Conservative dogmas which see schools as apolitical and unaffected by the larger social milieux are now being confronted by oppositional discourses. In articulating concerns about minority education in Euro-American contexts, there are many critical educational researchers and practitioners who see schools as 'contested public spheres' (Fine 1993, 682), as political sites for the reproduction of power and social inequality (see also Apple and Weis 1983). They see structural poverty, racism, sexism, and social and cultural differences as significant factors in the schooling outcomes of minority youth in particular. It is argued that the structural processes of schooling and education provide unequal opportunities and create differential outcomes, particularly for racial minority students and students from low socio-economic family backgrounds (see Willis 1977, 1983; Curtis, Livingstone, and Smaller 1992).

Critical educationists (Giroux 1983a, 1983b; Apple 1986; McCarthy 1990) have drawn attention to how schools function to reproduce the dominant ideologies of society. A focus on the examination of differential power relations within society, and how they implicate the processes of delivering education, has provided us with an understanding of how the ideology of public schooling works to maintain the status quo and to serve the needs and dictates of capital. This is a radical departure from early views that focused on family-school relations, conceptualizing schools and homes as sites and sources of student educational problems and pathologies.

While drop-outs may be seen as part of the culture of schooling, the factors which affect student disengagement still need to be articulated. Literature on the specific problem of school drop-outs is particularly extensive. Various factors, such as streaming in the schools, poverty, Eurocentrism, and discrimination have been suggested as influencing dropping out (Ministry of Citizenship 1989; Pollard 1989). However, until the 1990s, much of the analytical work tended to overgeneralize without delving into the specifics concerning various social groups in the educational system. Earlier efforts to understand the issue of school drop-outs also concentrated on statistical reports of drop-out rates without in-depth analysis of student perspectives as to why they stay in or leave school. In fact, studies of school drop-outs have generally been structural accounts that offer little insight into the students' points of view (see Trueba, Spindler, and Spindler 1989; Weis, Farrar, and Petrie 1989; Fine 1991). The lack of such insight into the experiential aspect of student disengagement, therefore, renders these studies superficial and speculative.

Lawton (1994, 2), in his latest examination of the drop-out literature, argues that current studies on the topic reveal that 'the generalizations characterizing earlier research rarely apply to specific subgroups. Males differ from females, francophones differ from anglophones; rural from urban, etc. As well, careful analyses of the process of dropping out ... indicate that the kinds of impact particular events have on the likelihood of one's completing school are usually contingent on other events and conditions.' There is an emerging awareness of the need to attend to racial, ethnic, and gender differences and specificities, as well as to explore the exact relationship between employability and dropping out.

In the Canadian context, much of the research data and scholarly writing that exist focuses on the 'problems' and issues of youth education in general. A general survey of environmental, social, attitudinal, personal, and economic factors that contribute to the early departure of students from school in Canada (see Statistics Canada 1991) confirmed the most common reasons cited by students: a preference to work, boredom, problems with schoolwork, financial reasons, problems with teachers, pregnancy, and marriage (see also Watson 1977; King et al. 1988; and Ministry of Education, Quebec 1991).

Hartnagel and Krahn's (1989) study in Edmonton looked at 'how the labour market may be related to criminal behaviour among school dropouts.' The study also found that a third of the drop-outs surveyed had been questioned by police and that free time and boredom characterize the lives of drop-outs. These 'combine[d] to increase opportunities for and temptations to engage in deviant behaviour' (Hartnagel and Krahn 1989, 440). It was revealed that the use and sale of drugs was as common among students as

drop-outs (see also Fagan and Pabon 1990). Two of the most comprehensive and recent Canadian studies on 'drop-out' are Tanner,
Krahn, and Hartnagel (1995), which synthesizes their longitudinal
work dealing with reasons for dropping out, the difficulties in
accessing the labour market, and the relations between premature
school leaving and 'deviant' behaviour; and Gaskell and Kelly's
(1996) edited collection on new policy perspectives on dropping out
and related practical issues.

In Ontario, a few studies have highlighted the specific problem of
minority youth disengagement from school, with an eye to strategies for intervention (Cummins 1989b; Natriello, McDill, and Pallas
1985; Wright 1985; Cheng et al. 1989). Radwanski's (1987) study,
focusing on the problem of streaming in Ontario and its effects on
Black/African-Canadian students, also identified school-related and
economic and personal factors as contributing to a student's decision to drop out. This influential report called for the elimination
of streaming. In their critique of the study, Allison and Paquette
(1991), Black (1988), and Townsend (1988) argued that Radwanski
had 'confused correlation with cause and effect' (Lawton 1994, 3).
Mackay and Myles (1989), in their study, also highlighted family
background (e.g., economic and educational status), personal characteristics and attitudes (e.g., age, gender, psycho-socio characteristics), academic achievement (marks, grade retention), and school
climate (e.g., culture and ecology) as significant variables in the
explanation of why First Nations' students dropped out of Ontario
schools (see also Mackay and Myles 1995).

Lawton et al. (1988) explored how the school system itself, and
social and maturation themes therein, work to place some students in a marginal position and eventually lead to their dropping
out. Questions of relevance of school courses, school attendance,
and disengagement from classes to 'drop-out behaviour' have also
been examined to varying degrees in surveys by Karp (1988), King
et al. (1988), and Sullivan (1989). The specific issues about 'transition' through grades have been explored by Hargreaves and Earl
(1990) and Hargreaves, Leithwood et al. (1993). Watson (1977) has
also discussed the specific reasons for leaving school for Ontario
school drop-outs. Finally, Quirouette, Saint-Denis, and Hout (1989,

1990) utilized a questionnaire to identify students at risk of dropping out, by asking about family characteristics, feelings of isolation, schoolwork, future plans for school, school interest, and the need for help from teachers. In particular, Quirouette, Saint-Denis, and Hout (1989) discussed intervention programs, including individual and group counselling measures and mentoring and peer counselling, for drop-outs and 'at-risk' students in French-language schools. Desnoyers and Pauker (1988) also surveyed some of the methods and programs being implemented by schools and boards of education to increase school attendance and to deal with the drop-out problem.

These studies generally highlight the need to address the genuine problems faced by students in the Canadian educational system. But, while many of the authors provide recommendations for reforms in the schools, they fail to adequately explore the questions of class, gender, race/ethnicity, power, and history in their discussions of dropping out and, particularly, how students' lived experiences and social realities have contributed to compounding the problems of racial minority education and school disengagement. We take the position that addressing questions of power, equity and social difference is crucial for ensuring student engagement and retention in schools, and for eventually achieving enhanced learning outcomes.

Daenzer and Dei (1994) point out that research in terms of race is still largely an unsettling issue for many Canadians. Yet much of the available research data do point to significant differences that Black and other minority youths experience in the Ontario school system (see Brathwaite 1989; James 1990; Solomon 1992; Henry 1992, 1994; Dei 1993). These critical educators and researchers draw attention to the need to examine the institutional processes of schooling (see also Lee 1985, 1994), thereby bringing to the fore how racism, discrimination, exclusion, and economic inequality contribute to schooling outcomes for Black youth. To varying degrees, the works of Brathwaite (1989), James (1990), Solomon (1992), Sium (1987), Little (1992), Dei (1993, 1994, 1995a); Dei and Razack (1995), the Working Group (1992), the Canadian Alliance of Black Educators (CABE 1992), and the Black Educators Working Group (BEWG 1993) draw attention to Eurocentric curricular practices, the lack of Black representation in teaching and top administrative positions, ineffective and biased assessment and placement procedures, tensions between dominant and oppositional minority cultures in the schools, and conflicts between diverse learning and teaching styles and techniques (see also Cheng 1995). Many of the research findings documenting Black students' alienation in Ontario schools correspond with literature on minority education in other Euro-American contexts (see Carby 1986; Oliver 1986; Jacob and Jordan 1993; Garibaldi 1992; Comer 1988; Amos and Parmar 1987; Fuller 1980; Fine 1991; Ford and Harris 1994; Alladin 1995). In fact, research in the United States is focusing strongly on alternative visions of schooling informed by success stories in minority settings and a critique of conventional schools (see Ernst, Statzner, and Trueba 1994).

Since the early 1980s, the voices of many Black parents and educators have intensified about the problem of student disengagement from school, and they have acknowledged a 'crisis' within their communities (see Board of Education, Toronto 1988; *Share* 1991; Brathwaite and James 1996). Some of the educational concerns that specifically affect Black youth were articulated in the Stephen Lewis report (see Lewis 1992) and also in the report of the Ontario Royal Commission on Learning (RCOL 1994). In the 1990s, state-sponsored and community-initiated research studies on Ontario education have affirmed minority student voices and questioned the absence of an inclusive school environment. Community groups such as the Organization of Parents of Black Children (OPBC; see Board of Education 1988), Black Educators Working Group (see BEWG 1993), the Working Group (1992), and the Canadian Alliance of Black Educators (see CABE 1992) have pointed out that the absence of an inclusive school environment makes it difficult for some youths to connect to or identify with the school. From 1993 to 1995, the provincial government, partly in recognition of expressed concerns and community pressure, undertook a number of policy initiatives (see Wright and Allingham 1994). Four of the most notable of recent government policy documents dealing with Ontario education are *Changing Perspectives: A Resource Guide for Race and Ethnocultural Equity, K-13 (MOE 1992), The Common Curriculum* (MET 1993a), *Antiracism and Ethnocultural Equity in School Boards: Guidelines for Policy Development and Implementation* (MET 1993b), and *Violence-Free Schools* (MET 1993c). These documents, for the most part, provide general frameworks within which school boards and schools can act. Also, the provincial Ministry of Citizenship (through the Ontario Anti-Racism Secretariat and in conjunction with some school boards) has initiated specific programs directed at minority youths who are not succeeding academically and are considered at risk of dropping out of school (see, for example, Ministry of Citizenship 1994). While, in theory, many of the provincial documents aim to meet the challenge of inclusiveness in schools, the difficult task of converting policy statements into concrete and practical action remains. More disturbing is that the fate of some of these policies, in light of the political shift to the right, is not clear.

Theoretical Approaches to Understanding School 'Drop-outs'

Lawton (1992, 1994) has synthesized the various theoretical positions, models, and frameworks explaining 'dropping out.' The fact that the drop-out literature is theoretically inadequate and impoverished is generally acknowledged. Lawton (1992, 1994) points out that Finn's (1989) 'frustration/self-esteem' model views dropping out as a developmental process beginning in the earliest grades. The model argues that students who do not do well become frustrated early in school. With time, their frustration can result in a lower self-image, which eventually leads them to drop out. Our criticism of this model is that it does not adequately explain why some students do not do well in school in the first place. The notion of 'low self-esteem' could be used to blame students and thereby mask the structural and institutional inequities and contradictions these students have to deal with that engender the phenomenon of dropping out. Therefore, 'self-esteem' may not be a useful concept for understanding the phenomenon of school drop-outs when it fails to acknowledge racial, ethnic, and cultural differences as well as issues of social class and gender.

The 'participation-identification' model is a distinct yet related theoretical approach to explaining dropping out (see J.D. Finn 1989). The model postulates that involvement in school activities usually results in identification and social attraction to a group (J.D. Finn 1989). Conversely, the lack of participation results in a lack of identification. It is argued that the likelihood of a youth successfully completing high school is maximized if the student 'maintains multiple, expanding forms of participation in school-relevant activities' (Lawton 1992, 20). Marginalized students can become isolated from the mainstream student body. They may feel alienated from the school system as a whole and consequently drop out (C.E. Finn 1987, J.D. Finn 1989). This model has some utility for understanding the impact of marginalization of racial and ethnic minorities in Eurocentric educational institutions, but it does not adequately address how and why visible minority students, for example, become marginalized. It does not account for why even those students who identify with the school system could still fade out because of the way external structural conditions are mediated within the school system.

Similarly, the 'deviance theory' of dropping out (see LeCompte and Dworkin 1991) argues that by failing to support and respect the existing institutional norms, values, ethos, and rules of the school, students run the risk of being branded deviants. Consequently, these students may be denied privileges and rewards that the institution accords to well-behaved students. With time, the 'deviants' internalize such institutional labels by redefining themselves in terms of their deviant behaviour. As they drift towards behaviours that offer their own rewards, rather than the institutional sanctions of the school, their oppositional behaviour acquires some legitimacy of its own. But because the school system does not tolerate frequent absenteeism, poor academic performance, and truancy, the perpetrators of such behaviours are eventually 'pushed out' of school.

The deviance model is particularly relevant for steering attention to institutional structures and processes that rationalize school decisions to 'push out' students who are non-conformists. However, it does not problematize how 'deviance' is constructed in society. This is important if we are to make the connection between the school and its policies and the wider social setting in accounting for school drop-outs. This connection is essential for understanding the school experiences of Black students. The policies of the school towards 'non-conformists,' towards those who act differently from the mainstream, or even look different, are a reflection of the social forces of society. Society expects the school to legitimize certain hegemonic and ideological practices, while delegitimizing others.

Schools can be seen, then, as a microcosm of society and the primary site of social reproduction. Schools create the ideological conditions necessary to replicate the extant social-class and power relations which maintain social order. However, for minority students, this entails replicating a position of marginality in which issues of equal access to opportunities and success are constrained by the same social and ideological factors which operate in the broader social context and serve to legitimize their subordinate status. These factors include racism, classism, discrimination, language barriers, Eurocentrism, alienation, and, in general, a perceived deviance from the status quo.

Other theories explaining school drop-outs include those that hypothesize a link between structural strain on institutions and the behaviour and attitudes of their employees and clients. LeCompte and Dworkin's (1991) 'structural strain and alienation' model argues that if societal changes reduce the fit between school and society, then teachers and students are likely to perceive their efforts and participation as purposeless. The outcome of such a situation is burn-out for teachers, and alienation and dropping out for students. The relevance of this model lies in the introduction of key concepts such as 'alienation,' 'powerlessness,' 'meaninglessness,' 'normlessness,' and 'isolation' to explain why students give up on school when their lived realities do not match the expectations that society and schooling have created (Lawton 1992, 21). Others studies, such as those of Manski (1989), Stage (1989), and Bickel and Papagiannis (1988), have utilized economic models of cost-benefit analysis in order to explain the causes of dropping out. Stage (1989) and Bickel and Papagiannis (1988) focused on local economic conditions, arguing that high-school students will more likely stay in school and graduate if there is a good chance of gaining employment and improving their incomes with a completed education. On the other hand, if students feel that local conditions make employment unlikely, regardless of education level, then there is a good chance of students leaving school prematurely.

These theories provide additional insights into students' decisions to stay in or leave school with reference to the rational calculations students make in light of their social circumstances. There are students who leave school when they realize they could be better off economically by doing something else. But even here, the narratives of the lived experiences of these students reveal the complex web of social, structural, cultural, and institutional factors that come into play.

We find Bowles and Gintis's 'correspondence theory,' espoused in their influential *Schooling in Capitalist America* (1976), very insightful in this regard, particularly in explaining the dynamics and social effects of schooling. This theory asserts that hierarchically structured patterns of society are mirrored in classroom dynamics. As Giroux observes, such a theoretical framework aids in 'pointing to the social relations of the classroom as processes that link schools to determinate forces in the workplace' (1981, 6). In their work, Bowles and Gintis (1976) proceed to focus attention on the school's reinforcement of social differences, such as class, among students. In examining the classroom, the authors aim to demonstrate how the institution of the school maintains that social differentiation among pupils (and by extension all people) occurs naturally.

Bowles and Gintis (1976) describe the 'selection and reward systems' operating in schools as 'the legitimation of inequality.' Students' expectations of success in life, and their cogitative attitudes towards institutions, are configured through differential treatment by school authorities and use of the curriculum. Students on the lowest rungs of the socio-economic ladder become accustomed to a limited role in society, while those students at the top become equally accustomed to positions of privilege and domination (see Sheth and Dei 1995). For Bowles and Gintis, these processes underline how the school is both a social organization where all students learn the attitudes essential for reproducing a patriarchal and stratified society, and a secure environment in which to apply these attitudes. From an early stage, students learn to view 'the order of things' as a rigid and therefore unchangeable pattern, and during the long schooling period, they also learn to respect and embody their particular positions in the capitalist social order. Bowles and Gintis conclude that schools reproduce the hierarchical workforce by teaching each member to accept, rather than question, his or her class location. Societal preparation for failure becomes sanctioned as individual inadequacy. Therefore to lack success in school is a personal and internalized fault of character.

Sheth and Dei (1995) argue that although the work of Bowles and Gintis (1976) is pivotal in informing educational stakeholders how schools manage and reproduce the social order, it is of limited use in forming strategies of resistance and transformation. The paradigm employed by Bowles and Gintis provided no hope of social mobility; persons in the upper social echelons will continue to preserve their privileges and exercise their power over persons in the lower social positions, who, in turn, have no choice but to accept an inequitable society. Furthermore, the authors failed to examine the practices of social stratification which are manifested through the manipulation of identities such as gender, race, and sexuality. As noted by Giroux (1981), the authors blatantly neglected the process by which classroom knowledge is mediated through the culture of schools. Teachers and students confer socially negotiated meaning to both the form and content of school indoctrination. 'What we are left with is a theoretical posture reinforcing the notion that there is little educators can do to change their ... plight. In short, not only do contradictions and tensions disappear in this account but the promise of critical pedagogy and social change disappears too' (Giroux 1981, 7).

An important consideration for this discussion is the role of culture as an influential mediator between dominant structures and the everyday life of human agents. This role, as maintained by

Bourdieu and Passeron (1977), adds context and complexity to the notion that schools only mirror the capitalist structures and logic of society. The authors claim that schools are relatively independent; they function with their own formal structures and individual cultures. They argue that schools, as institutions with such characteristics, are particularly capable of generating, maintaining, and regenerating the ideology of capitalist/bourgeois interests in society.

An examination of the views of Althusser (1971) and Bourdieu and Passeron (1977) reveals analogous accounts of schooling as a system which conveys the dominant modes, norms, and values of society, and which can therefore be considered a significant component of the 'ideological state apparatus.' Within such a structure, the school concurs with the dominant view and applies the vision of the efficacy of dominant cultural values. Given that within schools the valued, and consequently normalized, culture is that of the bourgeois, those students whose cultures most closely resemble that of the accepted class are predisposed to achieve more easily in a familiar environment. Following that assumption, the school has a perceived and actual function in recognizing and rewarding this 'cultural capital' as students endeavour to conserve or acquire it, and this is brought about through ideological conditioning occurring in both schools and society. The school provides the environment necessary for a reproduction of the social relations of production. The students who fail, or barely achieve, simply have failed to acquire the requisite cultural capital for success. In other words, students who commence their school careers with the valued culture of the bourgeois, in ambitions and masteries, and in similar family, language, and literacy patterns, have already achieved a 'knowledge' that other students will have little opportunity to access.

In the school system, standard testing procedures, entry/qualifying requirements, and diverse 'standardized' measurements of social and intellectual achievement contribute to the schools' pretence of impartiality and autonomy, permitting educational institutions to continue in their relatively independent positions within society's dominant power structures. Consequently, the ideological conditioning that takes place in society and schools allows schools to claim some air of 'objectivity' and 'equity.' Nevertheless, behind the façade of these practices, schools are achieving the diametrically opposite goals of partiality and inequality. When students are 'treated the same,' whether in a 'colour-blind' approach or in a way that negates the intersection of diverse social locations, the school abrogates its duty of encouraging all students to succeed by refusing to recognize that the difficulties some students face are the direct result of lacking valued cultural capital and social knowledge (Sheth and Dei 1995).

The most significant failing of the above mentioned theoretical arguments is that their proponents have ignored an important reality: that while students, teachers, administration, and staff are members of an institution, they are also actual subjects, and that although schools are institutions, they are also actual sites interacting differently with their members on the basis of intersecting socio-economic locations. In fact, race, gender, sexuality, and the trajectories of social differences are ignored in much of the analysis. Consequently, subjects who are meant to be studied, as *subjects*, become objects in isolation from class and other identities. The real and the actual become the abstract and the disembodied. In a fabricated world without multiple social locations, the struggle and resistance that operate on multiple levels are collapsed into a deterministic, structuralist, and singularly classist explanation of the process of education. The whole concept of grass-roots change and popular mobilization is summarily dismissed. When power is held only by those in the uppermost echelons, it becomes a reified and destructive force that loses any transformative dynamism. Without change, an analysis that operates on multiple levels is impossible. If class is seen as the only site of oppression, and that site is seen to be rigid and impervious, then there are no tools with which to fight the oppressions of racism, heterosexism, patriarchy, and ablism. Moreover, there are no tools to fight the systems of oppression and their permutations that are a reality for the students in the classroom and members of the broader society. Finally, the rudimentary explorations of sites of oppression by these theorists do not exhaust the usefulness of such positions in class analysis, and in theories of capitalist/bourgeois cultural domination. However, to examine schools to gain a deeper understanding of the school as a site of multiple oppressions and dominations, resistances and transformations, a more complex analysis is needed.

We therefore argue that for Black/African-Canadian youth in a multi-ethnic city, a grounded theory for understanding the causes of dropping out should build upon the insights provided by earlier theoretical approaches. Understanding the causes of dropping out must also include the concept of resistance as a factor related to student disengagement. Building a theory of resistance for students begins with an adequate definition of 'resistance.' We understand resistance to involve the attitudes, behaviours, and actions which challenge dominant institutional norms and practices, as a means to effect social and institutional change.

There is no one specific context for discussing the issue of resistance in this study, since it is manifest in many forms. Dropping out and the behaviours associated with 'fading out' of school (e.g., truancy, lack of interest and participation in school, etc.) can be seen as forms of resistance. However, increased student participation within school structures (e.g., establishing clubs, participating on student council, etc.), when engaged in as a means to effect institutional and social change, can also be regarded as a form of resistance. Even though engaging the system in order to change it runs the risk of being co-opted by the same institution it challenges, the vision of an alternative structure qualifies these actions as acts of resistance.

Some expressions of resistance can be identified in terms of 'ideological resistance,' or oppositional attitudes influenced by counter-hegemonic ideologies. As well, oppositional behaviours such as 'acting out,' adopting styles of dress which conflict with dominant cultural norms, distinctive use of language, and sometimes violence may be interpreted as practices of resistance when they are intended to assert the marginalized perspective and attempt to subvert dominant norms and values. Education itself is also a means of resistance, particularly in alternatively focused schools (e.g., Black-focused schools) or other sorts of private religious/

cultural schools where the introduction of otherwise repressed knowledge bases (e.g., African-centred knowledge) challenges and decentres dominant paradigms (Dei 1995b, 1995c).

Establishing a grounded theory for understanding the causes of dropping out is facilitated by analysing the narratives of students. In doing this, we begin to uncover how social difference, based on such dynamics as race, ethnicity, socio-economic class, and gender, restricts the educational and life opportunities of some students. We also learn how public schooling privileges and engages certain groups, while disengaging and disempowering others. In this report, though we centre our attention on individual students' narratives of lived personal experiences at school, as well as those of various focus groups, we do not lose sight of the larger macrosystems, and particularly the out-of-school political and economic forces, that structure these experiences.

Though educational and social researchers and practitioners continue to scramble for solutions to the drop-out dilemma, the voices and critiques of students and actual drop-outs, as we have stated earlier, have barely received attention. Their knowledge remains, at the very least, under-expressed in educational literature. As Sheth and Dei (1995) have argued, mainstream educational research has deemed it acceptable to study lived realities through textually transmitted documents without the need for actual subjects. We choose, by contrast, to include the views of the people we are interested in and are funded to study. Instead of starting with statistical information and prior theoretical constructs of acceptable social behaviour, we proceed by way of collecting material from those who have been labelled 'drop-outs' or 'at risk,' as well as from those – whether satisfied to be or not – who are still in school. We recognize that the school system is intent on resolving the dilemma of drop-outs, but is also incapable of making the necessary changes without dismantling the very structures that allow schools to function. Starting from a recognition of this double bind, we build a theoretical framework for understanding from the standpoint of those who are involved.

Our Discursive Framework

Our study has employed an antiracism discursive framework to understand and report on the issues of Black students' disengagement from school in the Canadian context (see Dei 1995c, 1996). The antiracism perspective interrogates the institutional structures of teaching, learning, and administration of education and how local communities (e.g., parents, families, community groups) interact with these structures. This framework acknowledges the role. of the educational system in producing and reproducing racial, gender, and class-based inequalities in society. Antiracism links the issues of identity (race, class, gender, and sexuality) with schooling processes. While the recognition of individual identities is fundamental to educational transformation, it is argued that for educational change to be meaningful, students' identities ought to be connected to the collective existence of the social group.

The antiracism perspective also acknowledges the pedagogical need to confront the challenge of diversity and difference in Canadian society and the urgency for an educational system that is more inclusive and capable of responding to minority concerns about public schooling. It also critiques the marginalization of certain voices in society and, particularly, the failure to take serious account of the rich knowledge and experiences of subordinate groups in the educational system. The antiracism framework sees schools not only as agents of cultural, political, and economic reproduction, but also as sites of contestation between groups differentially situated in terms of power relations. A critical ethnography that uses the antiracism framework reveals instances of resistance, from both students and educators, which challenge the prevailing culture of dominance.

Antiracism sees the task of achieving genuine inclusion as involving school administrators and educators developing a demonstrated commitment to power-sharing in schools where students, teachers, parents, and local communities are given effective joint responsibilities over the processes of delivering education. Within the Euro-Canadian/American educational system, inclusiveness means dealing foremost with *equity*: that is, dealing with the qualitative value of justice. Inclusion also means addressing the question of *representation*: that is, having a multiplicity of perspectives entrenched as part of mainstream academic knowledge. Furthermore, inclusion means that school and classroom teaching and instructional materials must respond to the challenges of *diversity and difference*: that is, the socially constructed intersections of race, gender, class, sexuality, language, culture, and religion in the school system.

On the Category of 'Black'

In our study, 'Black' has been defined as referring to those students of African descent who identify themselves as such. When the project began, two questions were often asked: Why is the study focusing on Black students? and, Does this research see Black students as a homogeneous group? One can interpret these questions as being contradictory. First, there is an implicit and mistaken assumption that the drop-out issue and the accounting factors are uniform for all students. There is a substantial body of literature that emphasizes a palpable difference between the educational experiences of Black and non-Black students (see Goodlad 1984; Jaynes and Williams 1989; Fine 1991; Garibaldi 1992; Kozol 1991). Second, while Black students are not a homogeneous group, we believe that there are some commonalities in the educational experiences of students born in Africa and the Diaspora, including those of mixed parenthood (Black and non-Black). A good share of the educational problems that these students have to contend with may stem from the exigencies of being Black in a White-dominated society. A significant development that impressed those of us who had the privilege to talk to the students of this study is how the students opened up and related some of their deep feelings to us after first appearing distant. No doubt, the fact that the interviewers were Black/African-Canadian facilitated this study as the students identified with the interviewers and were able to take us into their confidence.

Nevertheless, as this study revealed, the concerns of Black/

African-Canadian students vary to some extent. For example, Continental African students have concerns about the broad issues of language, religion, and culture. Students who have been schooled in the Caribbean complain about the 'social labelling' of Black students as 'troublemakers.' There are also complaints about the attempts by schools to place them in English-skills-development (ESD) classes. Questions of identity are raised by students born here in Canada and, particularly, to mixed parents. Students who speak with distinctly different accents and dialects point to intra-group discrimination and prejudices among their peers. By and large, however, certain themes and concerns do emerge from the analysis of the Black students' narratives which allow us to speak about issues in the collective, and consequently the term 'Black' is also used collectively in reference to African Canadians.

The term 'non-Black' is used in this book to refer to those students who were other than African-Canadian. Although we recognize the multiple social locations and diversity of students this implies, we have chosen to centre Black students and their experiences by using this reference. Where possible, we have identified by ethnicity the particular students who are quoted.

This book is divided into thirteen chapters. Chapter 2 discusses the methodological approach to data gathering and analysis and the challenges of doing school research. Chapters 3 to 12 examine in detail the Black youth narratives about school and out-of-school experiences, highlighting how these subjugated voices help inform our understanding of the drop-out dilemma. Specifically, chapter 3 looks at the social construction of the term 'drop-out' in the social and political contexts of Black students' understandings and interpretations of dropping out. Chapter 4 discusses educational factors, specifically school practices, that lead students to drop out of school. Chapter 5 examines the intersections of race, class, gender, and sexuality in the schooling experiences of Black youth. Chapter 6 analyses students' views about authority, the exercise of power, and the role of respect in schools and their implications for students dropping out of school. Chapter 7 explores issues involved in the perceptions Black students have of teachers, teaching styles, and teacher expectations, and how these factors relate to students' engagement and disengagement from school. Chapter 8 moves the discussion of disengagement to concerns regarding the curriculum offered and the ways in which students negotiate it. This chapter also explores the notion of the 'deep curriculum'; that is, all formal and informal aspects of the school environment and the intersections of culture, environment, and the organizational life of schools. Chapter 9 follows the previous discussion to examine in detail the related issues of how students communicate their concerns about identity and representation in schooling.

The topic of constructing alternative and inclusive knowledge is discussed in chapter 10, in the context of students' voices that speak to questions about Black heritage and history, Black and minority teachers, and African-centred forms of education. Chapter 11 examines how students perceive the involvement of the local community and parents in schooling and education, and the relevance of such involvement in addressing the problem of youth leaving school prematurely. In chapter 12, we interrogate students' voices about the possibilities, visions, and limitations of educational and social change. chapter 13, as the concluding chapter, ties up the basic ideas and arguments of the book and posits an alternative and critical theoretical framework for understanding and reconceptualizing 'dropping out.'

Chapter Two

Research Methodology

In this chapter we will outline and defend our general research methodology and research process. We begin by exploring the potentials that qualitative research methods presented in the design stage of our study, and in the resulting methods of data collection and analysis. We then outline the specific ethnographic methods of interviewing, observation, and surveying employed in the general research process, including preliminary research objectives and the determination of both the number and profile of informants. After laying the foundation of the research, we detail the considerable process of gaining entry into schools and school boards. Following issues of entry comes a discussion of ethical concerns, particularly in relation to research which involves young participants, an issue that was revisited throughout the research process. The collection of data is then discussed, including an account of the process of interviewing and observing our participants. As an integral element of this process, we needed to consider our research tools and our role as researchers, and we discuss these considerations throughout this chapter. Finally, the analysis of the data collected and the methods we employed in carrying out this work are outlined.

Designing the Study

Why Qualitative Research?

As has been mentioned in the previous chapter, one of the primary objectives for this project was to bring the voices of 'drop-outs' and high-school students to the centre of our research. We felt that this research should go further than to produce a statistical account of the 'drop-out' phenomenon. Students, 'drop-outs,' parents, and other concerned adults were all seen as stakeholders in this issue, and their thoughts, feelings, and ideas were seen as crucial to developing a research methodology compatible with our theoretical background.

We adopted qualitative research as our methodology because of, as Glesne and Peshkin state, the 'openness' of this type of inquiry and how 'it allows the researcher to approach the inherent complexity of social interaction and to do justice to that complexity, to respect it in its own right' (1992, 7). In terms of specific conceptual and methodological departures from most quantitative research, Glesne and Peshkin discuss (among many other relevant points) the rejection of an 'objective reality, primacy of method, detachment from subject and manipulation of data. Qualitative method instead recognises that reality is a social construct in which complexity and context of the emerging data must be considered; the subject, not method should be the primary focus' (1992, 7; see also Hitchcock and Hughes 1995). However, we also understand that such so-called 'soft' research, especially ethnography, is not intrinsically a more 'caring' method than quantitative research. As Davis argues, 'the combination of "what counts as science" and "what counts as newsworthy" may mean that [it] is as masculinist in its orientation' (cited in Burgess 1985, 83).

Notwithstanding the approach taken in this study, we recognize that quantitative research can be a socially profound strategy to render subordinated visible groups in society and that it could be a preferred mode of inquiry (Eisner 1991, 5). Unfortunately the statistical significance of Black 'drop-outs' may carry more weight with educational administrators than individual stories of struggle. Studies which rely on statistics to portray a picture of 'drop-outs' do not provide – and they are not meant to provide – either the researcher or observer with the reasons and actual experiences of those involved. The qualitative research approach has allowed us, as researchers and members of various communities, to explore this complex issue from various perspectives, taking into account the intersectionality of representation and identity (Matsuda et al. 1993, 113), which would be difficult if not impossible to express in numerical terms. Our theoretical base demands that such inter-sections of race, class, gender, and other means of oppression can-not be reduced to a tally of competing claims. As opposed to placing statistics at the centre of our research and working to contextual-ize the data with narratives and conclusions, we first listened to the 'stories' of students, teachers, and parents, and related these stories to larger issues behind the decision to leave school early. Therefore, our ethnographic research gives a stronger voice to the collective struggles of our subjects, and brings to the fore the inter-sections of many complex issues. We believe that a qualitative re-search method is the most appropriate method for this endeavour.

Qualitative research allowed us to demonstrate decisively that the 'drop-out problem' cannot and should not be conceptualized in a simplistic manner. Instead, we needed to consider the histor-ical and present socio-economic structures of White domination in our society. Further, we could not simply look at how the dom-inant society affects the 'drop-out,' but had to examine also the strategies of survival employed by students, 'drop-outs,' their fam-ilies, and communities in their interactions and relationships with the dominant power structures. We began with the students' own views and accounts and approached the issues from their per-spective. By connecting students' narratives to each other and to wider social issues such as racism, classism, sexism, and homo-phobia, we have aimed to represent the complexity of Black high-school students' experiences. The qualitative method enabled the voices of the participants to inform significantly the resultant inter-pretations and theoretical development. We chose to allow the narratives to guide our analytical process. By centring the students' narratives in our analysis and working from these experiences to develop a theoretical understanding, the students themselves have played an integral role in the creation of this knowledge. At all times, we have attempted to portray the experiences of high-school students in a manner which respects their views of their own situ-ations.

Methodologically, the qualitative, and particularly the ethnographic, approach has the advantage of preserving the individual stories and highlighting some of the common threads of a shared set of experiences. In terms of a traditional positivistic approach, critics could argue that this study lacks a statistically representative sample. In response, we challenge such critics to provide a group of similarly situated Black youth whose responses would be radically different from the two hundred students who were interviewed for our study. Even if many other students contravened the spirit of our two hundred young informants, their narratives, besides being stories, are also political statements and indictments of an existing structure, representing, at the very least, the views and experiences of a critical and articulate minority. The lives and experiences that became our data must be read as interpretations from the standpoint of the informants.

The random selection of informants to cross-reference the students' narratives serves to mitigate against some of the effects of self-selection, thus reinforcing the internal and external validity of the research. The message was clear from all sources: Black youth experience exclusion and racism on many levels in school. The evidence from this research does not seek to answer how it is *representative of* the school experiences of all Black youth; rather, it seeks *to represent* those experiences. In our study, we seek to present a multiplicity of voices while leaving open the possibility for other voices to be heard. It is both a narration of social realities and a challenge to other researchers. Openly documenting the number of informants involved and the variety of their responses has given us both confidence concerning the study's capacity to represent the social worlds of Black youth, and an awareness of its limitations in capturing every nuance of those worlds.

Methodology and Participants

The specific qualitative methods that we adopted were interviewing and observation. We also administered brief written surveys to the students we interviewed with specific questions regarding personal characteristics and their respective socio-economic situations as well as their opinions on school issues. We believed that in speaking directly to the stakeholders involved in the daily experience of high school, we would most effectively portray the issues involved in the decision to 'drop out' of school. This process involved gaining access to several school settings, as well as enlisting participants.

After securing the consent of the respective school boards, the initial research approach began in May 1992, when we earmarked the latter part of the month to visit schools to collect basic data on activities, programs, enrolment, and retention rates for the last five years. Part of this body of data was obtained at the school board level in order to gain a general understanding of the official perceptions and statistical realities of students 'dropping out.' The summer of 1992 was spent contacting 'drop-outs,' 'at-risk' students, and other students in Ontario public high schools for interviews. The initial research objective (1992–3) was to individually interview a total of forty male and female Black students, from grades 10 and 12, in each of four selected Toronto schools. We also planned to carry out detailed ethnographic observations of the schools and classroom interactions, and to conduct focus-group interviews with students at a future date

By the end of the first year, we were able to reach our established target of forty students in two of the schools, and over twenty students each in the other two schools; as intended, we conducted three focus-group interviews with students. In addition, over two dozen students from other Metropolitan Toronto schools were contacted through our connections in various communities, as well as twenty-one actual school 'drop-outs' and students designated 'at risk,' some of whom have since returned to school. Separate focus-group interviews were also conducted with 'at risk' students through three other sources: a provincially funded program run by a board of education, a student summer job program, and a student/youth program in Toronto.

In each of the schools in which we conducted our research, we worked with a project coordinator or contact person. These individuals were responsible for identifying students we were interested in interviewing and arranging both the meeting place and schedules. In each school, students were selected to provide a representation of both sexes, and grades 10 and 12. The criteria for selecting grade 10 students at 'high risk' of 'dropping out' included below-average marks, poor attendance or inadequate accumulation of credits (see Ziegler 1989; Waterhouse 1990). Grade 12 students provided valuable information about their reasons for staying in school and their abilities to adapt to the system. The difficulty in identifying enough suitable students from these two grades led us to include students from other grades (i.e., grades 9 and 11, and Ontario Academic Credit [OAC] level). With respect to the grade designation of the students, we have generally focused on the total credits accumulated as an important criterion.

In the second year of the project (1993–4), we continued to interview Black students from the four high schools involved in the project. By the end of the year, a total of 150 Black students had been interviewed from the selected schools for the project. Additionally, we conducted four focus-group meetings of ten students in each of these schools. Surveys had also been completed with these students. In the second year, we completed three basic research objectives. We interviewed fifty-five Black parents, caregivers, and community workers for their views on public schooling in Ontario, and specifically for their solutions to the school 'drop-out' dilemma. Secondly, we spoke with forty-one teachers, including some school administrators, about their views on the education of youth, the problem of Black student disengagement and 'dropping' out of school, and the solutions to the problem. Thirdly, we interviewed fifty-nine non-Black students individually and in groups in each of the four high schools to cross-reference the narratives of the Black students. The principal investigator conducted further ethnographic observations of school/work roles, gender roles, division of labour, as well as student-peer and student-teacher interactions. (For survey and interview questions for each group, please see Appendices 1–9).

Teachers were selected to provide a representation of individuals from diverse racial, ethnic, and gender backgrounds. Among the teachers chosen were those teaching history, English as a second language, science, mathematics, and physical education (including coaching staff). School administrators, including principals and some vice-principals, heads of departments, guidance counsellors, and school psychologists were interviewed. We were careful to ensure that the pool of interviewees consisted of both young staff and those with extensive working experience in the schools.

The study sample of Black parents, guardians, and community workers was chosen to reflect gender and family differences, as well as socio-economic backgrounds within the possible informant group. Canadian-born and non-Canadian-born parents were interviewed. Parents and community groups with a long history of contact with the school system were also interviewed and afforded us a valuable insight into the experiences of community veterans in interacting with the education system.

Gaining Entry

We approached several school boards in Metropolitan Toronto to request permission to conduct research in their schools. This was in most instances a standardized procedure which required that researchers complete a form which asked for a research proposal and an outline of the research methods and activities. However, as the principal investigator was required to make extended defences of the project before the research committees of some boards of education, we were often frustrated by the delays in getting the project under way. When one school board refused permission for access to their schools, the reason cited was that the board was conducting a similar study. We were later dismayed to learn that the actual reason for being denied access was not the one given.

In general, as will be subsequently discussed in the section on data collection, the research in the schools ran smoothly. The principals were helpful and cooperative, and the contact persons were more than diligent in ensuring that we felt comfortable in the schools. The contact persons often spent considerable time and energy in facilitating our work by arranging the interviews with students, locating students, and finding private space in already crowded schools where we could conduct our interviews. Our contacts also distributed and collected information letters and consent forms for the project participants. In light of such courtesy, we attempted to cause minimum disruption in the general school operations and daily schedules of both teachers and students.

Ethics

Because of the young age of many of the participants in our research, and educational research in general, priority must be given to concerns of ethics, including, but not limited to, issues of consent and confidentiality, the vulnerability of our subjects, questions of exploitation, and the responsibility of the researchers to disseminate our findings. As Troyna and Carrington argue, both the practice and theory of antiracist research should be 'informed by the same principles' of antiracism, such as 'commitment to social justice [and] equality' (1989, 219). Consent forms were completed by students if they were of legal age, or by parents/guardians for younger students. Information about the study was included with the forms for participants and their parents/guardians to consider prior to agreeing to participate. Although the students who participated in this study were all adolescents and not children *per se*, we still needed to be aware of their vulnerabilities. Most of the students were quite candid and revealing in their discussions with us, a result either of our abilities as researchers or of their need to speak on these issues, or a combination of these and other factors.

Another area which merited considerable attention was confidentiality. All participants were promised confidentiality, and we took every measure to ensure that this promise was kept. In this text and elsewhere, participants are referred to with pseudonyms, and any revealing characteristics have been altered or omitted. School boards and individual schools also remain unidentified to protect students and teachers. Confidentiality was an issue which sometimes surfaced with the informants, most frequently with students who for obvious reasons were concerned about commenting on their school and on specific teachers. In all cases, confidentiality was promised and maintained.

In most cases, students did trust us to handle the information respectfully. We needed to consider seriously the explicit and implicit responsibility placed on us by the students' revelations. On account of their age and their position in the school system, students are particularly susceptible to exploitation by research. Next to ensuring their anonymity, of primary concern was reporting their views in a reflective and appropriate manner. Many students wanted to know how this research would impact on the school system and their school experiences in particular. We could only share with them our plans for reporting our findings and the hope that our conclusions would reach a wide audience. In working with any research participants, and students and marginalized youths, in particular, researchers must consider their vulnerability in terms of appropriation and distortion of the experiences and knowledge they shared.

In certain instances, we realized that the students were opening up to us either because they rarely had occasion to be heard on these topics and/or because they shared certain identifiers with the researcher. Some of the students shared views with the researcher which they probably would not have, had the researcher not been of the same racial group. Although this experience gave us the possibility of acquiring accurate information from the students, it also made us more careful about reporting their views at the same level of accuracy. As Finch argues, when addressing a case of women interviewing other women who are less privileged, a high level of rapport built on commonality may lead the participants to share more information than they normally would, and consequently leave themselves open to exploitation (cited in Riddell 1989). In these cases, we needed to be especially aware of the information the students were sharing so as to ensure that it was handled appropriately and used as effectively as possible to achieve positive change.

Data Collection

Designing the Interview Questions and Collecting Ethnographic Data

In designing the research, we envisioned particular issues which we wanted to address, and these priorities guided our interview questions. We structured our questions according to the group being interviewed since we needed to ensure that our language was such that participants could easily understand the questions being posed. The questions we eventually used were pilot-tested with a group of youth who shared similar backgrounds and characteristics with those we planned to interview for this study. At times, we became aware that it would be necessary to have participants define certain terms to ensure that we were clear on the meaning that they attached to their own language. For example, we asked all students to define the term 'drop-out,' so that we could put their perceptions in the appropriate context.

In some cases, we posed several questions on the same general theme in order to develop fully the participants' responses and to ensure that we were gaining a full account of their views. We designed the questions in a manner which we hoped would reduce any 'leading' of the participants to give an anticipated response. Overall, we found that centring a few questions around all the major issues we wished to explore was an effective method of conducting interviews.

The project included an ethnography of the schools involved. We conducted field observations of school culture, work roles, and gender roles, as well as of student-peer and student-teacher interactions and classroom activities. Some of the researchers attended classroom discussions and observed the varied interactions that take place in the daily life of a school, while at least one researcher was designated to be present at important school functions, such as opening days of the school term and graduation events. Furthermore that designate was permitted to observe and speak, on occasion, at staff meetings and Parent-Teacher Association meetings.

Reflections on the Research Process

In this study, the research process encompassed a wide variety of activities, from interviews in various settings and with various groups to organizing a forum for youth to speak at our university. We look back on all of our endeavours with satisfaction and some anxiety. We experience joy and satisfaction because we have heard the voices of 'drop-outs,' students, parents, and teachers and have sought to represent their concerns, dreams, and aspirations. However, we are also fully aware of the hurdles we had to go through just to begin the study. In our respective roles as interviewers, ethnographers, document reviewers, and data analysts, we all have something to tell.

Two repeating occurrences and a unique one stand out in our minds: first, the intense emotions seen in the faces of the youth as they spoke about the challenges of going to school; second, the repeated expression by students at the end of focus-group discussions that they wished such events were more frequent in their schools; and third, at a scholarly conference on school 'drop-outs,' the surprise expressed by a colleague about how articulate the students and 'drop-outs' were in discussing their concerns.

We are grateful for the students, school 'drop-outs,' parents, and guardians who took time to come to our offices at the Ontario Institute for Studies in Education (OISE) for an interview. More than once, a mother and her whole family came to OISE for interviews. In fact, one mother came with prepared notes for the interview and, pointing to the interviewer, said, 'Son, I don't want you to miss a word.' Then there were the students involved in the provincially funded summer jobs programs, including those from 'Goals for Youth,' who came to OISE for many interviews and kept asking when would they be invited back. One school principal, having missed an appointment at his school, graciously came to OISE to speak to us. We also encountered many parents who called us (when the youth took home the informed consent form for parents' signatures) to find out more about the study. Some of these parents would commend the researcher for initiating the study. At one point, a group of Black students interviewed for the project were invited to share their thoughts and ideas with OISE faculty, students, and staff at a public forum. One female student was initially apprehensive about appearing before a university audience. At the end of the forum, she remarked, 'This place is not all that they make it out to be.' We will surely be seeing this student enrolled in a university in the future.

Within the schools selected for the study, there were the usual frustrations associated with beginning research. For example, interviewers would have to wait for some students to arrive for the interview. Yet quite a few times, a student would arrive for an interview bringing a friend who had heard of the study and wondered why she/he had not been called for an interview. A few students were at first reluctant to speak freely and would offer brief responses to questions. It took a little bit of 'ice-breaking' for these informants to open up to the researchers. It was all part of the feeling-out process. Students wanted to know about the 'politics' of the researcher. Some students asked if the study was going to be of any benefit to them, noting that they had in the past expressed their concerns and, in their view, no meaningful action had resulted. Several times students wanted some assurance that their voices would be heard this time around. Other students wanted to know the practical benefits of the study in terms of improving their schooling and education.

Interviews with some students were very painful and at times emotionally charged. Some students broke down as they recounted details of their experiences. There was one particular moment in a focus-group interview when a student identified a mate in the group as her role model and idol. The expression of surprise and the tears on the face of the individual who was identified will not be soon forgotten. On another occasion, a student refused to identify the person she looked up to in society. This was because, as she put it, this person was in the focus group and she did not want her to feel 'too proud.' The student then broke down and cried when telling us how much she admired this individual.

The study also had an emotional toll on researchers. We often took the students' experiences to heart and became concerned about the implications of this research. If the reader feels that the remainder of this book is overstocked with quotes from our participants, we worried about keeping our commitment to the students and ensuring that this time as many voices as possible would be heard. It was also difficult when we realized that the students were opening up to us in ways that perhaps they normally do not do in the school setting. We needed to be particularly cautious in respecting their privacy as we spoke to other students and school personnel.

Students also told us that they did not have the opportunity to discuss social issues, particularly racism, in school. Frequently, the focus-group interviews we organized were the only times they had an opportunity to discuss this topic with peers. For both Black and non-Black students, dialogues about race developed into heated discussions. The researchers often left the school after these group sessions feeling that they had only scratched the surface and that these students could have contributed much more, if given the opportunity. Finally, we often returned to our 'centre of academe' feeling that we had not 'done enough' for our participants. Through the dissemination of this data, we hope we can begin to give something back to them.

Data Analysis

Analysis of the narratives collected from students (Black and non-Black), 'drop-outs,' teachers, administrators, and parents involved a two-step reading process. Using a software program designed to sort qualitative data, transcripts were coded and recoded according to interview structure and emergent themes. The participation of four research assistants in the analysis made it possible to have a number of different readers of each file and to gain general familiarity with the data collected.

Research data from students, teachers, school administrators, parents, and community workers was cross-referenced, and focus-group meetings were used to cross-check our interpretations of individual and group narratives with the study participants. Research data was analysed qualitatively and quantitatively to reflect general trends, and particularly the impact of gender and social difference on the issue of student disengagement and the process of 'dropping out' or 'fading out' of school. Through triangulation we have been able to compare individual narratives and show both general and distinctive trends.

The preliminary reading of the transcripts involved coding the files according to the questions asked in the interviews. Students interviewed were asked a series of questions pertaining to their perceptions of 'drop-outs,' school experiences, and their overall vantage point in society (see Appendices 1–9 for a complete list of interview questions). The responses to these questions were coded according to the particular framing, so that the context for any segment is immediately discernible. Once codes were entered in the computer program, searches for particular combinations of codes by variables could be conducted. Variables attached to student files included gender, age, grade, stream, and place of birth.

The searching of files was completed primarily by looking for quotations, in combination with each of the question frames, that were considered representative, salient, compelling, or notable for other reasons. In this way, a generalized understanding of students' responses to each question was established and themes highlighted. From this examination, a broader synthesis of themes in the narratives, as well as the way in which the process of disengagement was constructed by students, were established in focus meetings of the analysis team. The process of theme coding was accompanied by additional tracking of student responses to some of the questions. Our quantitative summary has allowed numerical values to be attached to some of the issues addressed in the analysis, such as the importance of having Black teachers and guidance counsellors, whether or not students shared a sense of commonality with other Black students, positive and negative expectations for the future of Black youth in the school system, and so on.

The in-depth analysis of narratives followed a flexibly structured framework, which allowed the words of the students, parents, and teachers to direct the coding. Particular themes emerged which informed the development of a 'theme code set.' The cross-referencing of themes with question frames was useful in providing a context for understanding the relationship between two or more issues. For example, if some students emphasized aspects of their religion when asked about their identity, claims about the construction of identity through religion would be strengthened in that the connections were made by students, rather than being generated or solicited by the interviewer.

We approached the analysis of data in a collaborative manner. This approach brings with it many benefits and perhaps some pitfalls. Working as a collegial team, with each member characterized by differing socio-cultural and/or racial locations and ideologies, can be challenging, especially when each researcher exercises a relatively equal level of input in the project. Discussion and debate regarding significant issues in the findings are invaluable to the final product and are perhaps the greatest benefit of this approach. We found that by working as a group, the study was enriched by various points of view and different areas of expertise. Giving each member a significant role in the analysis of the data allowed us to conceptualize the outcomes from multiple vantage points, thereby adding a complexity to our conclusions and deepening the layers of our analysis.

The narratives which follow are the result of our research endeavour. We attempt to portray the issues through the words of various stakeholders in education, particularly 'drop-outs' and students. Through the use of qualitative research, we have captured the emotions and experiences of students as they interact with the education system. We believe that through this process we have respectfully represented the compellingly powerful experiences and views of our participants.

Chapter Three

The Social Construction of a 'Drop-out': Dispelling the Myth

The narratives assembled in this ethnography draw from experiential frames of reference to give meaning to the term 'drop-out.' The collective meaning which emerges is a composite of behavioural traits, attitudes, and socially constructed notions which are often at odds with one another. These notions speak to the fact that the term 'drop-out' represents different things to different people, all of whom speak from particular vantage points. The various perspectives which emerge emanate from specific ideologies and world-views, including some which challenge the 'conventional wisdom' regarding drop-outs and others which reinforce standard misconceptions. By employing race as a factor, the stereotypes and stigmas of dropping out of school take on different meanings and are seen to affect students in specific ways.

Students were asked specifically to define a drop-out. Black and non-Black students generally agreed that the term refers to someone who stops coming to school. However, some students also included in their definition of a drop-out students who are still officially 'at' school, but who are involved in a process of 'fading out' or disengagement. These students were characterized as skipping classes, hanging out, 'acting out,' and not being involved in the formal aspects of the school. These behaviours often represent the first stage in a process of disengagement, yet many of these warning signs are ignored or inappropriately addressed by school agents. In this way, the term 'drop-out' does not adequately capture the students' experiences of schooling and why they leave school prematurely. The term 'fade-out' may be more appropriate because students may be there in body but not in spirit.

The question of whether students who change schools may be considered drop-outs also became relevant. The implication of the question is whether failing in a particular environment qualifies as 'dropping out.' Student narratives were unanimous – a drop-out is someone who completely disengages from the system, not one who changes environments. Students who transfer to different schools were understood generally to have experienced failure or other problems at the previous school – conflicts with administration, teachers, or students – and were seeking an alternative environment in which they could succeed. In fact, when students actively seek out alternative school environments and succeed, this serves to validate their assessment of the problems they felt they were facing previously.

The ways in which students framed their understanding of why some students drop out of school can be related to certain ideological positions. Some responses conceptualized drop-outs as 'push-outs,' implicating outside forces such as adverse economic conditions, realities of the social structure, and personal problems, all of which conspire to force individuals out of school. Kin, a grade 12 student, was clear about the existence of barriers which compel some students to drop out:

> Drop-outs are ... students who have some kind of personal problems or anything socially that doesn't allow them to actually continue school or even work. They can't, whatever the problem may be, they can't actually continue school. *They have no other choice.* (File W01: lines 24–32)

Other responses provided examples of individualized and meritocratic world-views in which individuals are implicated as the sole architects of their success or failure. These views can be said to form the basis of popular notions or what is known as the 'conventional wisdom' regarding drop-outs. Suneel, an OAC student, framed the decision to drop out as a free choice, not a reaction to circumstance:

... it's like if ... you drop out, it means that you don't want to come
to school or you choose not to come to school. And *it's up to you*, it's
your decision. Nobody won't force you to go. (File B04: lines 22–8)

Conversely, some students isolated factors related to the notion of a
'hidden curriculum,' that is, the attitudes and behaviours of teachers and other school agents which may affect a student's decision to
leave school. Fema, a Black grade 10 general level student, identified interpersonal relationships as a factor in the decision-making
process:

I understand that lots of people dropped out because some of them
are saying how much a teacher don't like them and stuff like that.
(File D27: lines 11–14)

Fema addresses the powerful effect of the interpersonal relationship between teachers and students and the repercussions which
can occur if this relationship is perceived to be negative.

Coupled with ideological factors, it becomes apparent that
'drop-out' is a loaded term and commonly embodies an aetiology.
When causes are connected to individual shortcomings, they contribute to negative stereotypes and the stigmatization of leaving
school, rather than implicating the school and society as part of the
problem. When race is accounted for as a factor, these stereotypes
are seen by Lea, another grade 10 general level student, to contribute to the low expectations held for Black students:

I feel so angry; I get so bitter inside for them because it's like this is
what people expect of some Black people, that they can't accomplish
nothing. They can't be a doctor or a lawyer ... they're not capable.
They're ignorant, as 'they' put it. They always say we're ignorant,
and it just, it makes us look so low. (File W17: lines 100–20)

The anger expressed here is empathetic and directed, not towards
the drop-outs, but rather to their predicament. This young woman
not only identifies the negative stereotypes associated with dropping out, but highlights how those stereotypes are connected with

racial and cultural biases. In other words, for a White student, dropping out may carry the stigma of perceived failure but it is not automatically ascribed to racial or cultural factors, which is what is understood to occur when the student is Black. The preceding quotation is evidence of how the stigma associated with Black students who drop out affects even those students who remain in school, since it legitimizes perceived notions of the inferiority of all Black people. Therefore, the negative stereotypes and social stigmas carried by Black students who drop out affect not only themselves but, in effect, the status and perception of all Blacks in society.

Students expressed a range of feelings from sadness to empathy to anger. In response to the question of why students drop out of school, students frequently began with statements like 'It's too bad, I feel sorry for them.' Many students spoke in terms which did not blame drop-outs, but rather empathized with their reality. Lesline, an OAC level student, shared her insight into this reality:

> I don't scorn them, because I feel my friends ... would be considered drop-outs. But because I know them, I understand that there's politics involved when they say you are a drop-out or when you decide to. Some people, they're bored, and you say that's not a valid reason, but after being bored for two years and you haven't gotten let's say eight credits, and ... you're like, 'I'll be in school longer and longer and it'll get more boring and more frustrating' ... a lot of friends have left because of that. Some people leave because they just can't, they can't find themselves in school ... (File O03: lines 73–95)

Lesline talks about the need to understand the reality faced by students and the importance which that understanding has for legitimizing their experiences. The references to not being able to 'find themselves in school,' and to the sense of 'frustration' and 'boredom,' reveal the emotional and psychological conditions which are seen as contributing to the process of disengagement. These feelings are understood as the result of the 'politics' of schooling, in which students who are unable to conform to the demands of the education system feel marginalized and eventually fade out of school.

The narratives addressed varying problems facing students. Financial concerns, 'family problems,' pregnancy, problems in the school related to racism, relationships with teachers, lack of academic success, and how some students simply cannot cope were identified as the primary issues affecting the lives of students. This reveals an identification with the complex and varied experiences of disengagement, both through personal experience and association.

When students talked about the future for drop-outs, it was frequently associated with negative activities such as dealing drugs, hanging out, collecting welfare, and so on. Yet at times some students mentioned the positive outcome of getting work, despite not having finished school. In this regard, a practical understanding of how drop-outs might assess their immediate future is expressed by Susan, an OAC student:

> They don't think after high school they're going to have anything else so they want to go pursue something that will give them some economic benefit right now. (File B19: lines 24–8)

Despondency over future employment prospects reflected an understanding of the changing realities of work in late capitalist society. Students questioned the practical benefits of education in a limited and fluctuating labour market. At times negative and somewhat fatalistic attitudes about future options were expressed. In this context, the exploitation of short-term gains at the expense of long-term goals such as continued education appeared more pragmatic.

More often students were critical of abandoning long-term goals, arguing that drop-outs are myopic in not seeing the connection between work and school. Some students empathized with wanting to leave school but felt it was not practical. The repeated comment 'Even to be a garbage-man you need grade 12' among students still in school indicated their awareness that one had to 'play the game' in order to succeed. Education was understood as a means to an end rather than an end in itself. This understanding highlights the clear connection made between education and future economic opportunities.

Students were generally sympathetic towards drop-outs, empathizing with the disadvantage they feel drop-outs have in society, as a result of their lack of education. As Danielle, a Jamaican-born grade 12 student, indicated, these difficulties are compounded by the issue of race:

> I think it's sad and I think that [Black students] can do better. It's hard enough being the most obvious minority and having to live with that, but the lack of education will only hurt them more. (File D24: lines 139–45)

The discrimination and difficulty experienced in being Black is clearly described by this student as being intensified when a Black student drops out of school. Dropping out therefore creates a double impediment: racial discrimination compounded by a lack of education. As this student explained, Black students who drop out are regarded by some of their peers as following a course of action, whether or not it is of their own volition, which will serve to further disadvantage them within society.

Black students tended to speak about symptoms of disengaging rather than specific characteristics. They expressed a deep identification with the experience of not feeling as though they 'belonged.' Kenneth, a Carribean-born student in the advanced stream of grade 11, related the feelings of alienation felt by students who eventually drop out:

> Mostly it's just the person who's, like, being stretched out, stretching him or herself out, and saying that they don't feel like they belong. They don't feel like they belong in the school ... (File B07: lines 356–62)

The notion of 'stretching him or herself out' implies a certain incongruence of the reality of the student with that of the school and the pressures felt to conform. For Black and minority students this sense of not 'belonging' is often related to the centrality of White middle-class norms and values within the educational system (see Ogbu 1982b; Delpit 1988). An inability or unwillingness to conform serves to marginalize the culture and realities of minority students, and in effect the students themselves. When the interests of these students remain peripheral to mainstream education, the students themselves will feel similarly situated outside the boundaries of social acceptance. This process of marginalization can be seen to engender a school culture and climate that is perceived as unresponsive and excluding.

A few of the students interviewed had dropped out or had come close to dropping out. These students shared anecdotes and insights into their experiences. Wendy, a grade 10 advanced level student, discussed the feelings of dissonance and anomie experienced when she could not relate to other Black students after starting at a new school where the majority of students were White:

> After I moved up here, I didn't really like the area. I thought that I didn't really fit in because nobody was really the same as me. Even the Black students were different from me ... they were a bit more White to me than what I was used to and I just didn't really like the school. I didn't fit in ... I didn't feel like going because to me there was no reason to go. I had nothing to look forward to going there. (File R02: lines 1476–90)

Wendy expressed a sense of detachment from members of her own race and ethnic background who acted 'a bit more White.' This detachment addresses the paradox of cultural conformity, in which, as individuals become culturally and socially more integrated into the mainstream, they often distance themselves from members of their own ethno-cultural group. In this instance, the student feels a sense of double alienation, from mainstream society and from members of her own community who have conformed to the status quo. The importance of school culture and the social aspects of schooling therefore cannot be underestimated in terms of their impact on student disengagement.

Students who had not given serious consideration to dropping out cited family influences as the main reason for not doing so. Responses such as 'Oh yeah, I've thought about it, but my Mom would kill me' were prevalent when the students discussed their own situations. This suggests that parents and the values they hold are powerful deterrents to leaving school. People within the school (teachers, counsellors, administrators, etc.), however, were not mentioned as persons students could or would approach. In fact, students did not relate to them as people who they felt would care or try to intervene in a positive way. This view reveals the perception many students have of school agents and their inability to provide the kind of support students require.

The topic of disengagement elicited discussions of parental relationships, values, and responsibilities. Students talked about their connection to a parent and their desire to make that parent (and others in the family) proud. Many young males also spoke about being able to provide for their mothers in the future. As well, the limited opportunities experienced by their parents and how this affects their own motivation to stay in school was mentioned by male and female students alike. Rana, a grade 10 advanced student of Caribbean descent, stated:

> ... I'm just kind of holding back because of my dad ... he had a chance to get his education but he didn't really do that. He was supporting his younger brothers and sisters and stuff. And now today he's got a good job and everything but he could have done better ... So, I'm kind of, you know, just staying on. (File O30: lines 133–44)

Many students said they would not even discuss the idea of dropping out with their parents. Rather, siblings and peers, if anyone, were indicated as people they would confide in if they were thinking about dropping out. In fact, for all students, the people who they indicated would most likely serve as confidants were friends.

When those who have been through the process of disengagement from school conceptualize, interpret, and give meaning to the term 'drop-out,' they invariably do so from a radically different vantage point than do students still in the system. The latter, whether 'at risk' or not, talked hypothetically about what dropping out might mean, whereas for actual drop-outs, the years (or months) of experience after leaving school had put a different 'spin' on the meanings and interpretations they gave to the term 'drop-out.'

Drop-outs tended to discuss dropping out as a personal loss – as a decision which had resulted in lost time, lost chances, and/or lost status in society. In this way, their narratives do coincide with those of many of the students. Yet drop-outs tended not to blame themselves for dropping out and still maintained that their decision made sense at the time. They defined the process of dropping out as one of gradual disengagement from school, a process which, for some, began as early as grade 2. Drop-outs were able to reach back into their early memories of schooling to locate experiences that related to the beginning of their own process of disengagement. Jennifer talked about how racial discrimination and isolation laid the groundwork for her decision to drop out:

> ... it was in fourth grade ... I had a teacher, she blatantly did not want to teach me anything. And I was the only Black kid there in the school, in the neighbourhood, in the whole area ... yeah, she was something else. (File F03: lines 254–61)

Jennifer's comment also makes connections to the broader impact of the local community and social relations, and the alienation which permeated her experiences in and out of school. Later in the same interview, these early negative experiences are described as having had a constraining effect on her future aspirations:

> ... by the time I got to high school, I didn't think I was smart for anything so university was never, ever, ever in my dreams ... (File F03: lines 315–18)

This shows how low expectations, negative reinforcement, and alienation associated with dropping out are internalized and can place limits on self-esteem and ultimately life chances.

Students tended to say that drop-outs do not feel that school is 'for them.' Drop-outs echoed this sentiment as they talked about a drop-out as someone for whom the school is an unfriendly, uncomfortable, and unwelcoming place:

> They're not comfortable, you know, the environment that they're in is not really for them, and they're feeling sort of, like discouragement about not going to school anymore. (File F10: lines 60–4)

Here Robert exemplifies the personal and academic constraints that result from a negative school environment. The social aspects of schooling are therefore important to the level of students' satisfaction with their educational experience and can ultimately influence their decision of whether or not to remain in school.

Drop-outs tended to relate dropping out as a failure on the part of the school rather than as a failure on the part of the individual who leaves. Darren, a drop-out himself, spoke directly to this issue:

> I don't see them as people who failed. I see them as people that the system failed ... (File F13: lines 2594–8)

Perhaps because of a lack of confidence in the system within which they had once been marginalized, the drop-outs were concerned that their voices would not be heard. They, more than any other group interviewed in this study, questioned whether anyone would listen or truly respond to their concerns.

Non-Black students did not have a clear image or stereotype regarding drop-outs – anyone can and does drop out. These students also spoke of dropping out as a process, and among the factors they mentioned which they believed led to dropping out, the most notable was negative attitudes towards school. Peter, an OAC level student, was unequivocal in his opinion:

> People who don't want to learn, just don't want to be in school, they just decide to take a hike and leave. (File CG05: lines 10–12)

This type of response, which attributes responsibility for dropping out to the individual, who is someone who 'does not want to learn' or does not like school, was a common one for non-Black students. Whereas Black students were usually able to acknowledge certain outside forces which impact negatively on a student's ability to remain in school, non-Black students were less cognizant of such factors (e.g., racism). Although they might acknowledge that some students dropped out of school as a result of financial difficulties, their vantage point did not seem to equip them with a clear understanding of how systemic barriers may hinder the progress of those who are less privileged on the basis of their racial or ethnic identity.

The understandings and opinions held by teachers about the meanings and interpretations associated with dropping out of school and other related issues can be said to reflect different locations on an ideological spectrum. These views may be characterized as ranging from 'conservative' to 'progressive.' Although social location (gender, race, class, age, etc.) frequently influenced the ideological position held by individuals, it was not necessarily a determining factor. Generally speaking, older White males who described themselves as having life experiences which did not include close relationships with Black/African Canadians would be defined as being conservative. Conversely, younger, female, and non-White teachers, or White males who had had life experiences involving Black/African Canadians, had what we defined as more progressive attitudes. Conservative responses were consistent with a belief in meritocracy and denied the saliency of race as an organizing principle for differential treatment within educational institutions. They were similarly unsupportive of anti-racism and multicultural initiatives in education. More progressive opinions, however, usually reflected a deeper understanding or appreciation of Black students' experiences and acknowledged the need for more inclusive schools.

Teachers with more conservative views tended to conceptualize dropping out as a choice, made solely by students who chose not to be focused. They pointed to several other contributory factors, such as becoming pregnant, acting out generalized adolescent alienation, frustration as the result of not being taught the basics earlier on in school, lack of motivation, lack of a belief in the possibility of success, unstable family homes, and an absence of certain attitudes needed in order to succeed. In particular, these teachers saw dropping out as related to a societal attitude of 'taking the easy way out' or 'not taking responsibility.' They often spoke of the lack of a 'work ethic' in students, how students want instant gratification and don't realize that one has to work to get things.

Teachers expressing opinions corresponding with the conservative end of the spectrum recognized that drop-outs might 'blame the institution' for their lack of success but saw this blame as misplaced. Andrew, who had been teaching history for thirty years, referred directly to a faulty interpretation of responsibility on the part of students:

> You don't have to be responsible. And so I think they end up here, many of them without having thought anything out, without putting any effort into anything. And when they find that seven different teachers treat them seven different ways and there doesn't seem to be any consistency in that, then they look at the institution and they say, 'The institution sucks. It doesn't know what it's doing. Why should I be here? Why should I do what they say? They don't even know what they're doing.' And so they sort of give up. It's almost as if they come wanting to give up before they even start. (File T01: lines 472–87)

Here Andrew implies that drop-outs are somehow predisposed to having negative attitudes about schooling. However, this interpretation does not account for why these students have negative attitudes in the first place. It therefore holds the student accountable without first subjecting other factors related to schooling to the same critical examination.

Other teachers saw the drop-out dilemma as the result of inappropriate placement. They argued that students with a history of failure are frustrated when they come up against the reality of their failure. Some teachers suggested that certain students cannot function within the rigid structures of the school system and would do better in co-op programs. This explanation once again reduces the issue to an individual's failure to meet the demands of the system. It does not, however, confront the issue of whether the system has systematically failed the student. Thus, in cases in which individual ability or academic aptitude is of concern, this should be a demonstrated concern rather than a foregone conclusion.

Some teachers viewed the family as the key to a student's dropping out. The ability of a single-parent household to provide the necessary support to students was seen as problematic. It was frequently held that single parents have less time and often a lack of education, and that children in these environments take advantage of their parents' ignorance of the school system. The perceived dysfunctional nature of such families was seen by these teachers as a primary factor in student disengagement. While families in crisis are of concern, the drop-out problem cannot be reduced to this issue. Implicating the 'dysfunctional family' as the source of educational difficulties for the child, in a sense, divests the school from responsibility and fails to interrogate the difficulty many parents feel in engaging with the educational system. Parents from non-White backgrounds, in particular, often feel alienated by the school environment (Dehli 1994). Language difficulties and cultural notions which lead to feelings of intimidation by the authoritative structure of schooling, as well as a lack of minority representation within school administrations, are specific impediments to parental involvement. Therefore, in order to achieve a mutually beneficial partnership, schools must confront the barriers which distance home from school and create the means for parents to effectively engage with the school system.

A number of teachers described the drop-out as someone lacking the requisite work ethic needed for academic success – an individual for whom school is unimportant and socializing is of primary importance. For most teachers, the absence of discipline and respect for the school system was seen as a problem. Interestingly, this was a view also held by many students. Yet the feeling was prevalent among those teachers defined as conservative that there are plenty of support services of which students may choose to take advantage if they are experiencing difficulty – it is the student's choice. Disengagement, then, is understood as related to a lack of motivation and desire on the part of students.

These attitudes contrast sharply with the views of drop-outs themselves, who felt incumbered by the system and by the low expectations of teachers, rather than by their own sense of apathy. This explanation also does not correspond to the depth of emotion many drop-outs exhibited when discussing their decision to leave school. From the narratives of drop-outs, it was clear that it was not a decision taken lightly as some teachers may believe. In their narratives, teachers did not address what, for students and drop-outs, may be considered deterrents to accessing the of support services provided by the schools.

A decided minority of teachers, who were more progressive in their understanding of the difficulties facing Black youth, viewed possible reasons for disengagement as lodged in the school system. In this way, they conceptualized dropping out as a process, as opposed to an isolated decision based on individualized notions of failure. Although these teachers also tended to see dropping out as a specific choice, they cited reasons which included not only personal and family variables but school variables as well. Some of these teachers also noted that the schools are not adequately addressing the needs of students who feel that school is meaningless and boring. They felt that the problems students have outside the school are intensified by the lack of support within the institution.

For their part, as stakeholders in the educational system, parents see the drop-out problem as a major issue for the Black/African-Canadian community. They are concerned about their children 'making the grade,' and particularly about youth who no longer see education as a tool to achieve their life ambitions and dreams. When asked to describe students who have dropped out, parents used images which appear to reflect both systemic difficulties in the school system and individual issues with students. Marilyn, a mother, responded to the term 'drop-out' with the following:

It means to me that they're kids who the system has failed and it has turned them off of school ... because ... when you look at the kids who are drop-outs and they turn around and do something and then succeed at it, it means that they had the capability but it was not tapped ... If the system had provided the necessary nurturing for those kids, they would have made it. (File P04: lines 6–27)

Marilyn argues that the educational system has to address the students' need for nurturing and focus on identifying the abilities and potential of students. By addressing these needs, she believes the level of achievement for Black students would be positively affected.

The idea that more could be done to ensure that students complete high school is prevalent throughout the parent narratives. Amma, a Black woman who works with youth on a regular basis, interpreted the term 'drop-out' as referring to students who have somehow 'lost their way':

When I think about that person I think about someone who is ... alienated ... disillusioned ... frustrated. Somebody who has just basically given up in believing the school system can work for them or that it can make a difference. Yeah, when I hear that term, I put it in that context right away, in terms of issues ... I see it as something that is prevalent within our community ... as a matter of fact, some of the kids that I've come in contact with are some kids who are finished grade eleven, grade twelve and who are not even aware that they can go on beyond that, or that there's assistance for them to go on beyond that. It just boggles my mind that they feel, 'This is as far as I'm going to get.' (File CW1: lines 25–58)

Students who leave school early are seen by parents to be those who have lost interest in the school system for a variety of reasons. These students are seen, through a combination of their school experiences and personal lives, as having become disconnected with an educational system that does not strive to engage them.

The contrast that exists between the ideological vantage points of conservative teachers and non-Black students, on the one hand, and those of Black students, drop-outs, and Black parents and community workers, on the other, represents a clear dichotomy in the way drop-outs are conceptualized by these groups. For example, the conservative perspective tends to individualize reasons for dropping out and to point to factors such as negative attitudes towards schooling, lack of a work ethic, and low scholastic achievement. Conservative responses do not implicate schools or the educational system for contributing to the drop-out problem, except for a decided minority which cited some culpability on the part of schools and educators. The issue of race was not mentioned. While there may be a tendency to interpret such an omission as positive, it actually points to a disregard or lack of understanding of how issues of race can contribute to the process of disengagement for Black and other minority students. Although, ideally, race would not be a factor related to educational success, the students' and drop-outs' narratives show that it is.

Narratives from the other end of the ideological spectrum (most Black students, drop-outs, Black parents and community workers) generally highlighted alienation, failure of the school system, and lack of support within schools as being some of the preconditions for Black students' disengagement from school. It was felt that family values in the Black community were conducive to greater perseverance in school than suggested by those teachers who viewed drop-outs as the product of dysfunctional homes. While 'family problems' can certainly impact negatively on a student's school life and may ultimately affect the process of disengagement, this should not overshadow the positive effects of family ethics and values which many students carry with them into their educative experiences. Black students stated that it was concern for their parents and the thought of how the repercussions of their dropping out would affect their parents that helped give them the impetus to remain in school. While some teachers and non-Black students tended to locate the epicentre of the drop-out phenomenon within the family structure and within the individual themselves, drop-outs, Black students, and Black parents and community workers generally implicated racism and the inefficiencies of the educational system as the co-determinants of Black students' disengagement.

The fact that many Black students stay in school and complete their education 'successfully' gives the false impression that systemic barriers within the educational system do not exist or, at the very least, are overstated. Some students are successful in spite of genuine educational problems, and many do in fact give something up, specifically in terms of their identity, in order to 'succeed' (see Fordham 1988). The issue is framed in another way by Fine (1991, 7), who states in her study of drop-outs in an urban New York high school that for her, after 'uncovering layers of systemic, widespread school failure, the question was no longer why a student would drop out. It was more compelling to consider why so many would stay ...' The narratives suggest that once students get on the track of fading out (e.g., skipping classes, sitting in the back of class, hanging out in hallways, 'acting out,' being truant), schools often help them 'out the door.' These behaviours may be symptoms of a larger problem and can often tell us something about the process of schooling rather than simply about the individual. 'Acting out' and other forms of anti-school behaviour among Black and minority students is often viewed as a means of resistance to school authority (Giroux 1983a, 1983b; Solomon 1992; Willis 1977). It is important to recognize the limits of resistance theories and that all oppositional behaviours cannot necessarily be connected to defiance of school authority; still, an understanding of the socio-political implications of such behaviour among Black and minority youth does often lead to this conclusion.

As the narratives in this chapter have shown, understanding student disengagement involves redefining ideologically conditioned notions of failure and misapprehensions regarding 'drop-outs' through an examination of the lived realities of students who must contend with what Fine (1991, 6) characterizes as 'the rationalized policies and practices of exclusion' within public schooling. Contrary to the conventional wisdom surrounding the issue of student disengagement, Black respondents did not associate low scholastic achievement with dropping out. Dropping out was recognized as a process which had much broader social and cultural implications.

There is no simple cause-effect relation which characterizes Black students' disengagement from school. Dropping out is the final act of a series of school and out-of-school developments/experiences that define the student's ability to engage and disengage in a school's culture. Students drop out of school when it appears, in their view, there is no other appropriate recourse or action to take.

The following chapter delves further into the aetiology of student disengagement. As in the present chapter, the narratives of the drop-outs, students, parents and community workers continue to provide the frame of reference through which the dynamics of Black students' disengagement are explored and understood.

Chapter Four

Understanding Student Disengagement

This chapter will examine the various factors identified by students, drop-outs, parents, and teachers as contributing to student disengagement. The narratives point to the ways in which school structures and policies can facilitate a student's decision to leave school. It will further illustrate the difference between students who leave school prematurely because of pragmatic reasons, such as pregnancy or the need to work, and those characterized as 'push-outs': students who, for various reasons, feel forced out of school.

Student narratives are further examined in terms of the positive and negative experiences of school they relate, and the implications these experiences have in the processes of engagement and disengagement. Home, family life, and harsh economic realities have a decided role to play in whether or not school is the most viable option for many students. The perceived relevance of education is often preconditioned by these factors. For Black students, education in a racialized society carries specific challenges and can lead to differential treatment within schools. Race is a constant factor among many varying social and economic situations which confront Black youth and is a major frame of reference for the experiences of those in this study.

Finally, the phenomenon of re-entry or 'dropping in' as it was experienced by some of the drop-outs and parents interviewed will be discussed. This phenomenon holds important lessons in the reconceptualization of drop-outs and contributes to our understanding of possible strategies for change.

Accounting for Student Disengagement

When asked directly what factors students felt contribute to disengagement and dropping out, Black students provided a variety of responses. These factors were perceived as contributory and not seen as having a direct causal relationship. While 'problems at home' was the most frequent response given, students also talked about economic situations in which students must work to support the family, or parents work at more than one job to make ends meet. In fact, economic factors were the second most frequent response. Students also talked about drop-outs not living at home and therefore having to work.

'Family problems' was a phrase used along with 'problems at home' to bring up the idea of emotional problems that would keep students from participating in the school. When asked if dropping out was an 'easy' thing to do, Susan, an OAC level student, made explicit reference to this issue:

> If your mom or your dad are out of the house all the time, they don't know what you're doing, it's an easy thing to start. If the parents don't seem to care, it's easy to get away with. If they kick you out, then it's an easy thing to do because nobody's watching over you ... If you don't want to go to school, you just don't go ... If your parents make you go, then you're not going to drop out. (File B19: lines 64–77)

Susan speaks to the issue of how problems within the home can contribute to the decision to leave school prematurely, either through financial pressures or lack of support. Reference to 'family problems' or 'home' must be understood to contain a variety of issues: unemployment for parents or parents holding two and three jobs; students living independently and managing a home while attending school; students living with guardians or extended family until the family can be reunited; and, at times, conflict within the family.

It became clear that students see issues of the family as only one of a complex set of issues that affect students' disengagement from school. Kenneth, a grade 11 advanced student quoted previously, identified three main issues which implicate both the family and the school:

> ... the main three ... problems at home, the school's not teaching them what they need to know, and the racism. The racism, particularly, is the main factor in most schools. (File B07: lines 185–90)

Experiences of racism, whether stated explicitly or implied, were a constant theme throughout students' narratives. 'Pressure,' a term that was used frequently, seemed to underlie the complex web of factors that affect a student's ability to engage formal schooling the way it is presently structured. In a joint interview with grade 10 students Faye and Karen, 'pressure' was understood to involve issues of racism and alienation within the culture of the school:

> Maybe the racial pressure ... Also, I guess, if you're being, let's say, the sole Black person in school, it can be difficult ... you feel like a raisin in a glass of milk ... (File R01: lines 209–23)

This analogy illustrates powerfully the alienation felt by Black students immersed within dominantly White schools, and relates to the pressures associated with this environment which may eventually lead to dropping out.

Difficulty and pressure were among the most common responses with respect to the factors involved in dropping out. Difficulty in handling school pressures along with feelings of isolation were expressed by Blythe, a grade 12 student:

> Most of them, they're uncomfortable and they come to school and nobody knows what's going on, how they feel. They could be all alone inside. And they just don't perform at all. They just go to class and they just look in space and they just keep failing. And when the pressure becomes too much, they missed out so much in the class and they can't do nothing. They just drop out. (File D26: lines 390–400)

Pressure seemed to be a pervasive element of students' situations which ultimately caused strain and anxiety. Some students went on to refer specifically to issues of homework, other students or friends, their economic situation, relations with authority, and rules. It appears that this inability to cope could not be overcome despite the existence of school support systems which are designed for this express purpose.

Various references to the behaviours of teachers were also among the five most frequent responses to the question of why students leave school. 'Schools pushing them out' and 'not being encouraged' were other explanations given for why students dropped out. Karen and Faye's discussion above continues with suggestions that the school is not doing enough to encourage students:

> I don't think the teachers provide enough encouragement towards students, particularly Black students. Whereas in my situation, I know who I want to be, I know where I want to go, so I know about myself as a Black person, so I don't need their encouragement. I know where I have to be and I know where I have to go. (File R01: lines 470–9)

Race is inextricably tied to these shared experiences and, in this case, to students' relationships with teachers. While the above student's confidence in her identity is expressly stated, other students confirmed long histories of school experiences which served to undermine their self-esteem and self-confidence. A grade 11 student, Charlene, reflected on such experiences of her friends:

> I think that they're discouraged and they feel like they can't make a difference if they go ... they feel like they're not part of it, that they're different, that they can't learn ... A lot of people were told that they were stupid in elementary school, especially a lot of my friends and ... they hear it so much it's like a self-fulfilling prophecy. You just hear it all the time and their family doesn't say anything like, 'No, you're not' and so they just say, 'Okay, I'm not smart, I can't do it.' (File R05: lines 480–502)

In the above, Charlene implicates both the school and the home in terms of responsibility for the perpetuation of these self-images. She also speaks to the perception of differential treatment among Black students which lays the groundwork for a history of negative school experiences. Lack of encouragement by teachers and family serve to compromise personal and cultural self-esteem. The result, a diminished sense of confidence in one's ability, can therefore lead to a sense of fatalism in which, as these narratives show, students begin to internalize negative self-concepts and feel that the demands of schooling are beyond their capabilities. This sense of hopelessness is commonly stated as a precursor to disengagement and must therefore be resolved in order for students to succeed.

Another common response involved how teachers and administrators take up school policies in ways which appear counterproductive to keeping students in school. The practice of being sent to the office for being late and then be kept for anywhere from ten to thirty minutes with other latecomers was an example frequently cited. Students suggested that this practice only exacerbates the situation by forcing students to miss a greater amount of class time than if they had been allowed to stay in class. Similarly, the practice of suspension for skipping class was also mentioned. Students indicated that once kids get on the track of 'fading out,' by skipping class for instance, the school helps them 'out the door' by suspending them.

A large number of Black students identified specifically, and often immediately, that the absence of Black history/Black culture could be a reason for dropping out. Frequently this was related to the process of disengagement through an understanding that these students became bored with what they were learning at school. Black students often felt that for them, the Eurocentric nature of the curriculum had a lack of relevance. Willis, a grade 12 student from Africa, noted the problem of relevance, particularly with respect to history:

> ... maybe they get bored or ... Like, okay, I take history and I don't
> like the way my teacher teaches history, he never explains to us the
> [real] history about Blacks ... So, maybe that's the reason ... they

drop out, because they think they don't learn anything. (File W26: lines 64–73)

Willis speaks to issues of teaching styles which are not inclusive and partial accounts of history which exclude the contributions and experiences of Black/African Canadians. According to Willis, denying legitimacy to the Black experience in Canada can contribute to the process of disengagement. It is interesting that while the issue of curriculum was specifically addressed later in the interviews, students made this connection when asked why students leave school. The school was seen as unable to engage students and, in turn, students were seen as unable to make relevant connections between their education and their everyday lives. The student narratives revealed that racial issues and a Eurocentric curriculum play a large role in discouraging Black students from pursuing their education. Descriptions like those provided by Willis also demonstrate that when students do not see themselves or their interests represented, they develop a fatalistic attitude about themselves, their education, and their future.

The school practice of streaming, particularly 'colour-coded streaming,' that is, streaming which is structured along racial lines, was also cited as a reason for students disengaging from the system. Victoria, a drop-out who had returned to high school as a mature student, talked about how this practice not only negates self-confidence and contributes to the perpetuation of negative racial stereotypes, but also affected her decision at one point to drop out of school:

I can tell you the reason why I dropped out! ... The school that I went to, they made me feel like I wasn't smart enough to do the stuff. They told my parents to send me to a technical school. They treated Blacks like we had no brains ... and that the Chinese were smarter, the Whites were better, so I just said, 'Forget it!' (File W33: lines 19–41)

It seems clear that when low expectations for Black students are juxtaposed with positive evaluations given to other racial groups, it compromises not only personal but cultural self-esteem. When these negative conceptions are internalized by students, despondency and a sense of fatalism towards their educational futures set in.

Among other factors, pregnancy was also a frequent explanation offered for why students drop out of school. This factor seemed to be understood as a final step when re-entry into school was unlikely. Interestingly, the issue of pregnancy was not framed in terms of how it affected males. It was framed as an individual issue which affected a female's ability to pursue her education. Acknowledgment of pregnancy as a factor in dropping out was much more pervasive among the young women interviewed – 80 per cent of the respondents who recognized pregnancy as a factor were women. The issue of male responsibility and accountability was left unaddressed.

While Black students tended to isolate specific factors associated with disengagement, drop-outs tended to talk about dropping out in a more holistic fashion. They tended to construct dropping out as a gradual disengagement process in which students are simply not given support and encouragement for schooling, particularly by school agents (teachers, guidance counsellors, and administrators) but also by friends and parents. Drop-outs tended to view teachers and guidance counsellors as having given them little support for what they actually could do, as having communicated low expectations and little interest in their work.

Invariably, drop-outs cited what they saw as their Blackness as mitigating against encouragement, high expectations, and continuous support on the part of school personnel. While students in the system tended to generally concur that dropping out might be easy, drop-outs themselves emphatically and unanimously declared that the process was not only easy, but assisted. That is, drop-outs tended to describe how family, teachers, and guidance counsellors, along with other factors in the school itself, facilitated the process of disengagement and made the act of dropping out easy.

Drop-outs also discussed how schools, particularly school personnel, could not be relied upon for support to stay in school. Sometimes, to the contrary, school personnel might encourage the student to decide to drop out. Mary Jo, a drop-out who now works in a law office, described what happened when her family experienced a crisis – the physical abuse of her mother and then the 'break-up' of the family. She recalled that it was only her 'in-school' behaviour that was noted:

> I really needed someone to talk to but was afraid of the consequences. I was hoping one of my school teachers will pick up my home troubles and spare me. While everything was taking place, I was being criticized openly for slacking in my school work. But no one was asking me why. (File F11: lines 54–62)

Here, Mary Jo refers to what is perceived as an unresponsive school system which she feels is all too willing to condemn her 'slacking' yet is seemingly unconcerned with what may have caused the difficulties in the first place. Such behaviour should, on the contrary, be interpreted as an early warning sign for students who are beginning to 'fade out' and may eventually leave school altogether.

Drop-outs included as factors contributing to their decision to drop out becoming pregnant and being assured flatly that school under these conditions was out of the question and that flexible times could not be negotiated. Another commonly cited factor, as mentioned by Mary Jo above, was not being able to articulate the intensity of family problems to any school personnel and never being asked why they were having problems. In looking back on their experiences, some drop-outs mentioned feeling that if they shared their family problems they might be labelled as coming from 'another pathological Black family.'

Tory, forty years old and a former drop-out who had returned to school and was now pursuing an undergraduate degree, described a rift between her school and home experiences which she could not negotiate. Together, the feeling that she couldn't talk about her home experiences at school, and that not much was expected of her, made it easy for her to 'slip through the cracks.' She went on to explain:

... home problems were not for the school neither were school problems for the home ... I was an abused child and I remember running away from my foster parents to hang out with friends and roam the streets. I didn't think it was advisable for me to bring my personal problems to the authorities at school ... There was an unwritten code that the school was separate and distinct from the home and that you leave your home problems outside the gate of the school ... Sometimes too, because the school system has such low expectations of Black students, you say to yourself, 'Why bother?' (File F04: lines 41–64)

This 'unwritten code' may be understood as part of the 'hidden curriculum' of schooling through which the attitudes and behaviours of teachers and other school agents convey specific messages to students. It is clear that many Black students feel that these messages are often conveyed through a climate of preconceptions which are fuelled by racial stereotypes such as the notions of 'the pathological Black family' as referred to above or Black students being underachievers. Not only do such attitudes generalize a negative understanding of the Black community, but they act as strong deterrents against Black students relating their problems to teachers or guidance counsellors, who they presume will be evaluating them in light of these misconceptions.

It has been noted that the narratives of drop-outs provide a more holistic view of the problem of disengagement. Central to this view is what could be called a 'network of disinterest,' that is, a sense that nobody is interested in, cares about, or has worthy expectations of the drop-out. Drop-outs almost unanimously see the intersection of inaction and an apparent uncaring and discouraging attitude on the part of those who should have a vested interest in their education and well-being. Thus, a network of family, school, and community which could help them remain in school is absent.

In the following quote, Valerie, a nineteen-year-old mother, describes making a plea for help to a school guidance counsellor who she hoped would help her to negotiate a solution to her problems, so that she could remain in school:

I made an appointment and I talked to them ... I'm going through a major period right now and it's very hard for me in school and I don't want to drop out ... but at the same time I needed a bit of the weight lifted ... I don't know what to do, I don't want to quit school ... I was wondering if I could do correspondence, anything, and they were just like, 'No, no, you have to be in school.' And the hours aren't flexible or anything ... it wasn't even the flexibility I wanted, it was more like a support, just knowing that someone was there ... (File F15: lines 463–96)

In the end, Valerie acknowledges that it was personal support more than academic counselling which she needed. Instead, she was only confronted with another uninterested party, and eventually she did drop out.

In the context of a focus-group meeting, one drop-out described this generalized sense of a lack of interest and asserted that the people who did try to dissuade him from leaving school were actually drop-outs themselves, rather than teachers, school administrators, or parents. In effect, the only secure part of this potential network were students who had already disengaged from the system and understood his experience:

... no one told me to, like, drop out of school. But my parents and people, the way they were acting, and my teachers and everything, that pushed me to drop out of school ... Other people I know were mad because I dropped out of school ... people that dropped out themselves tell me it isn't worth it and stuff, but I did anyways. (File F05: lines 576–91)

It is this type of disinterest and lack of support on the part of friends, family, and school that often leads to the student feeling 'pushed out' and denied any other recourse.

Non-Black students cited many of the same, generalized reasons for dropping out: personal or family problems, economics, boredom, difficulty with school work, or difficult relations with teachers. The following are typical responses:

They have problems at home. They can't handle class work. People they hang around with, stuff like that. (File CG7: lines 5–6)

Maybe they want a job, maybe they're having family problems or maybe they can't keep up with their school, problems with teachers. (File CG8: lines 6–7)

Many of the responses seemed to place the decision to drop out on the student, individualizing the issue. The fact that non-Black students did not mention issues of race or the differential treatment of Black students shows a lack of recognition of the very factors which inform the daily lives of the Black students who were interviewed. This disjunction between the perceptions of the two groups highlights the different realities each experiences both within the schools and in society in general, and it also indicates how separate must be their social frames of reference. Positionality, therefore, becomes relevant to how the process of student disengagement is interpreted by students from different racial backgrounds.

Parents raised many of the same issues as Black students when they considered why students leave school early. Among these issues were concerns regarding the curriculum, the lack of Black history, the absence of Black teachers, and the streaming and labelling of Black students. Parents acknowledged that in some cases students' personal lives can also make it difficult for them to stay in school, particularly when it appears that the school system is not responsive to their concerns.

Most teachers tended to locate factors contributing to dropping out as being either within the student's character, the character of the student's family, or the student's earlier educational experience. More than any other group, they tended to place the blame for dropping out squarely on the shoulders of the student. While students, drop-outs, and parents saw disengagement as a process, teachers tended more to see it as a specific 'choice not to participate' made by a student. Some teachers also saw society as responsible, critiquing North American culture for allowing students to believe the best things in life are free. A lack of responsibility on the part of students was also noted.

The most salient feature of teachers' responses concerning why students drop out of school was the way in which some drop-outs were constructed as being socially and academically deficient both within their families and in their values and attitudes towards education. This view, in fact, allowed many teachers to excuse the educational system and their part in it from any sense of accountability.

A minority of teachers did feel that students were 'pushed out.' A few teachers noted a 'cycling down' of teacher expectations for particular students who are labelled 'troublemakers' on the basis of the lists of suspensions and expulsions which are available either in records or by word of mouth. Such lowered expectations for some students, they maintained, can result in what amounts to self-fulfilling prophecies. These few teachers noted that the school system needs to look at strategies to get these students back into school.

A few teachers also cited the nature and environment of the school itself as being problematic for Black and minority students. They identified a number of factors in the school environment which did not reflect the students, their history, or their culture. They talked about students who felt they did not fit in, and they judged the schools as unable at certain junctures to effectively support these students. It is notable that teachers who felt that the school system was in part responsible seemed to have hope that schools could intervene to prevent or reverse student disengagement. In contrast, those who blamed the students, their families, and the previous educational experiences of the students seemed at a loss to find hope for change. Therefore, by situating themselves, as educators, somewhere outside the drop-out dilemma, the notion of transformation also seemed to be outside their scope.

While the issue of streaming was absent from teachers' evaluations of why students drop out, it was identified by Black students and Black parents and community workers as a primary factor in Black students' decision to leave school. Streaming was described as a process which can result in limited life chances and low self-esteem and self-confidence. Lack of encouragement and low teacher expectations were seen not only as compounding the

effects of streaming, but also as adding to already negative stereotypes of Black students.

The fact that many teachers' understanding of why students drop
out contrasts so sharply with the responses of drop-outs themselves is evidence of what these students describe as an unresponsive school system. Students who were fading out of school
felt deprived of the support needed to get back on track. Personal and family problems were compounded by the lack of interest
among teachers and other school agents. Moreover, students felt
that their situations would be viewed within a climate of pre-
judgment fuelled by negative racial stereotypes which made con-
fiding in teachers or guidance counsellors difficult. This situation
speaks to the need for more Black teachers not only to serve as
role models, but also to provide the personal support and guidance which is otherwise lacking. Finally, from the various narratives it becomes clear that there is an identifiable need to sensitize
non-Black teachers and support staff to cultural issues which are
critical to students' experiences within the school.

Experiences of Black Students in the School Environment

Students consistently mentioned that they felt their experiences
within the various facets of the school culture were directly related
to their level of academic achievement. For example, Bill, a student
identified as 'at risk,' talked about how his achievements in sports
gave him a position in the school which he could not gain within
the classroom:

> I was the only Black guy in the classroom and didn't get heard most
> of the time, [my] ideas didn't get heard. But ... in sports, and I
> excelled in that, even if they didn't want to hear me they'll hear me
> anyway 'cause I was usually at the top right, so they had no choice
> but to hear me that time. (File A07: lines 672–85)

For Bill, sports activities were the only situations within the
school context where he was able to be heard, yet this did not necessarily compensate for the invisibility he experienced within the

classroom. The issue of invisibility was strongly correlated to race in the student narratives. In the above quotation, Bill illustrates his need to gain social empowerment in areas where he excelled in order to be accorded a voice, something he felt as a Black student he was otherwise being denied. Even though the above was related as a positive experience, it still contains very negative undertones.

In the context of a focus-group meeting, one student related the experience of feeling empowered by confronting the discriminatory practices of a teacher:

> ... the class was very integrated ... It wasn't such an important class ... sewing or whatever, so we used to talk a lot and the teacher used to get angry and then she started to segregate us. She started to put all the Blacks at one table and all the Whites at one table. And I asked her, 'Why do you do that? Don't you think that you're causing ... some sort of rut in the class?' And whenever our table talked, she used to get angry and [whenever] that table talked she never used to say anything ... I got angry at her, but in a civilized way, and I told her, 'You should change this because it doesn't make you look good. If you're not prejudiced then don't make us think that you are.' And then she integrated us again. (File A03: lines 1287–1350)

Having a sense of agency about what happens within the classroom and feeling as though she was a part of what eventually unfolded in the class was clearly empowering for this student, particularly in terms of addressing what she saw as divisive practices on the part of the teacher.

Other students related the importance of having relationships with other Black students and found these social experiences to be among the most pleasurable. Rana, a grade 10 student, described an occasion when she felt a strong sense of belonging:

> The most pleasant experience at school was one lunch time ... in the basement, there's one part where these White students hang out, there's the other part where nobody, like it's pure dead. So, one day at school everyone was at the patty shop and we went down-

stairs in the basement, someone brought out some music and everyone's dancing and having fun and everything. (File O30: lines 983–93)

This quote also illustrates how social segregation based on race has a great deal to do with common cultural interests, and therefore should not necessarily be seen as a divisive element within the school culture. In this way, students need to be able to express their interests and identities without being labelled.

For many students, extracurricular activities, particularly sports, represented positive aspects of school life which kept them motivated to attend and made the process more engaging. Some students commented that certain classes also made the school experience more enjoyable. Lesline, an OAC level student quoted previously, commented on the teaching style of certain teachers:

I really like my English class 'cause the teacher gives something back to the class. She's very open. She's White and says, 'You know, White people have done some really bad things.' I've never found a teacher who's ever said that before, that Europeans have devastated the world. But she'll come back and say, 'There's good and bad in everybody, and I acknowledge the fact that this happens to Black people or to people who are non-Whites' or whatever, and she makes a class fun. And she treats you like an adult. She treats you, not like you're 13 years old. (File O03: lines 1187–1204)

Lesline's positive evaluation of the class was contingent upon the attitude and pedagogical practices of the teacher. Teachers, as the narratives have shown, are an important factor with regard to student engagement. In this case, it is the willingness of the teacher to discuss, openly and critically, issues of race that inspired the interest and enthusiasm of the student.

For many of the students, negative experiences of school were related to differential and unjust treatment at school. This treatment was most strongly and most frequently related to issues of race. Examples of such treatment involved teacher/student relationships as well as relations with peers, both within their own group and outside it (i.e., with White students). In this context, students spoke of harassment by other students, getting into seemingly unsolvable conflicts, and, at times, having conflicts treated in unjust ways by teachers or administrators. Bill, who identified a positive experience of school above, related to this issue:

> ... grade ... 11 or 12 ... everything was [going] along fine, I was doing well and ... [the teachers and principal] thought that I was like a leader, a peer leader for them ... Then ... one day, and I hear the teacher talking about 'All the niggers, they always cause trouble. These damn niggers, they're so many of them now. What are we going to do?' Hearing that, and then hearing them when they talk to me when I'm either at a wrestling match or something like that, it's totally different. It's like a big shock. And if [I go] to them and say, 'Well, I heard this. What's going to be done?' And nothing gets done, that was a pretty big let down for me. (File A07: lines 694–714)

Being confronted by racial epithets by those who are in positions of authority within schools is a particularly disillusioning experience for students, yet having such indignities go unresolved is even more frustrating. Consistently, the narratives of Black students and drop-outs have shown that racism exists unchecked within schools, and even when incidents are brought to the attention of school authorities, just and decisive measures to address the problem are lacking. This may be particularly true when teachers or other school agents are the perpetrators.

For some students, school was their initiation into the experience of racism. Elizabeth, a university student, commented on the use of racist language as part of her growing awareness of racism:

> I just remember being called jungle bunny very often and ... the whole three years was an unpleasant experience for me ... it made me understand that this thing called racism really exists. (File R07: lines 1094–1104)

Other students spoke of the interracial schisms which exist among the student body. Rana spoke about the seemingly mutual suspicion and distrust which exist between Black and White students:

> My most unpleasant time at school was when me and one of my friends were walking down a hall and there was all these White boys and White girls and they start talking their language and laughing ... you get that sense from them that they're talking about you ... that's why, there's a lot of splits, because in our school, a lot of White students, they don't care ... I guess they're picking up from their parents or something. They're not trying to make things easier for one another, they're just making it worse. (File O30: lines 994–1012)

Tensions with non-Black students and having to be on the defensive were also mentioned as unfair. Sheryl, a grade 12 student, commented on these tensions and the lack of understanding felt by Black students:

> ... everybody's like jumping down your neck ... maybe they can't relate. Maybe other students ... don't understand because they're not Black students. So ... they're, like, 'Well, that doesn't happen to us so I don't know what you're talking about.' (File W11: lines 1190–1208)

Again this refers to the need for interracial and intercultural channels of communication to help bridge the gaps in understanding between the various groups.

These sorts of negative attitudes can therefore translate into an environment which is counter-productive to social and educational goals. The sense that the various existing interests within schools seem polarized is evident in the following scenario related by Sandy, a grade 12 advanced student:

> When we were starting the club, it was really horrible ... [At one meeting], we were just talking about a police shooting. The next day the school just 'exploded.' We got called into the office and they're saying, 'You cannot have this in our school. If you want to

have a Black club, you're going to have to rent the room after five o'clock and you have to have it somewhere else because you wouldn't like it if we had a White racist club.' We just had to go through a lot of red tape to have this club. I was going to give up. That was the worst experience. (File R06: lines 1769–86)

When the interests of Black students are absent from the school's agenda, their desire to pursue these issues collectively, as in this particular situation, are then hindered by the school administration. This sends a powerful message to Black students that their interests are devalued and have no place within the system.

Still in the context of discussing school experiences, positive and negative, students also expressed concern regarding the lack of Black teachers and administrators. As Beth, a grade 12 advanced student, explains, the lack of minority representation in these positions leads Black students to the conclusion that there are glass ceilings on the ladder of social mobility for Blacks in society, which in turn serves to circumscribe their aspirations for the future:

Our administration is all White ... it goes back to the drop-outs' point of view for reasons for dropping out, if you look at that and ... you can see that the people in power are all White and ... you might start thinking that there's no place for a Black person there. You aren't seeing any role models ... You might say, 'Blacks can't do that; Blacks can't make it that far, so why am I bothering because with this school system I'm not gonna make it anywhere.' (File O04: lines 558–605)

Again, a sense of fatalism is evident in this student's evaluation of how the differential relations of power among Blacks and Whites in society are mirrored within educational systems and how this leads to the understanding that 'Blacks can't make it that far.' Without role models, many Black students will likely feel themselves similarly situated in positions of indefinite social and economic subordination.

Overall, the issues raised by students which related to negative experiences within school included teachers' inability to deal with race, lack of Black teachers, arbitrary exercise of power, interracial conflict, and lack of role models. Clearly, the centrality of issues related to race in the lived experiences of Black students and the inability or unwillingness of teachers to address these issues within their pedagogical practices greatly affect a student's sense of belonging and encouragement. Their dissatisfaction lies in the Eurocentricity of educational institutions, which excludes the needs and interests of Black and other minority group students.

Re-entering the School System or 'Dropping Back In'

Some of the students who drop out do in fact 'drop back in' under different circumstances. Some students return to their former schools, but the majority find alternative institutions for their education. A significant proportion of the drop-outs interviewed were themselves in the process of trying to drop back in, or had already returned to school and had moved on to postsecondary education. The drop-outs who were in the process of 'dropping in' were, without exception, experiencing continued difficulties in that process. In particular, women who had dropped out because of pregnancy were receiving little support from the school to continue in the context of the challenges of motherhood. For these women, there was no one to talk to at school about how to balance the responsibilities of motherhood with the demands of schooling, and they also cited the lack of flexible time and space considerations.

Interestingly, both male and female drop-outs who had returned to school noted particular situations in which they felt they were treated as adults and found a curriculum which actually included them. Some of these students mentioned teachers and subjects, particularly Black history and Black teachers, that made them feel like they were finally learning about themselves. As well, alternative schools were positively mentioned as offering more options and, in particular, a curriculum which allowed discussion about social issues and personal experiences.

Most drop-outs found that the pain and the stigma associated with dropping out made them feel less intelligent and mitigated against their return to school. Natasha, age twenty-eight, left school when she found out she was pregnant. When asked whether she regretted having left school, she responded:

> I don't know whether it is regret or something else. I rather resent the lack of support for me to finish my education. That's what I think it is, not regret as much but the resentment ... (File F17: lines 234–42)

It is significant that Natasha speaks in terms of resentment for the lack of support in her past educational experiences, rather than regret, since to speak in terms of regret would imply that dropping out was a decision she could have made differently, rather than a response to a situation for which she felt there was no other recourse.

Many parents were currently returning to school after having left high school early. Their decision was based on several factors which were both personal and economic. On a personal level, they wished to serve as role models for their children and feel more confident about themselves. Economically many of them believed that by pursuing an education they would gain better employment opportunities. Anita, a former drop-out who was now attending university, explained her reasons for returning to school:

> Why did I go back to school? Well ... you see women getting in their mink coats and their cars and their house ... And you see commercials telling you, 'Stay in school. Go back to school. Get an education.' And then you see other people that you've known, that you didn't think they'd do it, they're going back to school. And you say to yourself, 'What's wrong with me? Why can't I go back to school?' So I think the motivation came from seeing other people going back to school and accomplishing. (File P06: lines 390–407)

The fact that many of the Black parents who were interviewed were former drop-outs accounts for their very insightful responses throughout the study, but it is also indicative of how entrenched this problem is in the Black community. The persistence of the drop-out problem in the Black community is in part a result of the failure of the educational system to meet the needs of Black youth and the challenges that face them. However, as the narratives have shown, there are multiple forces which can conspire to create the social, economic, and emotional conditions through which student disengagement can occur. Home, school, and societal conditions are all implicated in the process to varying degrees. Students spoke of the pressures they encountered while in school. Some were problems carried over from their home and family lives, but many centred on the institutional practices within schools which are informed by the politics of race and social difference.

The narratives speak clearly to the feelings of disempowerment which Black youth experience within the framework of a Eurocentric school system. Low expectations on the part of teachers and the differential treatment they felt they received as Black students were key factors in many students' decisions to leave school prematurely. The following chapter further interrogates race as a factor of student disengagement and examines how the articulation of class and gender also inform the delivery of education.

Chapter Five

Intersections of Race, Class, and Gender

Race, class, and gender represent the basis for some of the multiple social identities which students bring with them into their educational experiences. Positionality is an important factor in locating the experience of individuals within both schools and society. Schools are specific sites where social location can mediate educational outcomes and the reproduction of status roles in society. Race, class, and gender, then, are inextricably linked to how social realities are experienced and negotiated.

This chapter explores the intersections of race, class, and gender as they relate to the realities of Black students and to the issue of student disengagement. However, we do not attempt to confine the discussion of how race, class, and gender intersect in the lives of Black students to this chapter alone. These factors provide social, political, cultural, and ideological vantage points which are inextricably linked to the issues associated with student disengagement and are therefore pervasive themes throughout the book.

Race

In terms of race, some students spoke about positive experiences related to being part of the Black Heritage Club or similar clubs and organizations, and also about various moments when they felt a sense of pride about being Black. For the most part, however, students focused on negative experiences, racism being a pervasive theme throughout their narratives.

Differential treatment by teachers, but also by students and administrators, was frequently mentioned as occurring along racial lines. The experiences which students recounted often related to teachers treating some students differently than others. Sheryl, a grade 12 student, spoke about the difference between positive and negative attention:

> White people seem to get positive attention, meanwhile we're getting negative. Like, 'Stop talking and do your work' ... And, [for] the White people [it's] just, like, 'Oh well, she got 100 and she da, da, da' and all this stuff ... (File W11: lines 495–501)

The issue of differential treatment was also emphasized in terms of the lack of positive recognition being accorded to Black students. Bill, a student identified as 'at risk,' talked about the constant reminder of negative treatment, even when success was involved:

> If I was White ... with the athletic stuff that I did ... I would have got so much recognition more at school than if I was Black. Even though I did do well in that, there was still a negative side towards it that was pinned on me. No matter how good you did there was still that part of you, well, you know, 'He does get in trouble sometimes.' If I was a White kid they would overlook that ... (File A07: lines 801–19)

Students also spoke of teachers and administrators singling out groups of Black students as responsible for disobedient or disruptive acts. Within the classroom, students often mentioned being segregated, being picked on by teachers, being stereotyped, and so on. In the school hallways, the biggest issue for students was being singled out as a group and labelled as 'troublemakers.' Some of these features of the school environment were observed during the course of conducting ethnographic research at the four high schools participating in the study. Segregation during recreational times – for instance, in the cafeteria – was a particularly salient feature of the school's culture. Black students were observed socializing together, while White students socialized with

Whites, Asians with Asians, and so on. Black students were further divided into affinity groups based on ethnicity and language; for instance, Somali/continental African students and Jamaican/ Caribbean students. Some gender segregation was also noted within all groups.

Directly addressing the issue of Eurocentrism in the school, students spoke about their inability to relate to the curriculum. The issue of Black history, raised in many different contexts, was also a direct response to the question of students' experience of being Black in the school. Angie, an OAC level student born in the Caribbean, spoke about superficial attempts to include Black history in the curriculum:

> Canadian history, I did not learn anything about Black people ... in the past two years, we have improved in our geography ... but we don't really learn about the cultural background ... not even the people, but just the city or the country. Basics, nothing deep ... I would like to know more about my history, yes, a lot more. I think I need to know a lot more than I know. (File W06: lines 573–88)

This response speaks to the general need for greater ethno-cultural equity in education. It also addresses specifically the need to create a space for African-centred studies in order to legitimate the experience and histories of Black/African Canadians, and to create a more globally oriented curriculum for all students. Creating an inclusive school environment with diverse centres of knowledge serves to make the process of schooling more relevant for racial and ethnic minority youth and enriches the overall scope of the curriculum. Education in this sense serves as an equitable forum for the social, cultural, and academic needs of all students.

Where this sort of environment was lacking, schools were described by students as hostile places full of interracial tensions. Explicit examples of name-calling, derogatory comments, and, in some cases, violence were cited as part of the experience of race within the school. Some students talked about the frustration they felt in seeing no consequences for White students when they engaged in racist language or activity, something they interpreted as just another example of Black students' subordination within the system.

The ideological positions of teachers were very apparent on the question of race. Most teachers claimed not to see colour, but to see only people. These teachers felt that they treated all students the same, regardless of race. They felt that it was important to treat all students equally and not to give preferential treatment of any kind to students who are racially 'different.' These teachers saw racism as a social problem that should not dominate the agenda of schools or even be dealt with in the school. Furthermore, they felt that the majority of teachers are colour-blind and that this was demonstrated by the way teachers teach. Some of these teachers stated that stereotypical ideas about Black youth are represented in society, although not necessarily within the school. As such, they saw it as the responsibility of the community to deal with racism.

The fact that teachers expressing this ideological position felt that racism should not be addressed may be evidence of their own discomfort with dealing with the issue, but it should not be an excuse to disregard the reality faced by Black students in the schools as well as the community at large. To view schools as being somehow separate from the community, as some teachers stated, fails to acknowledge the function and role of schools as integrally related to society.

A number of teachers also said that it did not matter whether the student was 'orange with purple polka-dots,' they would still be treated the same by teachers. Yet some teachers and administrators, less rigid in their denial of the school's responsibility to deal with racism, felt that the way to deal with diversity was by trying to assist every student to learn and to validate the experiences of all students within the school context. Brian, a high-school principal, saw this as an integral part of the learning experience:

> It still presents all of the basic challenges of trying to assist every student to learn as much as possible. The difference is that it involves knowing more about the background and the experiences of students ... to bring all of those backgrounds and experiences and

also things like custom and religious aspects as well into play in some way, or at least to allow all of those things to be validated in terms of the school system. (File T17: lines 74–87)

Some teachers understood the disadvantage of race as a limited background in terms of literacy for certain groups of students. Others felt that English as a second language or non-White racial characteristics allow students or parents to receive 'special treatment.' Following the same logic, these teachers were noticeably frustrated in 'having to hear' about racial issues. Some teachers felt that prejudice is a fact in society, but it is the responsibility of the individual to deal with it, by speaking up and identifying racist teachers. These teachers felt strongly that the school system is based on equity and that accusations of racism in the school can be a cop-out – an excuse for personal failure. As well, these teachers felt threatened and sometimes angry when they were referred to as 'the enemy.' One teacher expressed a desire to not have to 'feel guilty' because of the past, and a need to be viewed as part of the solution. Some commented that people seem to be searching out controversy by 'crying racism,' a practice which 'gets tiresome.'

Some teachers felt uncomfortable with the word *Black* and with the practice of citing difference. One teacher claimed that students feel the same way and do not really like to deal with issues of race and difference in the classroom. They noted that racism should not be an issue: if there is a problem, they felt, it should be addressed as a problem, not be made into a racial issue. These teachers also tended to note that there is a great deal of anti-White racism, and racism within groups, and they were inclined to see students as responsible for racist incidents involving students. Other teachers who share this perspective tended not to see a connection between low expectations as conveyed to students and possible subsequent failure on the part of the student.

It must be taken into account that the views of these teachers on the subject of race, which are so vividly in contrast to those of Black students, come from an equally different vantage point. While Black students approach the subject of race as a part of their everyday lived experience, many teachers are only able to see race from the position of White privilege. Without a subjective knowledge of racism, they react in response to their own position with feelings of discomfort, avoidance, and resentment of being made to feel guilty.

Some teachers tended to reduce racism to a process of name-calling, rather than seeing it as a wider systemic issue. A few teachers noted having heard racist comments being made about Black students by other teachers. Barbara, a White high-school English teacher, acknowledged the perpetuation of racist attitudes by some teachers:

> I've heard the comment made generally before ... when I hear words like that pop out of someone else's mind, I write them off. Unfortunately, I don't think that even as educators and facilitators of knowledge that everyone has that idea themselves or carries that ideal within themselves. There are some individuals here that do not embrace education and learning and are not open and are racist and that does continue on. (File T21: lines 527–43)

More progressive teachers, who were in the minority, felt that lower expectations were conveyed to Black students in the schools in subtle and perhaps unconscious ways by teachers; that is, as part of a hidden curriculum. They cited, sometimes reluctantly, behaviours on the part of colleagues which they felt exemplified these lower expectations. In particular, they noted that Black students seem not to be encouraged by the schools to go into math or science, and that it is difficult for Black students to express themselves within the schools. They also noted that Black students tend to be placed in the lower streams. These comments were corroborated through ethnographic observation in the high schools, where it was noted that very few Black students could be found in either science or math classes. A number of 'visible minorities,' however, could be found in ESL and ESD classes and lower streams.

Mira, an East Asian female teacher, mentioned hearing racist comments about students of colour which she felt were shared with her because she is not Black:

And because I am not Black, they think they can say it to me and I will accept it. And other teachers who are not of colour have actually said something to those teachers, that [it's] not funny, that [it's] racism. (File T24: lines 249–54)

Thus while some teachers react against open racism, others maintain different sorts of biases. For example, the same teacher discussed the perception among some teachers that minority students who are smart are seen as a threat:

I think they are treated unfairly and almost like they're dangerous, and that scares me because I felt the anger as an adolescent and I was always angry. Because when you're smart you see it, and you will get angry at fifteen, you know! And I was angry at fifteen, but no one treated me that way. (File T24: lines 271–81)

Such fears may be grounded in ignorance and perhaps an unwillingness to see minority students transcend certain perceived boundaries and expectations. It was also indicated by some teachers that there is preferential treatment accorded to White students in various ways, such as more tolerance of their mistakes or of other problems that develop among the White student population.

In summary, we can say that students generally perceived some teachers and administrative staff as making racially offensive remarks. When asked to elaborate on their assertions, Black students would recall specific incidents. In many cases, students did not complain to school authorities. This created the false impression that those sorts of problems did not exist and therefore there was less chance of a resolution. There was also a general inability among teachers to distinguish between individual racist acts and institutional racism. In this sense, race provided a vantage point for teachers' experiences and also informed the ways in which they understood the social realities of their school environment, and the effect certain policies and practices had on students. Black and ethnic minority teachers showed a greater understanding of how social difference structured the organizational life of schools, as well as how Black students were often subject to differential evaluation and differential treament by teachers themselves.

While many teachers cannot directly attest to students' complaints about racist remarks, they nevertheless admit to isolated incidents, and a few point out that the school is not immune from the sentiments of the wider society. In fact, many teachers did not see any problem with articulating a 'colour-blind' approach to education. Parents, by contrast, pointed out the existence of denial on the part of some authorities when it comes to acknowledging there is racism in the schools. Many parents saw this as a stumbling block to undertaking proactive antiracism measures in schools.

Class

When students talked about why they were staying in school, despite the pressures, alienation, and disengagement they experienced, an explicit connection was made between education and future employment and ultimately social class. Steven, an OAC level student born in Jamaica, stated:

> Say I go to school with this person for like 18 years, then ... ten years down the line, he's like a lawyer and I'm a garbage man or janitor. I'm gonna feel stupid and dumb and I'm gonna say, 'We went to school together and, look, he's somebody and I'm nothing.' (File B21: lines 902–12)

Students made this connection between education and work consistently throughout their narratives. In many cases, this understanding of the economics of schooling seemed to be the single motivation that kept students in school. Most students demonstrated an acute awareness of the social consequences associated with a lack of education. Again, some students were able to look at their parents and the hardships they endured because of a lack of education. They related this to what they currently saw as their parents' relative lack of power within the school.

Most students talked about issues of class in a superficial manner in terms of clothes and material possessions. Others spoke of economic, social, and cultural disparities which translate into different kinds of pressures for social mobility. Some of the students felt that rich students might feel more of this pressure from their parents, while others felt that poor kids, especially if they are Black, have to work a lot harder in school in order to succeed. Carlton, a grade 12 student from a working-class background, addressed this issue but also implicated race:

> A child of poor parents, they've got more pressure on them because the parents are always telling them to work hard ... especially if you're Black because they say, 'Oh, the White man don't have to worry about it because there's always jobs for them to get.' You may be Black and you have the same qualifications as they do, but they're going to get the job. And for rich people it's, like, even if it's Black or White, they probably don't have to work as hard because their parents will probably get ... a job for them in a company or something. (File W36: lines 269–89)

Carlton highlights the complex relationship between race and class and how he perceives this reality within the framework of a racially stratified society. The articulation of race and class is exemplified by his understanding of how these factors differentially empower students in the school system and reproduce the disparate social and economic relations within society.

From another vantage point, class was discussed in terms of the time a parent has available to offer support to the student. Trevor, an advanced level student, was sensitive to the different value of time to different parents:

> I think that parents on the poorer side wouldn't be able to push their students to do that because they're probably out working all the time. But the rich parents, they're there watching, they're home, like, maybe at five o'clock. They are able to do that. (File W03: lines 502–10)

Trevor specifically addresses the different opportunities parents have to provide support to their children. This situation is seen as a fact of life wherein realities are circumscribed by socio-economic status and reproduce the conditions for success for some while limiting the chances of others.

Students expressed a clear vision of the complexities of social class in both school and society. Some students indicated that poor students were subjected to different treatment, in general, by teachers. Victoria, a grade 12 student, was explicit on this issue:

> I think they could achieve the same thing but the poor student would have to work harder to get the same treatment. (File W33: lines 375–8)

Rana also discussed the issue of differential treatment but in this case named the issue of race as well:

> In our school the rich ones are kind of the hippy girls and the hippy boys* and ... the teachers are always so nice with them, and always, 'Oh, you did so well on your tests' and stuff. But to other students, they just hand them their test, don't tell them nothing, just kind of give them a dirty look or something, you know. (File O30: lines 552–64)

Here, race and class are understood to provide the basis for differential treatment of Black students in both school and society; for instance, White students being accorded more encouragement and support by teachers than Black students. Class, then, is a frame of reference which, when linked with race, can provide a double sense of alienation among some Black students who see themselves as both socially and economically disadvantaged.

Many non-Black students indicated that while they were bored with school, they realized the importance of a high-school education in attaining their future goals, which, for the most part, included college or university. Non-Black students mentioned that if they were to drop out, they believed they would have 'no future,' that they would probably end up 'working at McDonald's' or being

---

* The term 'hippy' refers to students who have adopted the outward appearances of the 1970s hippy culture. 'Hippy' students are generally White and from the middle class.

on welfare. Not only did they predict this was the future which awaited those who dropped out, but at times they were able to give examples of people they knew who ended up in these situations. They saw clearly the connection between school and work, and often relied on this understanding to keep them focused in school. Melissa, a grade 11 student, felt that if she left school early her goals would be

> ... pretty much demolished. I'd end up working at a job that I know
> I wouldn't be happy in. (File CG02: lines 262–4)

Non-Black students felt strongly that their future goals and social class were completely contingent on their continued success in school.

Parents expressed beliefs similar to those of the students regarding the connection between education, employment, and current social class structures. They stressed the idea that education is important to their children. In some cases, parents themselves were in the process of returning to school to complete their education. Their decision to return to school was often linked to their desire to be an example for their children as well as to their own personal growth, rather than being a decision based solely on social class mobility.

Parents were well aware of the difference which education could make for their children's future, but they were also aware that young people could be greatly influenced by the systemic racism which they witnessed in their daily lives. Dena, a mother who has worked extensively with youth, spoke about how the issue of collective mobility among Blacks may be reflected in a student's decision to leave school early:

> I know of students who drop out because when they look at the
> issue of educational aspiration and how that is linked to employ-
> ment, and they look within society and see that their own people
> are not attaining jobs, they are unemployed, and they themselves
> have got an education, they feel that the educational system is not
> just, and regardless of whether or not they have an education, they

will not gain employment ... they've reached the point that they do
feel 'pushed out.' (File P30: lines 10–21)

Lowered aspirations betray a sense of fatalism towards the future,
fuelled not only by the existence of racial and social class hierarchies in society, but also by the recognition of the same disparities
existing within the educational system.

A high percentage of the drop-out sample discussed an intersection of economic factors related to dropping out. A significant
issue was the rupture of the school and work linkage that they
felt. That is, many drop-outs stated that since they were already at
the basic level in the streaming hierarchy, it just didn't make sense
to continue with school. Realizing that school was not going to
lead to university and professional jobs or high status was seen as
a deterrent to pursuing education for these students. Some stated
clearly that earning money at a job was preferable to 'feeling stupid'
in basic classes.

For drop-outs, then, the practice of streaming 'fixed' their
future prospects to specific socio-economic opportunities. Streaming was understood to limit their ability to transcend their socio-
economic status and class backgrounds, and thereby represents a
process of reproducing the extant social class inequities in society,
particularly along racial and ethnic lines. Being denied access to
social mobility led to a profound sense of disempowerment for
these drop-outs. They felt a lack of control in determining the
course of their educational experience and described being constantly given messages of inadequacy. This disempowerment
made school a lower priority than getting some sense of power
and control over their lives as members of society. Jennifer
affirmed her decision to drop out based on the issue of empowerment:

When I left school, I left a situation that was very negative and I put
myself into a situation where I was able to get some power, get
some control over my life – figure out who I was and where I was
going ... I don't regret dropping out of school (File F03: lines 1409–
19)

Jennifer explains the importance of sacrificing the long-term goal of education in order to assert her own sense of self and power. Leaving school is not perceived here as a failure to succeed but rather as a choice to abandon a socially oppressive experience.

Drop-outs experienced situations of social class discrimination in school which they described as being embarrassing and belittling. In a focus group, one drop-out clearly remembered a discussion of welfare which exemplified this treatment:

> ... something that happened in the class, about people on welfare, [the teacher] pointed out a kid in the class that was on welfare, and she said, ... 'Oh, I'll work my butt off to go and give you welfare ...' (File F05: lines 1292–9)

Such demeaning experiences occurring within the classroom must be seen as destructive to students' morale and self-esteem. These messages lay the psychological groundwork for students to disengage from school in order to be liberated from the source of such negative experiences.

Teachers tended to discuss class in terms of family finances, which can make it harder for some students to stay in school because of lack of money for supplies and other resources, or require the students themselves to work. They also mentioned that in poorer, and specifically single-parent, homes, less support was given to students. While a few teachers mentioned that they thought students were given more attention by teachers if they were privileged, this was not the view of the majority of teachers.

Therefore, the issue of poverty must been seen to have a significant impact on the educational success of students as they negotiate satisfying immediate economic survival needs and receiving education that has no apparent or immediate material gratification. The economic concerns of students serve as a distraction from education. This barrier is experienced in very specific ways for Black youth from low socio-economic family backgrounds.

Students, parents, and teachers generally acknowledged the impact that economic hardships have on schooling. Black students, in particular, felt that the school environment 'favours' rich students and that rich and powerful parents have much influence at school. Current harsh economic realities mean that students who find jobs want to hang on to them and continue to work while going to school. While it is possible that the current unfavourable economic climate may influence a few students to stay in school longer or drop back in, there are other students who find these conditions to be legitimate grounds on which to question the relevance of education.

Gender

In terms of differential treatment by staff and faculty, male and female students noted that there is heavier surveillance of Black males and that they are more likely to become the object of discipline. Some female students could not respond to gender differences in their own experiences but spoke about the treatment of Black males. The following comment by Charlene, a grade 11 student, summarized the complex set of pressures which are felt by Black males:

> I think Black guys have it worse ... the teachers and all the fight people come to fight the Black guys and you have to act like you want to fight even if you don't want to fight ... And, you're pushed to just do sports. And if a Black guy's smart, they don't admit it, they don't want to talk about it ... They just want to just do enough to pass to be like the rest of their friends, just wear the clothes and that's it ... if you're Black and you're smart it's usually female that'll admit it, not male – it's awful. (File R05: lines 1237–54)

Charlene speaks of the pressures young Black males face in terms of violence, both inside and outside of school. She also refers to stereotypes which affect young Black males to the extent of their internalization of these notions, particularly around issues of success in sports and the minimalizing of academic success. Sheryl also addressed the problem of stereotypes, but went further to talk about the lack of support and recognition of Black males who are excelling:

I think Black males have it harder because they're stereotyped, they're all bad ... I guess, like, they see a couple who are just like messing around, or whatever, and they don't take note that there are some people over here who are doing good ... It's not fair. I don't know why they just can't treat the person who's doing good, treat him, don't just keep putting him down or whatever, and don't put the people who are doing bad down. Tell them, 'You shouldn't be doing this.' Talk to them, and not just, 'Go down to the office.' [But] then they suspend them. I mean, that doesn't do anything. You're just doing a favour for them. (File W11: lines 217–45)

The issues of recognition and encouragement raised in this response directly address the role of the school and also make an explicit connection with dropping out. Reiterating the effect of stereotypes, a young woman speaking in a focus-group meeting of only female students also made the connection to role models and talked openly about 'living' race, and the differences of that experience along gender lines:

When you're a Black male, you're already, you don't have to do anything, you know. You could be a good student, you could be a good father or whatever, [but] when you're out on the street, [you're seen as] a criminal ... a drug dealer, whatever, you beat your wife, you have several children and you don't take care of them. It doesn't matter what you do. I think it's a little easier for Black women ... our role models have changed, and stereotypes, it's just such a big part of our lives as a race. And it's hard for us to connect with our men, and it's hard for them to connect with us and with themselves. So I think it's a little harder, I mean, we're working on it. We're working on ourselves and I think we're reaching this point of evolution and leaving our brothers behind. (File D05: lines 338–72)

While this student sees progress being made for young Black women, the inability to connect with young Black men highlights the disjunctures in their realities and experiences. This young woman also relates the difficulties of attempting to transcend negative stereotypes which stigmatize and malign individuals on the basis of race.

Negative perceptions and stereotypes associated with Black males operate for the most part in terms of inter-group relations; that is, between Blacks and other social groups, in particular the dominant White culture. Negative attitudes towards Black females often seemed to be perpetuated by Black males – an intra-group phenomenon. While Black females were able to identify the sources of Black males' oppression, the Black males interviewed lacked the same insights into the subordination of Black females, particularly how they themselves are implicated in that process.

Both male and female students did recognize the fact that female students are harassed in the hallways of the schools, and that this is often by Black males. This harassment included verbal and physical intimidation, and was even described as violent:

> F1: I think, Black guys, it's not only, everything they do is violent, because if they're talking to you, they're like ...
> F2: 'Bitch!'
> F1: ... and like, 'What's up baby? I want to talk to you.' It's aggressive and it's violent. Everything they do is violent.
> F2: Yeah. (File O08: lines 2397–406)

These young women complain about the treatment they receive from male students within the school. Black female students feel a deep sense of disrespect from Black male students and when discussions about the issue were raised in focus-group meetings, the exchanges were highly charged. Interestingly, males felt that females who are treated in this manner bring it on themselves – in their behaviour, dress, and speech. Their position was that the young women did not respect themselves. They were unable to recognize that by blaming Black females for creating their own problems by their manner of dress and behaviour, they were subjecting Black females to the same sort of stereotypes as those constructed around Black males which centre on the same sort of superficialities. This behaviour demonstrates their lack of regard for the subordination of Black women and their inability to recognize their own complicity.

Gender politics within the Black community have created schisms between Black females and males. One young woman in a focus-group discussion talked about the fact that the harassment had become so extreme that she avoids spending time with Black male students:

> I don't talk too much to [the males] because some of them, you do talk to, and it's, like, you pass and you say, 'Hi,' 'Bye,' and the next time they see you it's like they want to touch you all over your body. And if you tell them no, it's like, 'Oh, you think you're this, you think you're that, you think you're better than people.' So I really don't talk too much to them. (File D06: lines 749–59)

The perpetuation of negative attitudes and behaviours on the part of Black males towards Black females is seen, then, to undermine the unity of Black students.

Young women also complained about the double standards which exist and how these allow young men to escape responsibilities towards their female partners. This issue of being unable to enforce male accountability was discussed by Black women with regard to pregnancy in a female focus-group meeting:

> F1: Yeah, but that's only when they're young. When a woman, when she's pregnant, nobody's going to say anything.
> F2: Yeah, but just because you're young, so you're a ho if you have a baby? When a seventeen-year-old or a sixteen-year-old or whatever, maybe, that doesn't mean she's a ho, that doesn't mean she sleeps around.
> F1: Yeah, it could be an accident, right?
> F2: ... but I'm saying, they'll call a girl a ho ...
> F3: But, she didn't do the job alone ... It's like we did it by ourselves.
> F1: Exactly. (File O08: lines 2301–16)

It was felt generally that women's sexuality was under intense scrutiny and that men's sexuality and sense of accountability were not an issue. While these are issues that reach beyond schooling, the school's role in addressing them was never raised.

Gender bias in channelling students was also identified as an area of concern for both male and female students. Black males were seen as more likely to be channelled into sports rather than academics. The lack of legitimacy and support given to women's sports was criticized, as was the channelling of women into paths which ghettoize them in specific segments of the labour market. At the same time, young women felt discouraged from taking maths and sciences as requisites to alternative and often male dominated career choices.

The issue of inclusion was also raised by Black female students in terms of curriculum. Sandy, a grade 12 advanced student, specifically addressed the absences of Black women in the curriculum:

> Maybe it gets Black women even more, if you're dealing with gender. I took a Canadian literature course and we did poems by mostly White males and we had the odd White female but we never ever had Black women be mentioned. Like you hear Malcolm X, but you wouldn't even hear Angela Davis. Like you would never hear anything about Black women. (File R06: lines 1468–79)

Sandy demonstrates a clear understanding of the complexities of knowledge production with respect to issues of race and gender, and of how such omissions legitimize certain Eurocentric and patriarchal forms of knowledge, while delegitimizing others. Further, the way in which students interpret and relate their experiences as either males or females is inextricably linked to race. Students' expressions of these experiences demonstrate that gender remains a crucial variable in the construction of inequality for Black youth.

Matters of sexuality also included issues of homophobia. During focus-group discussions, homophobic comments from students were heard. These comments were made either in response to the mention of a particular person or incident, or expressed in the form of a greeting when a student arrived late to join the interview. Homophobic comments were also made when students complained about teachers who have the habit of touching students.

Teachers frequently noted that there were differences in terms of academic encouragement along the lines of gender among various cultures. Some teachers specifically noted that some non-Western societies play a strong role in giving messages to female students in terms of what they cannot do, and that teachers have a difficult time negotiating this. Hugh, a high-school history teacher, expressed his frustration in dealing with what he considered to be restrictive cultural influences:

> ... any non–Western European background, ... the girls have this whole societal thing that seems to be laid on them as to what they can do and what they can't do, and it's a real hard thing to fight. (File T04: lines 1330–40)

The tendency here to refer to female students from 'any non–Western European background' as being bound to the same cultural codes of conduct is a misinformed and essentializing statement, and betrays the propensity to regard non–Western European cultures as being somehow sexist or misogynist. Such ideologies not only demarcate clearly the social boundaries between 'us' and 'them,' but they also negate the cultural differences which exist among these groups. Ultimately, then, non–Western European cultures are evaluated in terms of their non-congruence with Western values. While Hugh addresses the tensions involved in dealing with the issue of sexism within the context of culture, labelling the issue of gender discrimination as somehow foreign is problematic and, in effect, allows teachers to avoid confronting the nature of sexism within the context of their own attitudes and behaviours.

Also implicated by the narratives of teachers was the socialization practices of the family. A number of teachers felt that schools should help girls develop skills, so that they can develop their potential as opposed to succumbing to pressures of family and society. Hugh continued here to explain how this would involve working with parents:

> I think that what the school can do in terms of helping a lot of the girls who are facing family pressures to do one thing, and their inclinations and skills lead to another, is to help the kids develop those skills, not in opposition to their parents, at least overtly but in

terms of letting them know, 'Yes, I know you're under this kind of pressure' … try to communicate with their parents, help them to develop strategies for dealing with the problem they have at home, so that they can reach their own potential. I don't think it's a matter of taking one of the girls under your arm and helping her put an application into an out of town university… (File T04: lines 1344–60)

The idea of creating partnerships between the home and school is important, and is a step towards negotiating these tensions. However, there must be some caution not to place the blame exclusively outside of the practices of the school system. Without implicating the school, the issues of gender bias in education are left unquestioned and the school's contribution to their perpetuation is ignored.

Finally, while some teachers complained of sexist behaviour on the part of the male students towards females, in general, and cite specifically that some students do not hold female teachers in high regard because they are female, it is significant that no teachers remarked on different treatment or experience of Black males. The interpretation of the issue of sexism in the school remained within particular confines. A more sophisticated understanding of the complexities of race and gender was not common among most teachers.

The social positions of race, class, and gender must be understood as locating individuals within a social, cultural, and economic hierarchy. They contribute to the multiple identities which students bring with them into their schooling experiences, and they are subject to the multiple forms of oppressions which accompany them. Race, class, and gender must be recognized as the basis for according individuals and groups in society positions of respective power and prestige or marginality and subordination. It is within this oppositional dynamic that the struggle for equal opportunity in education is marred by inequality of access.

The need to come to terms with these issues was difficult for many of the teachers interviewed to recognize and accept, yet the reality of the same issues was very clear for many of the Black students who confront them on a daily basis as part of the politics of exclusion. According to Michelle Fine (1991, 13), the needs of today's society mandates that 'questions of equity must focus not on educational access, but on educational outcomes.' The two, however, are inextricably linked. Educational access is mitigated by disparity centred specifically around race and social class, and these factors in turn, along with gender, inform the educational outcomes for specific groups in society. There is no way, then, to separate the politics of social identification from schooling and the delivery of education. Race, class, and gender are variables which produce specific forms of identification and define oppositional spaces from which to confront racism, classism, and sexism within the structures of both schools and society.

Chapter Six

Authority, Power, and Respect

All students have 'problems' dealing with school authority. However, it is apparent that Black/African-Canadian youths are generally having a 'tough time' dealing and/or coming to grips with authority structures in the school system. They perceive these power structures as intended to subordinate them further. Problems of authority, power, and respect are interwoven throughout the narratives of the students. Students generally related issues of authority and power to teachers and administrators in the school, as well as to police. Consistently, Black students linked issues of authority and respect. They held firmly to the belief that authority figures (e.g., teachers, principals) must respect them in order to wield authority over them. Black students seemed more concerned with who was exercising the authority and what was the relationship of authority figures to them than the actual content of those figures' actions. They believed that authority figures, despite their position, should treat everyone with respect in order to be respected and accepted by others. Often, Black students felt frustrated by discipline or decisions put forward by those in authority which did not take into account issues of respect.

It is interesting to note that parents were not mentioned in discussions of power and authority. When parents were discussed, it was not within this frame of reference. Teachers and their way of handling authority and power were a key issue for students. In a focus-group meeting, two young women highlighted the frustration experienced by students in this regard:

F4: You know, they always have to be right, and if you, like, get sent to the office, they're not going to believe you, they only believe the teacher.

F2: Because the teacher's authority. It's authority. (File D04: lines 733–9)

As in the above, students frequently constructed authority as a sometimes arbitrary means of control and power.

While many students spoke of reacting negatively to the institutional power structure of the school and its dominance, some students employed behavioural tactics that constitute part of a 'culture of resistance' which is anti-school. It is not coincidental that many of the students who fade out of school also exhibit what school authorities see as 'problem behaviours' (e.g., truancy, acts of delinquency, or even disruptive behaviour).

Students' experiences with 'authority' within the school system do not appear to get explained to them. They feel frustrated at their inability to participate in resolving conflicts and feel that they are silenced. Susan, an OAC level student, articulated the experience of feeling devalued by authority while at the same time feeling an obligation to respect authority:

> I think what wasn't fair is ... where the teacher is worth more than the student ... like the teacher's a god or something ... I mean, I think you should respect them but, if they do certain things to you, then you should be able to say things back ... If ... they get in your face ... what are you supposed to do? You're supposed to just obey them. (File B19: lines 784–801)

Susan is referring here to the lack of institutional recourse available when dealing with problems related to specific teachers. This concern points to the need for channels of communication to be opened through which students feel safe in registering their grievances and can be assured that their concerns will be given equal consideration with those of the teachers.

Many students did not feel that teachers were concerned with the interests of the students. Without genuine concern, they felt that they did not owe teachers any respect. Lack of respect from teachers, they felt, was variously indicated by insincerity, derogatory references, lack of interest, encouragement, and support, and negative attitude. In a focus-group meeting with continental African students, one student drew a comparison between teachers from his school in Africa and those in Canada, specifically around the issue of respect:

> Yeah, we used to, we used to respect our teachers from the bottom of our hearts, not like from neck up. You know, here ... you are not really respecting the teachers ... You're just pretending to ... it's lip service ... [an] artificial smile ... But back home we were respecting our teachers because they were ... trying to encourage us to get a good education. (File W02: lines 1693–714)

The disjuncture between this student's experience with teachers in Africa versus those in Canada makes it clear that within the continental African cultural context, the issue of respect is something to be earned through actions and behaviour, rather than an inherent feature of a position. It is also clear that respect is something which is expected to be reciprocated; in other words, it is a two-way street.

Students found the lack of discipline to be a major problem in their schools. They complained about the lack of respect in the school system, whether between teachers and students or among students. Black students, in particular, articulated a position that the discussion of discipline cannot be conducted outside the context of a mutual respect between those who wield power and authority and those who do not. They generally perceived the school system to be more interested in maintaining authority and discipline than in providing education. In such a context, students are less cooperative with teachers who are seen to be disrespectful to them and uninterested in their welfare.

For drop-outs, the issues of authority, power, and respect represented the disparate power relations which exist within schools and were thus seen as areas of resistance. Many males and a significant number of females stated that 'contrary behaviour' or acting out is a response to racist acts, or to oppressive behaviours on the part of the school itself. In particular, male drop-outs discussed their rage, thoughts of violence, and the need to act out against a system which they feel diminishes them. Male students still in the system, however, tended to have a less detailed and introspective understanding of their experience. This is possibly because drop-outs have had more time to reflect on their past experiences in school, while those still in the system may lack the emotional distance needed to put some of their experiences into perspective.

In the context of a focus-group meeting, one drop-out recalled a disturbing incident in which issues of power and authority went beyond the boundaries of acceptable behaviour:

> ... and we were all together and he called us a bunch of niggers, so we looked at him. Everything's okay, cool, we didn't say nothing, because I knew that was his last ... I wanted to kill him, but we just walked out. The next day I get suspended, just because I say I'm going to kill him. (File F05: lines 1126–38)

If accepted standards of mutual respect, decorum, and fair conduct between teachers and students do exist, the incident just described breaches every level of this code. It is obvious how justice was meted out differentially in this instance. While Black students were suspended for threatening the teacher, the teacher's racial epithets and provocation during the incident remained beyond reproach. This example demonstrates how the abuse of power and authority on the part of the teacher was supported by the school system, and with a lack of structures in place to provide advocacy for the rights of the student, it becomes apparent how this power can be perceived as oppressive and arbitrary.

Most non-Black students suggested that the discipline in their schools is not very strict and laughed at suggestions to the contrary. Non-Black students felt that they and other students were not deterred by the level of discipline at their school from committing certain infractions. They felt that discipline should be stricter in some ways, especially in classroom control, since insufficient control of the classroom by the teacher makes it difficult for those students who want to learn. These students did not feel that suspension was an effective means of punishment. For instance, in the case of 'skipping' class, most non-Black students felt that being given more time off through suspension might encourage some students to continue this behaviour. All non-Black students reported having skipped classes either occasionally or more frequently with few or no consequences. Non-Black students felt that the discipline at their schools, although lenient, was fair and administered equally to all students.

Opinions of teachers on the issues of authority, power, and respect represented particular locations on an ideological spectrum. There were teachers who felt that some of the problems involving racism were a result of the different ways in which Black students resist authority in comparison with White students. They mentioned receiving or experiencing anti-White comments from Black students in school. Some of these teachers related such comments to experiences of racism they assumed these students had undergone at the hands of other Whites or even White teachers. Others attributed them to racism against Whites.

Some teachers tended to refer to violence and Black youth. It was their belief that standards are the same for Black and White youth and that low expectations do not exist for Black youth. They felt that standards for numeracy and literacy are too low, and that students who do not meet these standards simply have to work harder. The teacher was then seen as an authority figure in this process who has to be the judge, thereby setting up the possibility of becoming the object of student dislike.

Other teachers felt that discipline problems had to do with students defying authority for particular reasons. These teachers tended not to focus on issues involving authority, power, and respect but talked instead about other facets of school related to disengagement, particularly the curriculum and teacher-student relationships. Some identified markers which they felt signalled a student's feelings towards school: forgetting a pencil or coming in late.

Across the board, teachers noted that students call certain teachers 'racist.' This fact was interpreted in various ways. While some saw it as a means of acting out, others saw it as related to the behaviour of teachers.

One teacher noted that other teachers tell her they are uneasy about approaching a group of Black students. She stated that there may be one 'bad kid' in the bunch, but that teachers may tend to view and treat them as if they are all bad. This tendency to essentialize or make generalized negative statements about Black students was identified as a common practice among certain teachers. Teachers exhibited frustration about issues of discipline and struggled with finding ways to hold students accountable for their behaviour.

It seems that shifting the locus of blame back and forth from teachers to students is indicative of a social and cultural schism within schools, where there appears to be little empathy or understanding of one position for the other. Another significant issue is the way in which authority is constructed within educational settings, often in an arbitrary and unilateral fashion. This approach can lead to feelings of disempowerment among students, many of whom have legitimate grievances and are left without any institutional means to effect change.

Some parents spoke about their own issues with power and authority in the school, and particularly how this has influenced their role as parents. Margaret, a Black mother, spoke of the difficulty in dealing with the school's and her own conflicting aspirations for her daughter. She mentioned that the school encourages her daughter to aim for goals which are based on stereotypes of Blacks. When asked if she felt that this practice 'undermines her efforts' as a parent, Margaret responded:

Of course it does because it really basically ties my hands at home, because if ... a child [says], 'Mom my teacher says that ...,' you tend to stand back and my flexibility as a parent becomes undermined. You don't want to challenge your child because you want to ... reinforce education ... Without education there is no power. There is no power. But it's how you use that education to facilitate the power that you hold within yourself. (File P01: lines 184–203)

Margaret refers to a duality within the notion of power, whereby the inner power of individuals can be either facilitated or constrained through education, and also to the role of educators in channelling that power. Margaret makes the point that the influence of school can often disempower and undermine the role of parents in the education of their children. Parents' ambitions for their children's educational future and the goals prescribed by the schools are often at odds, especially, as in this instance, where racial stereotypes are said to define the scope of these goals.

Amma, a Black community worker, outlined a profoundly disturbing scenario which captures many aspects of the often disempowering relationship some Black parents have with the school system:

> This is a young man who has just stabbed a White student over some racial incident. The principal sort of reported the end results of that tragedy. But the tragedy started way back when this [student] first entered one of the schools ... and the treatment that the student received through the principals, through teachers, through administrators, and not only the student, but also the parents of the student ... They [the family] are currently applying for landed immigrant status using a refugee claim ... The parents have been very active in school life, advocating for him on several occasions. One incident, he was late. The principal decided he was going to be suspended for a whole week. The parents were annoyed; he was upset. The parents went to principal. Principal says, 'I don't want to see you, I don't have time.' His teacher tried to advocate, [but encountered] the same kind of attitude that, you know the principal, 'I'm all powerful and if I say no, there is no negotiation.' But it's a whole series of things that led to this child being so alienated. He's watched this teacher who is supposed to have authority and some power trying to mediate on his behalf. He's seen his parents coming in, and nothing seems to happen. Eventually, the school decided that they didn't want him and for whatever arbitrary reason the principal decided that 'People like you we don't want in the school,' and he basically said that to the kid. The mother sent him to live with his sister and what happened was, he was in a class-

room and the teacher was talking about some incident with Black people and sport. That eventually led to some racial name-calling. The teacher didn't really deal with it in the classroom ... sent them to the principal's office. The principal didn't really deal with it either or react to it. You know, so this whole thing of being pushed around again, the White student threatened the Black student, Black student decided he was going to protect himself so he took a knife to school and when he was approached by the White student he decided to protect himself. So we see the end result and we wonder, 'What's happening to the little kids? Why are they becoming so violent?' (File CW01: lines 230–93)

The above provides the brief history behind what culminated in a violent racial incident. The background provides a context for what would otherwise be seen as a random act of racial violence, rather than a situation which was developing through a history of mistreatment and disempowerment within the school system. The question remains, though, whether this situation could have been avoided if intervention from parents, teachers, and guidance counsellors was accepted earlier on, and had there been an opportunity to negotiate an outcome which may have prevented the violent act. The principal's unilateral actions and unwillingness to consult other stakeholders served only to exacerbate an already volatile problem. Scenarios such as the above also speak to the need for alternative cooperative strategies to be employed to deal with conflict management, as well as to the need to interrogate the causes of such conflicts within the systems and structures of power in educational institutions.

The narratives collected call for a careful consideration of democratizing aspects of the school system. The disempowerment and injustice felt by students when power is seemingly arbitrarily exercised needs to be resolved in order to address the very real conflicts experienced in schools. Transparent processes in which various stakeholders are represented and have real participation are necessary. Various mechanisms are available to this end: open forums to discuss concerns, clearly defined school policies and procedures, commitment to involving students in the decision-making process, and student involvement in discipline decisions. There are many options available, and the creativity of different stake-holders, if consulted, is a valuable resource that schools must engage if they are to truly be accountable to their communities. In the following chapter, the issue of streaming and labelling students will be discussed. These practices and Black students' experiences with them also call for a more democratic approach to education.

Chapter Seven

Streaming and Teacher Expectations: Social Change or Reproduction?

As 'front line' workers in the education system, teachers were considered by students and parents as critical to the schooling process. Teachers' styles, personalities, and skills were closely scrutinized by their students, who looked to them for guidance and knowledge. They felt their teachers could make a real difference in their education, and, whether positive or negative, teachers' influence was seen as lasting. In this chapter, we examine how teachers' practices in regards to labelling and streaming are experienced by Black students.

Labelling and Streaming

Labelling students according to characteristics other than ability is one aspect of how labelling and streaming can impact negatively on a student's school success. How ability becomes conflated with personal characteristics is demonstrated through the narratives of Black students and drop-outs. In discussing school experiences, Black students repeatedly revealed instances in which they were subject to stereotyping. Often these stereotypes made a real impact on how they were perceived by others and how they began to perceive themselves. Streaming, some note, can be the process by which stereotyping and labelling become formalized by the educational system. Streaming students into different academic levels (e.g., general, advanced) has real implications for their educational chances. As mentioned in the Introduction, often minority and working-class students are targeted for admission to the lowest streams, ensuring the reproduction of social status through the educational system. Students who enter high school at the basic level find barriers and little encouragement to proceed to another stream, and eventually they realize their options are extremely limited.

Interviews for this study were conducted during the introduction period of the destreaming of grade 9 in Ontario schools. Although destreaming has been implemented since then, there is currently discussion of returning to a streamed system. Throughout the province, the destreaming decision was a controversial issue. Some teachers believed strongly in the need to separate students perceived as having different learning abilities in order to instruct them effectively. But most students supported the abolishment of the streaming process and believed that students could learn in any classroom where there was a real commitment to teaching.

Students, particularly those born in the Caribbean, complained about the social stereotyping of the Black male as 'violent,' as a 'troublemaker' and even as a 'criminal.' They blamed the media for this. Black female students also felt their male colleagues have it tough within the school system.

Almost 90 per cent of the students who expressed a position about streaming understood it as a practice which had negative implications for students generally and could be considered as a contributing factor to students' disengagement from the system. Some students were able to articulate clear connections between streaming and students' feelings of inadequacy and fading out. Beth, a grade 12 student in the advanced stream, was sympathetic to the experiences of students who are streamed into lower levels:

> ... there's a stigma with basic level ... the students in basic level are all [considered] stupid ... ignorant; they don't know what they're doing and they're there because they're below or inferior to the ones that are in the advanced level. Nobody wants to go through their life being labelled stupid or ignorant. It would be much easier for you to leave that. You know, leave all that crap behind and just say, 'Why should I go through this system where when people look

at me they associate me with ... stupidity and they think that I'm not gonna get anywhere in this world anyway? Why should I leave myself in a system like that? Everyone else is superior to me, everyone else is in advanced level.' People just want to get themselves out of a system like that and so they drop out ... (File O04: lines 293–318)

Some narratives recounted experiences of being 'placed' in basic and then having parents intervene to 'get me out.' These students spoke about 'how hard,' or even 'impossible,' it was to get out of the basic stream. The 'impossible' cases followed similar patterns, which involved the student asking to get out and hearing, 'We'll look into it.' Often the student was then left feeling caught in the bureaucracy and a witness to the inertia of the system. Finally the student would receive the response 'It's too late,' thereby being informed that there was no way to go into advanced after taking basic.

It is notable that some students said they were in the basic stream and later in the interview indicated goals for which the advanced stream was necessary (e.g., being a doctor, going to law school, etc.). Clearly, they had not been counselled or given the information required to make an appropriate choice regarding streaming. Samuel, a grade 12 advanced level student, cited a graphic example of the confusion concerning available opportunities:

The guy I'm tutoring, he's streamed into a technical environment, but he wants to be a lawyer. You can't really be a lawyer if you're going to a technical school unless you work really hard at it and ... get 90's. So I think once people see that, they get discouraged and go, 'Oh, I can't be what I really want to be because I'm where I am,' and then they just leave. (File O22: lines 237–49)

The existence of vocational, technical, and commercial schools, as well as collegiate ones, was often considered and named as an example of colour-coded streaming. This was how students described the process of streaming and the fact that many Black students were ghettoized within basic level streams. They perceived this to be the result of teachers' low expectations of Black students, rather than their actual ability. Aisha, also an advanced level grade 12 student, noted the lack of encouragement given to Black students:

> … there's a lot of students who are not encouraged … I see a lot of brilliant Black students who teachers tell, 'Maybe you shouldn't take advanced. No, it's really, really hard. You should take general.' And to me that person is brilliant. It's just that no one has encouraged them or told them to try harder or anything, and so they take the easy way out and just take the basic or take the general … that makes the ability in a person just dwindle. (File O09: lines 152–67)

In the following, Sandy also explained how stereotypical notions can impede the process of educational advancement for Black students:

> … in grade 8, I went to a majority Black school. Our guidance counsellor was telling, 'Well, when I look at your faces, I could see that not many of you are going to be going to university. So, there's no reason why you should be taking advanced. What you should do is just stick to the general and basic.' That's what he was telling a group of us. There were a lot of us there. And so, it's like the guidance counsellors and the teachers and everybody, they just push into the basic courses. And then, there's nothing after basic. You don't realize that until you get to grade 12. You know you can't do nothing with that … (File R06: lines 471–90)

For those students who share the above experiences, their educational choices are laid out for them with little opportunity to negotiate options. Despite the above student's experience, some students expressed the desire to go to schools which had a larger Black population because they felt there would be a higher level of comfort for them and more equitable treatment.

Many so-called immigrant students felt that the treatment of their cultural and linguistic differences as deficits was unfair and unwarranted. Despite having been previously schooled in English, students from the Caribbean mentioned being put back a year or placed into English-as-a-second-language (ESL) or English-skills-development (ESD) classes. Some talked explicitly about how it made them feel to be in class with a younger brother, for instance, while others talked about their anger at 'having to do things over.' What we see, then, is how negative evaluations are ascribed to language characteristics, such as speaking with a non-Canadian accent. Therefore, it seems that conformity to White middle-class cultural norms and standards of language has become one of the manifest purposes for schooling in Canada, with obvious and lasting repercussions for those who cannot or will not conform.

There were very few students who found that streaming is a good means of categorizing students according to their abilities; most of those who did were in advanced programs, which they perceived as an example of meritocracy in the school system. This group believed that you got what you worked for and did not see a process of differential labelling occurring.

Drop-outs tended to see the processes of labelling and streaming as being played out in the hidden curriculum – in subtle behaviours of teachers and guidance counsellors – as well as in the practices directly associated with streaming. Drop-outs associated stream-ing with disengagement from school, describing it as a process which resulted in a loss of hope for those placed in the 'lower' or 'non-collegiate' levels. Many students still in the system could not clearly define 'streaming' and had not formed an opinion on whether or not streaming was 'good' or 'bad.' However, in the drop-out sample, virtually all the respondents were able to define and judge streaming as a process which stripped them (and others) of any desire to be in school.

The feeling of being 'trapped' was emphasized when drop-outs discussed how their own self-perceptions were negated by the process of streaming. Michelle, herself a drop-out, emphasized the feelings of being limited and judged:

> … you're saying 'Oh my goodness, I'm so advanced, but yet I'm sit-ting here in basic. How is everyone viewing me?' And you want to get out. And it's just like trapping a fly in a jar, he will eventually die … (File F12: lines 628–33)

Almost all drop-outs discussed the process of streaming (as well as that of dropping out) as having significantly narrowed their options and chances for the future. In view of such circumscribed opportunities, Mike clearly denounced the process:

> There might be a thin line between advanced and general in reality, but then the consequences are so wide, so varied … So I don't really agree with streaming … you end up streaming right into society … (File F19: lines 1416–24)

In most cases, drop-outs were not fully aware of the consequences of streaming and of the impact it would have on their future options. The correlation between streaming and future occupational prospects, then, becomes part of a deterministic dynamic when being streamed in school means 'you end up being streamed in society.'

A story typical of those recounted by drop-outs was told by Denise, who felt that it was far too late for her to pursue her original goal, although she now felt this goal had at the time been quite attainable. With hindsight, she saw that she was, in fact, quite 'bright' and that her subsequent choices were constrained by the following encounter with a guidance counsellor:

> I went to guidance and I was told that you have to be very good at physics and [do] many years of university, and 'Oh dear, you'll be too old before you have kids.' No wonder I'm so confused. Because that was my ultimate. I was extremely bright when it comes to science and I couldn't understand why my focus was so shifted and why I did fashion designing. (File F08: lines 909–24)

This is a clear example of gender discrimination (with the insinuation that furthering her education would hinder child-bearing options), as well as of how lowered expectations for Blacks among school agents can limit and deny a student's potential and life chances. It also relates to how gender roles are stereotyped. Young women wishing to pursue sciences may be channelled into fashion design, in line with the ghettoization of women in specific sectors of the economy.

Examples of racism and the process of colour-coded streaming pervade the narratives of drop-outs like Mike:

> ... [the counsellors] direct them: the general's for the Caucasians and the basic's for the Blacks. Or you can tell the way they try to manipulate you, they think, 'Oh, [this class] is too hard for you, are you taking too much?' (File F19: lines 1071–6)

These comments point to the fact that all too often racial stereotypes preclude the equitable distribution of students into streams based solely on abilities. Black students are channelled into streams which are more in accordance with the preconceptions of teachers than with their abilities, desires, or interests. The outcomes of this process have also been articulated clearly as a loss of self-esteem, diminished hopes, channelling into inappropriate careers, or disengagement from school entirely.

Many drop-outs mentioned that they ended up in a 'streamed school.' Their parents, at the time, were not aware of this fact and could not intercede on their behalf. Denise discussed how this happened to her:

> My parents didn't realize that [it] was basically a trade school. I think because they were busy trying to settle in and do other things with the kids, because I'm not the only one. They didn't realize what the educational system was all about. (File F08: lines 169–75)

The role of parents as advocates for their children becomes diminished when they are not regarded as stakeholders and are not apprised of the school's educational policies and practices.

Teachers had very definite opinions on streaming. Some believed strongly that students in basic level were those who deserved to be there. They felt that these students could not cope with higher streams, and that it was reasonable to have different expectations for different students with different demonstrated abilities. Other teachers believed that work experience was essential to help the students in lower streams. They noted that basic level students and special education students tended to participate in co-op programs which prepared them for the world of work. They also noted that the lower streams are for students destined for certain occupations and who 'realistically couldn't be made into doctors.' These teachers felt that students with lower abilities would 'pull down the good' students if classes were destreamed, and the result would be dilution of the curriculum.

Some teachers had a strong belief that Black students are placed more often in the lower streams and intimated that this was because of lower teacher expectations. Some also noted that students at a lower level may feel badly about themselves, because they don't expect to be able to achieve at the same level as advanced students. Yet rather than providing encouragement, some teachers were reported to be condescending, teaching 'down' to the students.

Some teachers were able to recognize how negative stereotypes influenced their expectations of Black students. Catherine, a White art teacher, shared very honestly:

> I don't want to put myself in the position that I am above having these stereotypes, and it's not pleasant to admit them, but I have found them ... There was a Black student who won an award for something and I was surprised ... I'm quite sure that race entered into it, and that was very upsetting to acknowledge in myself. (File T33: lines 573–98)

These low expectations on the part of teachers, all of whom may not be consciously aware of them, translate into diminished opportunities for Black students, who are socially bound to these stigmas.

The question of whether different streams were simply the natural result of a meritocratic system, as many have indicated, or could in fact be attributed to other factors was raised by the teachers. The fact that many drop-outs return to higher education suggests that demonstrated ability is not always an indicator of individual potential.

From their perspective, parents saw too much labelling and social stereotyping taking place in the schools, often with direct and immediate consequences for Black students' sense of connection to the school system. In particular, some parents complained about the steering of young Black males into athletics and music programs.

Many parents spoke of labelling and streaming as ways in which Black students are led into the process of disengagement. They spoke of students being put back when they enter the Canadian school system and the negative impact this can have on young people. They also spoke of stereotypes which carry a heavy price for Black students striving to succeed in the school system. Wilma, a mother of eight children who have gone through the school system in Canada, spoke eloquently about some of these issues:

> What I find about going through the system is the stereotyping and labelling of different nationalities and races. If you were a Black student, one could look upon you as, 'Well, she's not going to be able to do well in grammar or writing – your abilities would not be as good or as efficient as one who was born here in Canada' ... once you were from a foreign country you [would] not ... be able to go through their school system, because of that. Because of stereotyping, kids fail because then the teachers put extra pressures on them which cause them to become more distant because their self-confidence and their self-esteem is gone, is taken away from them. If it's known that you're not going to succeed, then of course the person who's talking to them is ... not going to smile, to encourage you to speak more, or to encourage you to elaborate on the question they asked you ... (File P13: lines 12–38)

Jane, another mother, spoke of her own experiences with streaming in the Caribbean, and how, in her opinion, racism is the problem and not necessarily the practice of streaming:

> I have mixed feelings about streaming. In the West Indies streaming was done in that if you were recognized as above average you were put in a class with your peers who were also above average. You simplified the way in which the pedagogy was imparted. But we weren't fighting racism. If you were bright and you worked you were also

given a chance. So streaming for me has different connotations. Here in North America, it really means that my child, if I am not vigilant, will be put aside and will not be given the opportunity that his intelligence so richly deserves. So I mistrust streaming in this context. In another context, where ... race is not the basis on which the cookies are given out, I see nothing wrong with it. (File P12: lines 810–33)

In regards to standardized testing, Black parents recognized the need for more appropriate standards of measurement of students' academic achievement. Tania's narrative below illustrates the apprehensions and ambivalence that Black parents feel about school procedures which fail to acknowledge the differences in histories, skills, and privilege that students bring to classrooms. Tania is a Black mother of three children:

... I think sometimes it [testing] will allow the school to know where they are failing and where they need to develop. If you just go basically on what you're doing in the classroom then you may not know the strength of the students or where they're lacking, so it all depends on what they will do with the result of the testing. You know, will some kids be grouped and show up at one place, or are others going to be stuck in one position because they failed that test in grade 6 – that I don't really agree with, but if it's ... an assessment of where the students are going or where the school needs to go, then definitely ... I think in all fairness, I mean if you're doing [standardized testing] I would think it would be more a testing of what the kid has been taught and not whether the kid is astute or not ... the result of the test or how it's done should not be entirely up to the school system to decide, the community should have an input on what goes on. I think parents should be allowed to question it too. (File P08: lines 623–38; 649–76)

The responses of the parents, therefore, echo many of the sentiments of the Black students and drop-outs. The centrality of race within issues of streaming was seen as definitive. As one parent suggested, meritocratic principles cannot be applied in a society where racial disparities exist, as they are in effect corrupted by social and cultural biases which can preclude the just determination of students' abilities.

Parents were worried about the labelling and social stereotyping of Black youth and the consequences for their success at school. Many were troubled by classifications, including streaming in the school system. While most Black parents lauded the decision to destream grade 9, the majority of parents we spoke to wanted to see streaming abolished throughout the school system. Parents also argued that the provincial government should go further and directly involve parents and communities in monitoring students' academic progress. Conversely, the vast majority of teachers were opposed to the concept of destreaming.

Black parents believe in the need for more appropriate standards of measuring students' academic achievement. They generally recognize the value and relevance of standardized testing in mathematics and literary skills. They believe it is essential to know what their children are learning, as it is one way to make the schools accountable to their communities and 'taxpayers.' However, they caution educators and administrators about the importance of ensuring that these standardized tests and measurements are fair, and take into account all relevant facts in the assessment and evaluation of students.

Teachers, Teaching Styles, and Expectations

Black students believed that some teachers do in fact care about their students. But students generally were of the opinion that there is only a small number of teachers in their schools who make attending school worthwhile, and predictably their favourite courses were the ones taught by those teachers.

Clearly, if there is one area in which students show much emotion and anger when discussing unfavourable school experiences, it is the low expectations by some teachers of Black students' abilities. Students explain such low teacher expectations as part of the deeply held beliefs about people who are non-White. In interviews students would cite particular teachers making fun of students and making students 'feel dumb.' Low teacher expectations add to the bitterness students feel about the negation and devaluing of their experiences, histories and knowledges, as well as the contributions they bring to the school.

When talking about their favourite teachers, most students described specific styles of teaching. Teachers who answer questions in class (and outside of class) without making students feel uncomfortable, less intelligent ('stupid'), or as though they are wasting the teachers' time were commended for their abilities to encourage student participation in the classroom. Teachers who are actively helping the student to do better were also favoured, as the following comments by Debra, a Black grade 10 advanced student, demonstrate:

> The time they take – they give you your work, but then they show you why this work is important. And, when ... you don't get the perfect grade, they'll tell you why and how can you improve yourself so that maybe the next one will be even better. (File R01: lines 2416–22)

Beth, in grade 12, spoke of a favourite teacher in terms of the support offered:

> He is kind; he understands what I'm going through and he knows how to teach real well and if you don't get it, he'll make sure that you get it, that's to show that a teacher really cares, that you're learning ... (File O04: lines 328–34)

Favourite teachers, then, are those who demonstrate the belief that a student can succeed, or is able. In short, teachers who have positive perceptions and high expectations of the student are valued, as noted by Steven:

> She's encouraging. She always tells me ... that I could make it somehow, that I could be somebody. I always look at her ... I'm thankful for that. There's somebody that believes in me. (File B21: lines 256–65)

Students described favourite teachers often in familial terms or as being 'like a friend.' This is often connected to the description of favourite teachers as being supportive and accessible. Emily, a Black grade 11 student, gave the following description of a good teacher:

> They're the ones that let me feel ... [like] I'm doing something good. They're behind me, like a father or mother figure ... [If] I do something wrong ... I don't have to sit there and figure it out myself, they go, 'Come up here I'll show you how you did wrong' and try to change it. They're always behind you. (File W05: lines 569–83)

For many students with difficulties at home, the school often serves as a surrogate, where students hope to receive the attention and personal support missing in their lives. Teachers who took a personal interest in the students were highly regarded. Another example of this kind of interest was when teachers empathized with and took into account students' personal problems that could affect their school performance.

It is significant that students rarely described a good teacher as one who demands less of students or gives out good grades. Instead, good teachers were consistently described as having positive perceptions, high expectations, and the time, energy, and commitment to point out, and help students to correct, errors. Respect was regarded as an important issue, particularly in reference to best-liked teachers. Teachers who were described as respecting students were seen as being worthy of respect.

Teachers who were 'fun' and had interesting classes were also noted – specifically teachers who encouraged classroom discussion and seemed to be creating knowledge with their students rather than simply passing it on. Teachers who joked freely with students and had 'hands-on' work, such as research projects or experiments, were also appreciated. These teaching styles, moving far beyond the confines of the classroom 'lecture,' often seemed to involve interaction among people in a 'community of learning,' as noted by Beth:

> I like the way he makes an attempt to mix people up according to different backgrounds, that you learn as much as you can from

your lab partner. And, he also mixes people up according to the kinds of grades that you're getting. So he'll put a student who's doing really well ... with a student who's not doing so well and then he urges you to help that person out as much as possible. So you learn to help each other out. (File O04: lines 798–810)

Therefore, cooperative learning strategies seem to be favoured as opposed to traditional didactic structures. This underlines the importance of peer support in the learning process.

There was frequently a consensus among students at each school on the teacher identified as 'the favourite.' A number of students described grade-school experiences with teachers which still affect them and remain in their memory – an indication of how significant a good or bad teacher-student relationship can be.

When students spoke about teachers they disliked, differential treatment in the classroom was frequently mentioned:

... there's three Black students in my class, yeah, we sit together ... if the White kids talk and are making jokes ... [the teacher] is going to laugh with them. And if we talk, she's going to look at us and cross her eyes ... (File W30: lines 1153–61)

Students' perceptions of being reprimanded for behaviours deemed acceptable for White students support their feelings of subordination. Lower teacher expectations of Black students also contribute to the perception of their inferiority vis-à-vis White students. Aisha explained:

What she does in her class is that she says, ... 'You guys are stupid and you guys are smart.' That's what she's done every year ... My brother wasn't doing too well in the first term ... My parents wanted him to get a tutor, and there's a special tutoring thing ... My parents were willing to pay ... and wanted to get the tutor and [the teacher] made it really hard. So they came in and made sure he got the tutoring ... And then in class, they have this new pairs system, tutoring kind of thing, where older students who have spares come into the class and help the students. She would give everyone one tutor and she'd say, 'Here, you need two because you're stupid,' kind of thing like that … (File O09: lines 370–405)

Stories of teachers who 'belittled' students by telling them such things as they should be in a lower stream, or that they should work at McDonald's, were recounted with great emotion by many Black students, including Beth:

I really like to ask questions. That's how I learn … [But the teacher], she'll manipulate the question in such a way that I answer my own question and then she says to me, 'You didn't really need to ask that question. I don't want you to ask any questions if you don't need to.' And then I try to counteract by saying, 'But I really didn't understand,' and she says, 'Well, if you don't understand maybe you shouldn't be in enriched math. Maybe you should … take a course in plumbing.' She goes, 'You guys aren't very intelligent are you?' … It's horrible. She should not be able to treat us like that. (File O04: lines 884–906)

Edward, another Black student, cited similar derogatory and derisive behaviour on the part of a teacher:

… if you had a problem, [the teacher] would put you down. He would tell you, 'Hey, my daughter or my son could do better than this.' And I don't think that is right. If I knew someone had a problem I would go, 'Hey, do you have a problem? Maybe I can help you.' (File W40: lines 174–81)

Another student, Lesline, discussed the lack of interest with which they were confronted and saw this as a lack of willingness on the part of teachers to support their students:

I don't think that teachers are reaching out to their students. One of my teachers said, 'You know, whether or not you pass or fail, I still get paid.' (File O03: lines 1267–71)

Teachers exhibiting a condescending demeanour, then, alienated students, while those who took the time to provide extra help and had a supportive and nurturing attitude towards their students received high praise, and were also able to help students excel.

Teaching style was seen by students as an important factor in whether or not a teacher could engage the interest of their students. Some teachers were seen as boring. Students commented on teachers who did not allow for student input in the lesson. Victoria, a mature student, recounted the following:

> If you ask her a question, she tells you how long she's been teaching for, and it's like, 'I don't really care how long you've been teaching for, I just need your help.' And then she gets mad and if the students get her upset then she stops teaching and it doesn't make the rest of the class feel better. So, almost the entire class is failing. (File W33: lines 472–80)

Teachers who seemed to be doing the minimum amount of work required in the classroom were those who just instructed students to 'open your books' to such and such page number, and failed to actively engage students in the learning experience by eliciting their knowledge and experience and incorporating it into the classroom discourse. The role of teachers as facilitators in a learning experience was preferred by students to the role of teachers as the disseminators of information. Therefore, teachers who could make learning a relevant and egalitarian experience – that is, they were prepared to incorporate students' input and experiences – were regarded by students as being most able to engage their interest and elicit their best performance.

Students talked about instances when teachers did not consider students' interests and experiences. One example was a teacher who said, 'We won't talk about the Rodney King incident, because I don't know about it,' and then went on to talk about sports. Cultural insensitivity on the part of some teachers was also criticized, as shown by Susan's comments:

> She said this to the whole class, that AIDS came from Africa ... and like, there's all this kind of proof. (File B19: lines 486–95)

Teachers who do not allow critical thinking about the curriculum and teachers who do not accept Black students' statements about racism or Eurocentrism in books such as *Lord of the Flies* and *Huckleberry Finn* were also disliked by Black students. Sandy described a confrontation over this issue with a teacher:

> I had to do an essay on *Huckleberry Finn* and *Roots*, and I was writing that I thought Huck was racist just because of the things he said, and I backed it up and everything. And because I said that, [the teacher] didn't like it and gave me a really bad mark. And when I went to talk to him about it, he said, 'No, you can't say Huck was a racist because he became friends with Jim' ... I told him that the book offended me and he was, like, 'This book did not offend.' (File R06: lines 1072–88)

The unwillingness of some teachers to discuss students' attitudes on race, particularly as they relate to the curriculum, serves to further alienate Black students. These narratives have shown that in order to create an equitable and engaging environment, classroom discourse and curricular content must legitimate and include the concerns and experiences of all students. From the perspective of critical pedagogy/teaching, materials cited as offensive serve a viable pedagogical purpose and should be taken up collectively by the instructor and class for critical examination. Critical education and the fostering of critical understanding can only develop when students are accorded the ability to challenge and redefine the knowledge which is presented. Thus, teachers who are unwilling to divest authority over the discourse create educational environments which undermine the creative instincts and critical consciousness of their students.

Individuals in the drop-out sample also recounted falling victim to low teacher expectations, as was the ongoing case for many Black students still in school. They described how low expectations were conveyed through the hidden curriculum within schools. These expectations translated into behaviours and attitudes on the part of certain teachers and guidance counsellors which relayed messages of inferiority. Denise described the way in which the attitudes of guidance counsellors and teachers conditioned her thinking about her own 'potential':

> I blame ... my guidance counsellor, because, in so many words, she told me that I don't have the brain to do it. She wasn't overt about it, but that's the impression I got. And it's just like a disease, it stays in your brain, until you realize that 'Hey, there's a problem' and get it treated, it remains there. (File F08: lines 971–9)

This experience of constant discouragement is typical of the drop-outs' narratives. Drop-outs tended, more than students, to see the ways in which subtle messages from guidance counsellors and teachers had very real consequences in their lives. Many drop-outs discussed instances when counsellors told them to move into lower streams, take fewer challenging classes, or drop out of classes that they were finding difficult. While some of the students were able to identify teachers or guidance counsellors who had told them that they 'can do the work,' uniformly, drop-outs, like twenty-five-year-old Darren below, were unable to recall such instances:

> One of the teachers told me that I could drop math ... [so] me and my friend, as a matter of fact another Black guy ... dropped math and then ... the next [week] ... we seen that same teacher that told us to drop math talking to a White student saying, 'Don't drop math because if you do you might as well say good-bye to 87 jobs.' (File F13: lines 62–72)

Other examples of differential treatment on the part of teachers included 'chatting' informally with White students, but generally not including Black students in such discussions; and telling White students, but not Black ones, that they want them to achieve, that they believe they could do better, or that they are bright. While students tended to recall specific instances of these teacher behaviours, drop-outs tended to see these behaviours as typical and endemic to the school environment as they experienced it.

Other factors which drop-outs asserted make it easy to disengage include specific practices by teachers in the classroom, such as denying equal access to classroom participation:

> And you'll be surprised, you'll have your hand up for days and never be called ... (File F12: lines 1000–1)

Michelle here refers to the sense of invisibility some students reported feeling within the system. Being ignored or undervalued as a member of the class results in student alienation and contributes to the process of fading out.

Issues of conformity and acceptance were also seen as problematic. In speaking about teachers, Mike commented:

> One or two were cool. But they were like the rest. Cool only when you tow the line and do what they want. No one is willing to accept people on their own terms. You must conform. It was too much for me. (File F19: lines 212–17)

Incidents of 'veiled racism' – for instance, comments which carry implicit messages of racial differentiation – reinforced students' feelings of alienation:

> One day I was walking with this teacher and I thought, 'I know how they are, it's in their nature, but maybe she's one of those liberal Whites who will suppress it' ... it was hot outside in the sun, she goes, 'Oh you get tanned too don't you? I know, I have a friend who's brown and he gets darker' ... and in my head I go, 'I guess your nature must come true.' (File F19: lines 487–99)

Comments of this nature speak to the need to culturally sensitize the school community. The insensitive attitudes among school agents, as described by these drop-outs, are evidence of their lack of preparation to teach in a multiracial, multi-ethnic context.

The sentiments of non-Black students differed from those of Black students and drop-outs on the issue of differential treatment based on race. Peter, for example, had the following comments to make:

I think that education has no colour so those people who want to learn will and those who don't, won't. (File CG05: lines 596–8)

Tinh shared this view:

I think the teachers here are fair to all students. They treat every-body [with] the same respect. (File CG06: lines 108–10)

These responses were typical to questions regarding differential treatment of students by teachers based on race and also class. Non-Black students responded that the school administration and staff treated everyone the 'same.' The non-Black students believed that if someone wanted to learn and wanted to do well in school, they could do so through individual efforts. The individual was the unit of consideration in terms of opportunity and educational achievement; they resisted speaking in terms of groups.

Yet there were those non-Black students, like Brian below, who felt that Black students were subjected to different expectations by the school staff:

I think that the school system looks to the Blacks as inferior, that they won't know as much. So they expect them to have less grades ... I don't think that's right at all. I don't think that's fair. (File CG04: lines 918–25)

Even though these non-Black students were not the majority, it must be noted that there were still contradictions in many of their overall responses. For instance, a response like the above might be followed by a comment about equal opportunity. These students had not given the thought necessary to these issues to reconcile systemic racism with the daily practice they observed.

Most non-Black students described teachers they disliked as being 'boring,' and this spanned different subject areas. Most non-Black students said that the teachers they disliked did not appear approachable and were not available for extra help. Also, these teachers only seemed interested in the students' performances in that one class and knew nothing about the students' personal lives or personalities. Issues of fairness and equal treatment arose only with respect to the individual student as opposed to students as part of different racial and cultural groups.

Of all the groups, teachers spoke the least about teaching styles and expectations, although some teachers did discuss the ways in which lower teacher expectations contribute to the process of disengagement. These teachers also talked about the issue of expectations related to the race, gender, and class of the student. Some teachers were seen as being unable to deal with issues relating to racism and sexism. Some felt that the topics were suppressed in the classroom and at the administrative level because discussion of them often leads to conflict.

Parents, like Felicia below, expressed the belief that teachers have a vital role to play in the academic success of a student, as well as in the psychological and emotional growth of the individual:

> I think teachers play a great role in influencing or even socializing the children. And when they are negative or show negative attitudes towards students, you tend to lose your self-esteem and it makes you want to leave. (File P18: lines 110–16)

The role of the school as a primary agency of socialization is recognized here, as well as the pivotal role played by teachers.

Christine, a mother, emphasized the expectations that teachers carry for Black students and explained how these expectations are further prejudiced for Black students from a homosexual family:

> I think because I'm a lesbian that that has an impact on how she is perceived within the school system. I think teachers who know very little [about] lesbianism or who have their own ideas about what it means to have lesbian parents assume the worst. So they assume because you're a lesbian and especially because I'm a Black lesbian, that my child isn't encouraged to excel in school, that she may not have a study area at home … And so they assume that I wouldn't be involved in the system, I think, because I'm a lesbian and because I'm an out lesbian … Yes, I think that's the stereotype,

you know, that the child is coming out of an unstructured home ...
(File P7: lines 278–311)

Homosexuality and homophobia are seen by Christine as poorly
understood and inadequately addressed in the schools. Teachers are
perceived as making assumptions about the values and home environments of children of homosexual parents. The assumptions are
attributed to a lack of understanding of and exposure to the realities of homosexuality. This impacts directly on a teacher's ability
to relate to students who have this home environment, and can
lead them to convey potentially dangerous messages to students.*
Overall, parents stressed the need that teachers remain aware of
their influence and use it to positively impact on all students.

Obviously, it would be unrealistic to attribute all the failures
and successes in the school system to teachers. But we must take
careful note of the narratives in this chapter which suggest that
teachers wield a great deal of influence over the day-to-day aspects
of schooling. Students take to heart the experiences they share
with teachers, especially teachers who have shown themselves to
be concerned with students' overall welfare. By the same token,
teachers who are perceived as uncaring by students can have an
equally strong, or even stronger, negative impact on students'
educational choices. School systems must recognize the centrality
of teachers and encourage and enable them to take on their role in
a positive fashion. Teachers, of course, are limited in some degree
to the curriculum they must follow, and this topic is discussed in
the next chapter.

---

* As noted in the Preface, culture and politics are the intellectual companions of the
researcher. As such, it is because of her political and religious orientation that Jasmin
Zine is unable to support certain views expressed in this chapter and in chapter 8 regarding the validity of homosexuality as an integral part of schooling and of the antiracism
project. She believes that as a Muslim she is bound to a specific frame of reference
regarding this issue.

Chapter Eight

Curriculum: Content and Connection

This chapter will examine the relevance of curriculum content to the lives of Black students. Students unable to find relevance to their own lives in the curriculum find it difficult to connect with the educational experience. Black students see a lack of curriculum content devoted to their history and experiences. For example, Black students had strong feelings about how the inclusion of Black history in the mainstream curriculum would enrich their educational experiences. Students suggested that including Black history might mitigate the boredom experienced by some students. Debbie, a grade 10 student, made the following connection between a friend's decision to drop out and curriculum content:

> Bored, just bored; not getting what they want, like learning different things. I thought Black history would be good to learn but they don't teach that there in [her] school ... sometimes I think that's why she dropped out, because she wanted to learn Black history too. (File B23: lines 64–73)

In responding directly to the question 'What is important about Black history for you?' Kirk, a grade 12 student, stated:

> Because I'm Black. They're robbing you of your past ... And unless you have the interest and you could be in a group of people who have the interest that they want to learn, you're not gonna learn anything. (File O01: lines 1395–1418)

The exclusion of Black history, then, was regarded by these students as a clear deterrent to gaining a meaningful experience from
their education. Moreover, it was seen as 'robbing' them of a part
of their history and denying legitimacy to the Black experience.

Virtually all drop-outs felt the curriculum had not included anything relevant to their experiences, whether in the form of Black
history or in the form of an understanding of Black experiences in
general. There was a pervasive feeling of being systematically
excluded. Drop-outs recalled how in every class they experienced
exclusion, an absence of themselves in the curriculum. In fact,
drop-outs directly associated the lack of Black history with their inability to stay in school.

Denise, a drop-out, spoke of an African history class taken upon
returning to school and compared it to the curriculum as it existed
before she dropped out:

> The curriculum ... was one-sided, especially when it came down to
> history. There was never a mention of any Black people that have
> contributed to society ... I mean, everything, it's the White man that
> did. History is just based on the European Canadian that came over
> ... There was no mention of the Africans that helped build a rail-
> way, that ran away from the South and came up to Nova Scotia and
> helped work and build Canada too ... no mention of that. (File F08:
> lines 316–32)

Denise refers specifically to the absence of Blacks in Canadian history, a fact that contributes even more to Black students' sense of invisibility and lack of status as Canadians. Furthermore, it explains
how this exclusion places Black/African Canadians somewhere outside of Canadian history, rather than acknowledging them as an intrinsic part of it. Darren, another drop-out, spoke directly to the frustration and alienation experienced by Black students in this regard:

> It's like you're learning about somebody else's history. You're learn-
> ing about when they discovered America when things were good for
> them and when they did this and when they did that ... It started
> to take its toll on me after a while. (File F13: lines 397–410)

These drop-outs expressed the need for fundamental changes in the way history is represented. In a broader sense, they addressed the need for rethinking the efficacy of a strictly Eurocentric knowledge base in a multi-ethnic society and increasingly globalized world.

On the issue of inclusive curriculum, teachers, again, were divided by ideological positions of conservative and progressive. Some teachers did not believe in the notion and felt that including groups other than the 'founding groups' in Canadian history was unnatural, and not a part of the teacher's responsibilities. They expressed the sentiment that inclusive education was simply a response to pressures of 'political correctness' and felt that the curriculum should reflect Canada, implying that Canadian history basically went back to European contact and that 'minority presence' is recent and peripheral. Thus, these teachers believe that in trying to be 'all things to all students' the educational system will fail. For these teachers, labelling the curriculum as Eurocentric is unfair. The traditional curriculum holds values with which all should be made to identify and which are considered sufficient.

Other teachers were frustrated with the mono-cultural focus of education and discussed the difficulties with their independent efforts at making the curriculum more inclusive. Catherine, a White teacher quoted previously, addressed these issues:

> I am fairly new to teaching art history and it's all White European history and what I have to confess is that I'm still doing it, partly because I'm still learning it myself and I'm getting it across and all the while I'm thinking God, I've got to interrupt this somehow. And it is very difficult. I don't have the materials at my fingertips and I don't have the time at my fingertips … So all I end up doing is saying look at how White this is, look at how European this is, look at how we're not looking at what the Asians are doing at this time, what the East Indians were doing at this time, and I try to throw in the odd thing happening at the time but it's not on the curriculum, it's not part of the 120 key words they have to know so I can't spend time on it … I throw on a video now and then, I bring in some posters that a Black artist or an Asian artist has done … but I think

that's a little bit tokenistic, if there's such a word. (File T33: lines
286–327)

This teacher's narrative speaks to the need to broaden the scope
of the current curriculum to include the contributions of other cultures. It also deals with this teacher's sense of frustration in attempting to integrate this knowledge without proper institutional
support, that is, without the development of an inclusive curriculum. As is stated, this leads to tokenism when individual teachers
attempt to integrate their curriculum without the necessary time
allowances governed by course requirements. Therefore, this piecemeal approach to transforming and creating a more holistic curriculum is undermined by the institutional structures. However,
these constraints should not be considered valid reasons for not
pursuing educational change.

Other teachers were also critical of the middle-class, mono-cultural nature of school culture and values, and discussed how this
poses problems for students outside of these social boundaries. In
the following, Catherine's comments address some of the constraints:

> I think we have a very middle-class White environment. I think that's
> the majority of teachers, the majority of the focus of the curriculum.
> I think in terms of values altogether, it's middle-class and White. I
> think in terms of, for instance, what is acceptable noise level in a
> room or in a hall or in a cafeteria, that's a middle-class White per-
> ception. So I think there's a discrepancy for kids who aren't part of
> that. I mean I think there's a cultural discrepancy ... the whole way
> in which we, who are part of the dominant culture, have this ten-
> dency to think that what we do, what we organize is what's right,
> what's absolute ... and I think we are so oblivious to the ways in
> which we impose all of that, all those constructions, that we can't
> even give you all the answers of why the kids are dropping out,
> because we're oblivious to a lot of it. (File: T33 lines: 67–92)

Catherine situates the norms of schooling within the domain of
White middle-class society, and this contributes to the alienation

of non-White and lower-class students. She goes further to explain how this cultural hegemony can contribute to student disengagement for those who fail to fit in with the normative standards defined by White middle-class society. She also implicates teachers who fail to recognize the impact of systemic discrimination and social cultural exclusion because of their own immersion in the normalcy of Whiteness and the standardization of middle-class values and perceptions.

Other teachers felt that people interested in learning about their own heritage can do their own research. Some of these teachers felt that Black history is a part of Canadian history and is indeed taught. However, they noted that having a separate Black history class would be 'too exclusive' and would be less likely to be taken by other ethnic/racial groups. These teachers felt that a Black history class would create segregation and is unnecessary since no one really feels left out. As Fred, a high-school history teacher, stated:

It could be too exclusive. And then, you would have to ask how many other ethnic or racial groups are going to take the course. And ... are we building in, then, segregation within our school system? ... But I have never seen, in my classes, any student of any particular racial or ethnic origin reacting as if they have been excluded or don't have a role. And I'd like to think that we provide opportunities for everyone to succeed. No one is put on a limb and cut off because of who they are, their name or what have you. (File T07: lines 247–54, 264–72)

The argument put forward by other teachers to counter this view was that the issue is one of integrating as opposed to segregating, since minority interests are already peripheral to the mainstream discourse.

The inclusion of Black history was regarded by some as the result of special interest groups getting tax dollars in order to receive special treatment. Others perceived impediments to the integration of Black history to include the lack of materials, an inability to find junctures where it would fit the curriculum easily, and a lack of African or African/Canadian accomplishments in certain areas. Some teachers recognized the ministry directives that curriculum is to reflect the population of the classrooms, yet without the means to assess whether this mandate is being applied, they felt that there could be no accountability. Others acknowledged that Black students have a difficult time with their identity because of a lack of knowledge of their history. Gayle, a Black woman currently employed as a board of education officer, stated:

> I think it's difficult for them to even express themselves, because they themselves don't even know where they are coming from and anything about their history. The whole issue of identity and how that isn't reflected in their education, that is something I think the school system needs to deal with because the students themselves are not, do not feel a part of the school system. And, if they don't see themselves reflected in books or in the curriculum, they cannot express themselves. They don't know how to express themselves according to the images that they see on television. Whether it is through a magazine, that is the image that they perpetuate, and it is not an image that is created by themselves, but it's an image that is created by the media. (File T02: lines 836–57)

These teachers find that currently Black students do not see themselves reflected in the curriculum, and they tend to see inclusion as a challenge, a task to be taken up. Brian, a high-school principal, noted that Black History Month is only one month and that there is a need for inclusion year round:

> If it's one month, you sort of say, 'Now that we've done it this month, we can forget about it for another year,' and I don't think that makes any sense. We have to seek a lot of ways to be far more inclusive in terms of students' backgrounds. It's quite a challenge here given the range of backgrounds that they do have. (File T17: lines 677–80, 699–708)

Brian brings up the important issue of how confining Black history to one month can become a form of cultural and political containment, and diffuses the impetus towards a truly integrated education. Black History Month, then, can become an excuse to dismiss broader issues of cultural inclusion and equity – while it brings Afro-centric knowledge one step closer to the mainstream curriculum, at the same time it keeps it one step away.

Many parents saw a need for changes to the curriculum. The incorporation of Black history and Black heritage into daily lessons was a suggestion. Others simply wished the curriculum to be more inclusive of all students' lived experiences. As Christine, a mother, noted:

> They can expand the curriculum so that it's relevant to Black children ... they need to include things that have daily meanings for Black students, that things that they experience as they grow up are discussed in the classroom, that things that they experience at home with their families are discussed in the classroom. And I think I can go on to say that that's true for kids coming from not only a Black home but also a gay home or a lesbian home. (File P07: lines 317–28)

Christine sees clearly the need to validate the various experiences which different students bring with them to the classroom. The issue of children from a gay or lesbian home highlights the need for struggle against homophobia within the school system, particularly in making definitions of family and family life inclusive for all students.

Joyce, a Black woman who works in the community and who has experienced the Canadian school system herself, talked about the detrimental effect that not learning about her history and the contribution of Blacks has had on her and continues to have on other young people:

> For example ... I did Greek philosophy and Greek history. Now I, as an African person, if I had not done my own research, read on my own time, I would not have known that a lot of people who they were saying attributed the great works of civilization to Greece and Rome ... were African scholars ... Africans ... being portrayed as being born as ... Greeks or Romans. So, you see, when an African person goes to school, he does not see himself in the picture. He

does not see his people contributing anything to the advancement of civilization and therefore, he doesn't feel as if he has a place there. (File CW05: lines 475–95)

Gayle speaks of how, in her opinion, the curriculum is outdated and does not take into consideration the changing characteristics of the student population:

I think a lot of people who are responsible for the education for our children are locked in this time warp where they feel [that if] these kids are not learning, it's their [own] fault – it has nothing to do with me. They can't see the irrelevance of what they teach or the inappropriateness or how alienating it is. That's how I think the system was designed, probably sometime in the sixties ... not reflect[ing] the reality of what we have in our schools now. (File T02: lines 294–307)

The school system is therefore viewed as an anachronism, incongruous with the current social and cultural conditions, and therefore in need of transformation.

What is or is not present in textbooks and lesson plans is significant in the discussion of curriculum, but so also is the climate and tone of both the official and unofficial curriculum of the classroom, and the general conditions of school life, what we refer to as 'deep curriculum.' In other words, the deep curriculum encompasses all formal and informal aspects of the school environment and the intersections of culture, environment, and the organizational life of schools.

On the subject of the formal curriculum, students identified junctures where Black history is needed, where they have disagreements with Eurocentric curricula/texts, and where they feel unrepresented. These assertions were rooted in the daily school experiences of these students.

Drop-outs attributed weaknesses in the deep curriculum to an overall 'Whiteness' of the school system. To drop-outs, this 'Whiteness' is obvious, of course, in the formal curriculum. Denise, a drop-out who was particularly interested in science, noted that throughout her classroom experiences she was never taught about any Black scientists. When asked if it would have made a difference if, for example, Einstein had been Black, she responded with the following comment:

> It wouldn't have been in the book if he was. That's the thing, it wouldn't have been in the book if he was ... during Black History Week on TV [I learned that] the first guy that did a heart transplant was a Black surgeon. (File F08: lines 811–69)

For this reason, drop-outs often seek out other sources (e.g., media, community groups, books) outside school that will help them to develop a 'personal curriculum' which has more relevance for them.

While both students and drop-outs discussed how they, as Black students, need a formal curriculum which includes them, drop-outs furthered their analysis to highlight the reciprocal relationship between curriculum and school culture. Thus, from this more holistic vantage point, they were able to see the interconnectedness of curriculum, culture, and politics within the educational system and to link their lack of representation in the formal curriculum to their marginalization in the school itself:

> ... the mainstream kids ... they may not think of it, but when they look through all those books, they see a representation of themselves. And, somewhere in their little heads is, 'Well, I don't see someone who looks like so and so' ... the ridicule starts then, you know. (File F03: lines 568–84)

Mike added:

> So really, the curriculum, it's geared to Europeans – the way they think, the way they go about their lives. (File F19: lines 1561–2)

Lack of representation in the curriculum also relates to the sense of invisibility many Black students and drop-outs reported experiencing. This occurs not only through what they have described as an unresponsive school system, but also through not seeing themselves reflected in the formal curriculum. This is described as reinforcing the power and privilege of White society, and contributing, in a sense, to the colonization of other knowledges and experiences.

An ability to see the 'big picture' gave drop-outs particular insight into the schooling process and why it was that they eventually dropped out. For some, like Michelle below, this was linked to what they saw as the school's attempt to deny their identity and assimilate or reconstruct them according to dominant norms:

> Why did I drop out of school? Personally, I believe, high school especially, it's a processing plant. You walk in there in grade 9, and you are about to be processed and in the end you will come out a product, for lack of a better word ... the atmosphere lacks respect. It lacks principles, morals, values. I think it invades everything about one's character, totally breaks it down to then reconstruct another character. (File F12: lines 186–200)

Thus the attempt to deny legitimacy to the Black identity is perceived as an assault on personal and cultural sensibilities. In the following narrative, Lloyd explained how this often results in students dropping out:

> I believe when an African stops going to school, it is in part because he has too much self-pride and cannot stomach the system's moves to take that away. The school was successful in the past when some of our brothers and sisters were ... ashamed of their history and their roots ... I can see a person dropping out for the reason of declining self-esteem. I don't honestly think this is the case today. These kids have too much pride. When they leave school today it is because the system got them in other ways, yes, in other ways, man, but for sure not because of any lack of self-esteem. (File F18: lines 120–38)

Therefore, rather than associating dropping out with a lack of self-esteem, it is argued that it is precisely the existence of a strong sense of cultural pride and self-esteem among Blacks which schools seek to contain and which eventually forces students out.

Drop-outs cautioned, however, that it will take more than just equal representation in the formal curriculum to correct the situation. Given that the deep curriculum encompasses all aspects of the school environment, they suggested that many changes need to occur – everything from cafeteria food to teaching practices needs to be examined. Mike commented on the fundamental need for restructuring in the following analogy:

> ... you can't just ... drop a few in the pot. You have to dump out the pot, start from scratch and put the proper ingredients that were there in the beginning ... (File F19: lines 1612–20)

This analogy addresses the need to restructure the representation of Black history and to simply 'tell the truth'; that is, to incorporate Black history and experience as an integral part of the curriculum rather than as a token element. This, it was argued, could not be done by adding on to the existing knowledge base. It would require a rethinking of how history and the representation of the 'other' is conceived and presented.

Responses to the subject of the deep curriculum and antiracism education were influenced by the age and social location of the teachers; that is, their race, class, and gender. The responses of teachers were most consistent with those with whom they shared the above characteristics. A number of teachers claimed that antiracism education is not needed and maintained that the current curriculum is adequate to serve its purpose. Some believed that antiracism education is too abstract for high-school students. Others felt that this sort of education segregates groups and 'teaches kids the wrong stuff,' sometimes resulting in students 'crying racism' against their White teachers. This seems to be a partial attempt to lay blame on the students, rather than attempting a critical examination of one's own discriminatory behaviour or acknowledging one's own powerful position in society.

The following anecdote, recounted by Andrew, a White history teacher, reflects what some teachers felt as 'reverse racism,' or being discriminated against on the basis of White privilege:

> Like, I walked by a group of kids in the hallway ... and one of them

was a Black girl that I hadn't seen for awhile. I taught her last year
... I heard my name mentioned as I went into the washroom and
[when] I came back out ... [I] went up to her and I said, 'Hi. How
is one of my favourite kids from last year doing?' And, this other
girl, who was also Black, walked away because I had walked up.
And I said, 'Why is she walking away?' And this girl said, 'You don't
have to run away ... He's a good guy. He's okay.' And, I suddenly
realized this girl had walked away because she saw me as White
power ... I have to live with that kind of thing. (File T01: lines
816–24, 1115–41)

Some teachers, then, have a lack of understanding of their position relative to Black students. They feel maligned for being White
yet confuse this with racism, which refers to a system of advantage
based on race. Those whose race accords them advantages in society cannot equate their position with those who are disadvantaged on the same grounds. The reality of 'reverse racism' can
therefore not exist without fundamental shifts in the distribution
not only of rewards and penalties in society, but also power. There
would have to be a reverse in the relations of power and in the
hierarchy of privilege in order to validate claims of 'reverse racism.'
While the sentiments of these teachers should not be dismissed,
they speak more towards the need to create a culture of tolerance
and equity within schools which, at the same time, attempts to
bridge not only generational but cultural gaps. These sentiments
also speak to the need for antiracism and critical race education as
a requisite part of the educational system.

Understanding this need, a somewhat larger group of teachers
maintained that antiracism education should be implemented.
They see it as a tool which can empower all students by encouraging a global perspective in the class and by incorporating student experiences into the school system. In this way, the students
can relate to and have a vested interest in their formal education.
However, teachers complained that a lack of resources makes it
difficult to fulfil this mandate. Some, like Gayle, mentioned strategies such as finding resources in the community or from the students, and, as part of professional development, participating in

various projects which move them in the direction of inclusive education:

> I think it incorporates a lot of different things. I think, number one, antiracism education is geared at the empowerment of all students through antiracist teaching and practices and ... setting up the classroom in such a way as to incorporate the global perspective ... and dealing with things from a variety of perspectives and having students themselves participate in their own learning by understanding students' experiences and having them bring their experiences within the classroom and validating their experiences. (File T02: lines 683–701)

Yet, as these actions are still voluntary, many teachers remain ill-informed about antiracism education. Thus, as one teacher stated in regards to antiracism training, 'Those who need it, don't go.'

The impact of issues presented in this chapter goes beyond practices of labelling and streaming to the very identity of Black students. We will demonstrate in the next chapter how issues of representation impact directly on Black students' experiences of schooling. Black students' identities are challenged by the stereotyping and labelling evident in school practices.

Chapter Nine

Framing Issues of Identity and Representation

The issue of Black representation in the school curriculum is fundamental to developing an inclusive school environment. It is no exaggeration to say that Black students and parents are generally critical when discussing their reflections on the Canadian school system, particularly of the fact that not all world experiences are represented in classroom instruction, discourse, and texts. At the core of the issue of Black identity is the well-articulated concern that there are gaps in curricular content. Black contributions are not included with enough sophistication and centrality to reassure Black students that their race and the achievements of their forebearers are respected. These issues are integral to the notions of identity and representation.

The 'participation/identification' model proposed by Finn (1989) has significant implications for both representation and identity in terms of a school's ability to engage students who are not members of the dominant culture. It has been argued within the context of theories of social reproduction (Bowles and Gintis 1976) that school culture is a mirror to dominant culture in society. As such, when students find themselves in contexts where they are not represented, their expressions of identity and political decisions regarding conformity and resistance become sites of contestation. The issues are at times further complicated by differences within the Black student group (e.g., culture, religion, and language). Intra-group differences have an added impact for some students in terms of how they construct their identity and where they are able to find support within the context of the school. How students take up these issues within the school has implications for the extent to which they will feel willing or able to participate in and identify with the school. How students articulated their concerns over issues of representation and identity will be explored in this chapter with attention to implications for understanding expressions of resistance.

Black youths talked about the fact that classroom discourses occasionally speak to their lived experiences; the fact of being Black, a Black woman, a Muslim, or any form of a minority living in Canadian society. Students want their schools to reflect the communities in which they live. They want to be taught about their ancestral histories and cultural heritages. They also want a greater connection between what they learn in school and their actual lived experiences. Students who perceive a dissonance between their education and their lived experiences are more likely to disengage from the system.

At another level, and additional to these pressures and frustrations with the school system, there is also the constant struggle for Black students to maintain their individual self- and group cultural identities. Many times, students' actions do come into conflict, even with their peers. This is revealed in students' discourses about 'acting White,' about what it means to be 'Black' or 'African,' a 'Black male' or 'Black female,' as well as contestations about who is Black or not Black enough. Students attributed the struggle to negotiate their individual self- and group cultural identities to a very narrow school curriculum. There was some acknowledgment of the value of an event like Black History Month, but it is still viewed as a piecemeal approach to addressing questions of 'inclusivity.' The history of Blacks in Canada is discussed largely from the 'victim's stance,' as in slavery. Few educators highlight the moments and sites of political resistance in the history of enslavement. Furthermore, in the celebratory approach to Black History Month, when exceptional attention is paid to African-Canadian achievements, Black students and parents complain about schools ignoring the centrality of these experiences to Canadian history. It is little wonder that many non-Black students see Black history as only for Black students.

Most Black students found it difficult to discuss how they express their personal and cultural identities in school. This difficulty may have been partly a result of their general inability to fully comprehend the term 'identity.' This in itself suggests that the students are neither learning about self- and cultural development in the classroom nor consciously exploring them through other school activities. Occasionally, students mentioned a class in which they were permitted to discuss identity issues, but this was considered an exception. When students were asked how they expressed their identity within the school, they found it difficult to answer. As Kirk, a grade 12 student, noted, even when you have a means for such expression, there are limitations in the school structure:

> You don't have much opportunity to, unless it's in the clothes you wear and things … [and] the organization for Black students … but, if you didn't have that, like, take away that, there's nothing … you can't really express yourself. (File O01: lines 1508–23)

Students clearly felt that there were few structures at school which allowed them to explore their culture. In turn, the development of their creativity and sense of self-esteem tended to be hindered. Moreover, when they talked about having access to creative outlets, they also mentioned sometimes being made to feel guilty or a sense of wrong-doing. Sandy, a grade 12 student who has tried actively to engage Black identity issues within her school, recounted the frustration involved in legitimizing the attention paid to Black History Month:

> … when we were working on Black History Month, we got into so much problems … with the teachers and everybody else. And then, at the end of the year, all my teachers were saying, 'Oh, you got too caught up in Black History Month' … It's like all my marks went down because of Black History Month. So, my answer was, 'Well, if you had Black history in the curriculum, then I wouldn't have to forget about what I'm doing and focus on Black History Month.' (File R06: lines 1967–81)

Sandy critiques the relegation of Black history to appendix status within the regular curriculum and argues instead for a more integrated approach to incorporating Afrocentric knowledge and history into mainstream discourses. Attempting to contain Black history in this way ghettoizes Afrocentric knowledge and confines it to the margins of mainstream culture and discourse. The result is a negation of inclusive education. Sandy also argues that such a location within the curriculum limits the access students have to Afrocentric knowledge and forces them to compromise other courses in order to contend with the constraints placed on Black history.

Other students spoke about how their identity was stifled by a school system which demands conformity to the dominant culture. Of greatest concern was that the school not only fails to support students' personal growth, but it actually serves to silence them. Richard, a student considered to be 'at risk' of dropping out, noted:

> You couldn't express it … because you have to assimilate and you have to be like everyone else. So, you had to be like they be. If you didn't, then you're a troublemaker or you're the strange kid that's got this, you know, psychological problem. But even nowadays when you say it's more expressed, even still, you're looked upon as a troublemaker because you want to learn your identity and something other than [in a] class[room] where you feel … wrong. You don't feel it. And, you bring it up and … you're a troublemaker now because you're going against the school. So even though they say you can express yourself … it's not the same still. To me, it's all a big puff of smoke. (File A08: lines 761–82)

It is clear that the lack of tolerance for cultural differences within schools is mired with notions of deviance. Students who do not conform to standardized norms and conventions are labelled 'troublemakers'; a stereotype which is particularly difficult to negate once it is attached to race. The unwillingness to conform to the normative standards, codes, or conventions of the culture within schools or society at large can be seen as an act of resistance. This resistance is not simply teenage rebellion; it is a response to the oppressive conditions which constrain cultural identity and sense of self.

For many students, dropping out actually becomes an act of empowerment in order to maintain their self-esteem, which was otherwise compromised within mainstream schools. This form of resistance to assimilation and the need to preserve one's racial or ethnic identity are in keeping with the deviance theory put forward by LeCompte and Dworkin (1991), where the cultural non-conformity of those who look and act differently from the mainstream is viewed as antisocial and deviant behaviour. Consequently, these students begin to internalize these institutional labels and redefine themselves in terms of this perceived oppositional behaviour.

Although students had difficulty expressing details of their own personal identity, they were able to see several commonalities between themselves and their Black peers. Thus, while individual students may be feeling psychologically 'lost,' together they have a strong sense of group identity. Indeed, when asked if they felt they had anything in common with other Black students, 88 per cent of them responded 'yes,' with little variation according to gender or place of birth. They spoke of shared interests in music, clothing, sports, and community leaders. Black heritage clubs were also mentioned as a site where common bonds were fostered. As well, some students talked about their conscious choice to hang out with other Black students, regardless of whether or not they were friends, because 'We're Black,' 'We all understand each other,' and 'We have the same experiences.' Blackness is seen as an experience which is felt and understood, and which unites individuals. There is consequently a sense of 'us' and 'them.' Some students, like the two young women quoted below, admitted that they deliberately avoid having White friends on the grounds that these students would not be able to understand their experiences or give them support:

I hang out with mainly ... Black students and stuff. I don't really associate myself with any of the White students because ... I don't feel so loose with them and comfortable. I have to act, like, not myself. I have to be, like, you know, down played. (File O30: lines 335–42)

... sometimes when you go into the classroom, you look around and

see if there's any Black students and … sit down beside them …
There's just a need to, I guess, stick to each other and notice each other
… looking for another strength. (File R06: lines 1605–27)

Not only did students feel that there is strength in numbers, but
they also felt that they can be themselves and be 'recognized' in a
positive light among their Black peers. It is a feeling of comfort and
support that they do not get elsewhere in the school. Being unable
to express themselves fully in terms of their identity prevented some
students from hanging around White students. As one student in
a focus-group discussion stated:

… I want to be myself and show everybody who I am, but you
can't, you can't be yourself too much, you have to hide some of
your Blackness when you're around White people, because then
you become like an alien to them. (File O10: lines 691–704)

This student makes the claim that being around White people pre-
vents Black students from being themselves out of a fear of alienation.

Some students gave the impression that the sense of validation
which is derived from having Black friends made school a more
bearable experience and, literally, helped them get through the
day. This aspect of 'surviving the system' pervades their school
experiences. Indeed, Black students share strategies of coping with
each other which can be instrumental to their school success. Sandy
highlighted the centring of dominant culture within the school in
terms of which kinds of knowledge are validated and how this
impacts on Black students' sense of shared identity:

… we were going to write an exam … I think it was a parenting or
sociology exam. All the Black students were at one place studying
together, even though we didn't really know each other that much.
And some of them were saying, 'Oh no, I don't know if I'm going
to pass.' And then some of the Black students said, 'Just think
White. Think of the way White people raise their kids and you'll
pass the exam because that's what's going to be on the exam.' And

we felt a closeness because we know that we're raised differently.
(File R06: lines 2312–29)

This not only puts into perspective the disjunctures between family socialization patterns among Blacks and Whites, but more strikingly it highlights Black students' awareness of the normative value of Whiteness and the power that it holds within the curriculum; hence the need to 'think White' in order to succeed.

There is concern among some students, however, that feelings of commonality and racial group affinity may dissipate as students grow older. One student believed that Black people do not continue to work against racism once they have achieved some level of success and have fully assimilated into White culture. This notion was prevalent among some students, that cultural assimilation causes individuals to detach emotionally and psychologically from their group in order to garner acceptance and legitimacy in White society. Such assimilation is often perceived as a form of 'selling out,' as described by Douglas, an OAC level student:

> ... one thing we do talk about a lot is [Black] people who ... when they're forty, they've got a good wage and they're in a powerful position somewhere ... They're just the same as their White partners in terms of doing things we've got for the people. (File O02: lines 858–76)

The fact that students feel that a Black person must give up their personal and group identity in order to be successful reflects their situation in the school system. Black students were frequently well aware of how the differential distribution of rewards in society occurs along racial lines and related similar disparities in their school experiences as part of the same systemic oppression. Assimilation, then, can often be seen as an attempt by some Blacks to gain parity by conforming to the codes and conventions of the dominant society, often at the expense of their own cultural integrity.

There were other ways in which some students felt that they did not share anything in common with other Black youth. This is significant in that it ruptures the monolithic notions of Black culture and experience. Religion, clothing, dance, and values were all cited as sources of difference between groups of Black students. Language was a particularly significant element of division. For instance, Blacks from the Caribbean often speak English with a Caribbean accent, as well as speaking their own 'demotic' languages (Philip 1989, 18), which tends to create a barrier between themselves and Canadian-born Blacks, who speak with a Canadian accent. Similarly, some Canadian-born students feel that because they do not speak a 'Black dialect,' they are prevented from really fitting in with those who do. African-born students and Black students from other countries who are in English-as-a-second-language (ESL) classes feel more comfortable with their own language group than they do with the larger Black group. These observable differences may be exacerbated by the differential treatment that the students encounter within the school system itself. For example, those students who speak English but who have something other than a Canadian accent are sometimes put into ESL classes. Some students from the Caribbean also noted the decision to put them into English-skills-development (ESD) classes because of their English skills. A few so-called 'immigrant' students noted they had been held back a grade because of their language skills. For these students, language and accents are sites for discrimination at school. In a sense, they are perceived as inferior by the system, which then projects this image onto other students.

Intra-group differences among Black students were most explicitly expressed by students born in Africa and the Caribbean. In an all-female student focus-group discussion, the facts and realities of how these differences get addressed by students themselves were elaborated:

F1: I didn't know you guys, see, I was new to the place, to Canada and all, and it was my first day ... [you were saying], 'But I am not African!' – you were resisting.
F2: We're just glad you came.
F1: Oh my god, [I thought], I'm not going to talk to these people, you know? Because I never actually seen, you know, this was my

first time interacting with Jamaican people. I always spoke to African girls and my sister and African people. I never wanted to talk to you guys because I heard her say that, as if they hate us, you know? They hate us, that's it, you know?

F2: I must say, at that time I did.

F1: And I was so shocked, I don't forget it. It was one year and a half now, and I never forget.

F2: Because I was, I'll tell you where I was at that moment. I didn't want to be associated with Black people, with anything that has to do with Africa, because well, like I said before, what I hear was all negative things, and I think that they were all this, right, and I didn't want to be associated with.

F1: Girl, you couldn't fight that because you didn't even know.

F2: Exactly, because I don't know anything.

F1: I understand.

F2: But I started learning a little and little about myself, and I found out that, hey, that was all wrong. A lot of people, and I've made that comment to a lot of people, a lot of people now are frightened to see that I am the same person who used to talk like that, because I've grown so much. I've learned so much …

F3: There's been this huge evolution for all of us. I mean, we've all gone past a lot of things, together, and that's where, way back to the beginning, I mean, that's the importance of this group. I mean, we're all doing this all together. (File D05: lines 1440–1504)

The young African-born woman who opens the discussion talks about the resistance of the second student to her African heritage and identity. The discussion progresses as the students exchange very honestly their misconceptions and their educational and political development. The second student admits to having accepted stereotypical understandings of African culture and people. The first student supports her by pointing out that she didn't have the tools 'to fight'; that is, she did not have the knowledge. The group had developed a relationship over time and learned about each other, differences and commonalities, to the point where they were then able to talk honestly and continue to learn. This discussion provides an exemplary sample of the type of process that needs to occur for all students if they are to realize the misconceptions they carry and discover the knowledge which will provide them with understanding and help them to build connections across differences.

For students who are immigrants from Africa, particularly those from Somalia and Ethiopia, the issues of language, culture, and religion are of utmost concern. Muslim students, in particular, found it easier to formulate an identity through their religion. When asked if expressing his religion as a Muslim had something to do with expressing his individual and cultural identity, Thomas, a Canadian-born grade 12 student who had converted to Islam two years previously, replied:

> Yes it does because I think ... I'd like to say it's Islam but perhaps if anyone accepts a new religion and they're into it, then it's going to govern their life ... at least at the beginning. And Islamically, we're supposed to keep our culture and our identity except if some of that culture clashes with Islamic ideals, right, which isn't a problem with the Black issue. You're a Muslim before you're Black. (File O02: lines 925–35)

Thomas's layers of identity have been constructed in a way that gives priority to his religious identity. He does this, however, without renouncing his affinity to Black identity. Rather, he is adding another layer to the matrix of his personal identity.

When describing themselves, Muslim students talked about their food, clothing, and daily rituals, such as praying, which strongly link their everyday experiences and self-development to their faith. However, even though they have the support of a strong religious framework, they too experience a lack of support for their own personal growth within the school. They explained that their religion is not always recognized and validated in schools, both on an ideological level (e.g., the acceptance of their faith as legitimate) or on a structural level (e.g., spaces available for praying).

Some students recalled being outwardly discriminated against by other students, Black and non-Black, on the basis of religious expression. Others, like Thomas, found that while treatment by his friends hadn't changed, he had a sense that stereotypes were being applied to him because of his religious beliefs:

> The friends I had previously, I still have and they're still my [friends], I still hang around with them more than anyone else. I don't know. They don't tease me or anything like that. I'm sure they talk about me behind my back ... I know a lot of their prejudices about Islam ... [which are not brought] necessarily to the surface because they don't treat me any different. (File O02: lines 1036–49)

When students do express their identity through their religion, they also face challenges with their peers in terms of intra-group differences and peer pressure to conform:

> You have to be strong, you go, well it's a part of my religion, I can't drink, I can't eat pork, so that's it ... but most people have that peer pressure because they want to be cool, you know, so, and that's why they have to forget about the religion, they don't want to look like, you know, their background or something like that, so if they want to, you know, blend in. (File W31: lines 1290–97)

For Black students, then, who have spoken strongly about the importance of support from other Black students and group affinity, having their religious identity contested by that same group is an additional challenge to negotiate.

Not being 'Black enough' was a problem encountered by students in the higher academic levels. They felt that they are labelled as nerds and are penalized by other Black students because they do not fit into the Black youth stereotype of hanging out in the halls and of having poor study habits. During a focus-group meeting, one student voiced her disdain for those very students who 'act White':

> F4: Sometimes, it don't matter how White you look sometimes you have a little bit of Black in you. You are Black, so you're Black. They act Black, they talk Black, but acting like they're White ... I hate those people.

What's acting like White?
F4: They just act like White people, you know, like they're White. You know, they walk with, they only have White friends, you know, they listen to White people music, they don't know nothing about Black people music, they talk about that nonsense … and all like this, you know. They just act White. (File D04: lines 1211–35)

These barriers of difference can lead to a lack of solidarity among Black youth and consequently weaken the power of the consolidated group of Black students. This can also leave some Black students 'out in the cold' – neither Black enough nor White enough. They are left with no cultural group in the school to which they can turn for moral support.

The issue of Black identity also finds expression in the construction of difference along lines of 'shade' among Black students:

F4: Another thing too … you're a Black person calling them, 'Oh, he's too Black' …
F2: Yeah, I know. Shadism, thank you.
F4: … 'He's too Black.'
M1: Oh yeah, too Black…
Are you always talking about skin colour, or is it anything else?
M1: Skin colour. Skin colour.
F3: Well, yeah.
F2: And it could be the way that you act too.
F4: Or, something like, if you turned out the light, you'd never find that person, the way how he's Black. All that stuff.
F2: Shadism.
M1: You know what? Sometimes they're just joking when they say that, it's just a joke.
F2: But the thing is, it shouldn't be a joke.
F3: It shouldn't be a joke … The thing is, Black people have to learn to respect each other, you know.
F2: Exactly.
M1: Stick together. (File D04: lines 1112–49)

This example of intra-group racism highlights the divisive effect difference can have and the importance which students attribute to respect and unity in resolving these divisions and racisms.

School activities (e.g., yearbook committee, student council, various sports) were perceived by students as being dominated by certain races and/or nationalities, a factor which alienated other students and effectively discouraged their participation. For example, one student mentioned that although she wanted to play soccer, she did not join the team because she would have felt uncomfortable being the only Canadian-born Black in a team of Caribbean-born Blacks. This ghettoization of extracurricular activities can become entrenched within the informal structures of schooling when segregation is supported by the teaching staff and then maintained by the students themselves. For instance, if teachers encourage White students to be on the student council and Black students to be on the soccer team, eventually students will only be comfortable trying out for one of those activities. The result in this case would be that the Whites are found in the decision-making positions in the school, while the Blacks are relegated to the realm of sports.

If outlets of self-expression are lacking for Black students today, the situation for the drop-outs interviewed must be understood as having been more intense. The absence of this support no doubt contributed to their process of disengagement. As such, we found that the drop-outs interviewed had a more profound and deeply layered expression of identity. They described 'contrary behaviours,' such as skipping out, arguing with teachers, and even dropping out itself, as their response to being Black in an all-White system. They added that, contrary to popular belief, it was on these occasions that they were able to most significantly tap into their reserves of self-confidence and self-esteem. As Mike, an adult drop-out explained, it is submission to the system that eats away at the core of their identity:

> ... the system destroys their inner strength and character ... I have always maintained that we Africans have self-esteem ... We always had a positive image of ourselves and that's why the school system has tried over the years to deny us our self-worth. I know who I am.

I know where my roots are ... School didn't teach me that ... This ... is a big issue with some people when they say the kids lack self-esteem or what have you. It may be true for a few but we have to ask, 'Why?' It is the school that makes them lack that self-esteem. So the school should see the problem as its own doing, not the kids ...

Those who go astray are pushed aside and made to feel as if it is their fault or some personal weaknesses in character ... that is why they can't behave like everyone else. There is no serious effort to find out why some of us behave contrary to what is expected of us ... This failure gives me the impression that not many people care ... My philosophy of life is ... don't hang around in places and among people who are only interested in remaking you ... (File F19: lines 115–33, 170–84)

This view expresses the language of marginalized resistance from students no longer willing to be participants in what they see as their own subjugation. In this case, being liberated from the source of contention means disengaging from a school system which is perceived to hinder their personal and cultural growth and self-esteem. Yet it is important that they define this as an act of dissent rather than of personal failure, which they acknowledge is the popular conception of dropping out.

These sentiments were echoed by a number of drop-outs who felt that it is a struggle to maintain an inner identity in a school system that wants to transform and hence defeat them. Michelle, another drop-out, noted:

I think anyone with self-character, anyone who has an inner strength that nothing and no one can defeat, will most likely either be a drop-out or, if they attain an education, and they always bear in mind who and what they are and their culture and where they've come from, they will be a deadly weapon as far as society is concerned. (File F12: lines 462–70)

Drop-outs articulated the notion that differential treatment is a major commonality between themselves and other Black students.

They added, however, that there are also differences between themselves and these students. A major difference is that drop-outs put up more of a fight to retain their Black identity. As Mike further noted, they would rather drop out than give into the system:

> Well, I went to [school name], there was Blacks but they were too … how can I say, cultured. I mean, they were too 'runny runny,' you know what I mean? I'm just not part of that … They were imitating Whites and having some White person be their head, have them led on a string … I also went to [school name] … there were more Blacks there. Again … on the one hand they'd be cursing the White thing, but the next minute you see them buddy-buddy up with them, taking on their culture, dressing in the clothes they dress in … (File F19: lines 279–302)

Mike is critical of the hypocrisy felt to exist among Black students who attempt to follow the dominant culture. Thus, for students more strongly grounded in their own sense of identity, the need for some Black students to conform is seen to impede racial solidarity and is viewed with some contempt.

For the most part, however, comments on the similarities or differences of Black identity were either peripheral or absent from drop-outs' narratives. This may be because such differences are eclipsed by other, more pertinent problems. As well, for some drop-outs, the population of Black students in their school was much smaller than for those students presently in the system. The lack of a large peer group would mean that drop-outs had a weaker network of informal support within the school and therefore no source to validate their experiences or to help them to develop strategies to survive in the system.

While many non-Black students indicated that they do not feel it necessary to express their cultural identities at school, some nevertheless felt they did want to do so, but found that it was difficult. Erica, a White student, noted that one reason for such difficulty was that White students feared that any attempts to express themselves would be met with considerable resentment and rage by non-White students:

Well, because people would say, 'You're White. You're nothing because everyone knows about White history and everything cause that's what you learn in school.' So people just ignore it. (File CG09: lines 418–24)

Erica expresses a denial of the inequities in schools and an unawareness which is fed by a system that fails to teach students the true meaning of multiculturalism or provide the enrichment it could offer to their formal and informal educational experiences.

Like Black students, most non-Black students had friends who shared similar backgrounds to themselves. They admitted that this made them feel more comfortable because these students understood them. Again, this may be the result of a school system and society that tend to be mono-cultural and that do not encourage 'mixing.'

Many teachers found it difficult to describe commonalities and differences of students. This may be the result of cautious political positioning rather than ignorance – an attempt to maintain the position of cultural blindness. When discussing differences among students, teachers stuck to 'safe' and obvious traits such as language, rather than the more abstract and sensitive issues of culture, race, and nationality. Some teachers observed that those students who have difficulty with English or who have an accent are made to feel inferior and thus have more problems negotiating the school system and tend not to express their ideas in class.

Although there was reluctance to pinpoint racial and ethnic group traits, it was clear that many teachers could indeed identify such differences between groups of students. Most teachers were well aware that student peer groups segregated themselves by race. Some teachers were particularly insightful, remarking how this tendency to congregate in racial groups was a means of self-expression and peer support. Anne, an ESL teacher, noted:

... the [Black] girls in particular, they do seem loud! They seem louder than most ... to sort of risk stereotyping ... if you see the Vietnamese and the Chinese girls [in the cafeteria], they will all be sitting together ... and they'll be active, talking and so on, but you won't really hardly hear anything they're saying. And then across the way there'll be the Black girls and you will hear everything they say and … their conversation will be peppered with lots of 'fucks' and all kinds of things, you know, that are really offensive to a lot of people's ears … I have some theories. I don't know whether they're right or not, but I think it's real insecurity … In the classroom, I find them very, very quiet. Like in this room, a class of thirty I guess it is, with five kids Black, I find the Black kids are quieter than some of the others. So, it's only in this social group situation. To me, it's a reaction to an insecurity that they feel in almost every other situation. It's kind of a bravado that they feel they need to put up. (File T18: lines 582–605, 627–45)

Following Anne's analysis, Black female students feel intimidated in the classroom, where they are less free to express themselves. This may lead to getting lower grades and then being labelled as low achievers. The situation is not helped by teachers who believe that academic ability is an inherent trait that can be neither nurtured nor stifled, as voiced by Victor, a teacher with many years in the school system:

I think a lot has to stem from the individual. If somebody doesn't want to be motivated, you're not going to motivate them. (File T14: lines 187–90)

Many teachers failed to make the connection between classroom behaviour and the mechanisms in the school which hinder students' personal growth and identity. By focusing on the individual and not seeing broader issues of discrimination and inequity within the system, responsibility is placed squarely on the shoulders of those students who disengage from the school system.

Some parents also regarded language, culture, and nationality as sources of both student identity and discrimination. While such characteristics can help to foster a sense of self, as well as create bonds with other students, they can also be used by teachers as a basis of differential treatment, as Tania, a mother of three, noted:

Most [students] were actually born here and they have been referred to as immigrants. But they are not. They are Canadians ... My kids were born here and they're still referred to as Jamaicans. So the alienation is right there in the school where teachers are not seeing them as Canadians and are probably treating them differently ... (File P08: lines 840–53)

Some parents and community workers reflected on their own experiences in school. They talked about how it is difficult to express oneself in an environment which seems so 'foreign.' Francine, a Black woman and community worker, remembered how hard it was to relate to a fundamental element of school culture – her teachers:

I could see that young people ... who did go further than high school, seemed to have a certain comfort... this is how I saw these White teachers teaching ... they told these lovely stories about their children, etc. And I knew my reality was very different ... my mom gave me the piece that would have been missing otherwise. If my mom had not been there, the self-esteem piece would have been missing. (File CW02: lines 1251–66)

It becomes clear, then, that cultural incongruence can be fundamentally destructive to the self-esteem of those outside the dominant group. When Black students are constantly faced with the knowledge that their reality and experiences are not constructed within the dominant framework of cultural convention, they experience feelings of dissonance, which in turn can compromise the development of a positive self-image. As this woman finds, familial support is often necessary to fill the void one feels when one does not fit in.

The issues of identity and representation have been shown, then, to have significant impact on the extent to which students are able to engage the educational system. Various structures within the school constrain students' ability to express and develop both their personal and group identities. While students have asserted a strong sense of group identity, there still exist challenges at the level of intra-group differences for some students in terms of language, culture, and religion. Pressures to conform, particularly to the values and expectations of the dominant culture within the school, challenge the existence and development of the individual and group identities of students. Students respond to this challenge. For some, the response is to negotiate space for themselves within the extant structures. For others, this challenge and negation of identity can be the beginning of a process of disengagement.

It becomes important to consider, then, how issues of marginalization that have arisen within the mainstream school are confronted by students, and how being either within or outside the mainstream system is envisioned. There is an expressed need for students to have their racialized, gendered, and cultured identities validated. However, the question remains whether it is possible for students to develop culturally within the space which has been described in this chapter. To address these issues, we must turn to a deeper examination of the implications of Eurocentrism within the school system and the ways in which students negotiate these issues from their various locations.

Chapter Ten

The Colour of Knowledge: Confronting Eurocentrism

The issues of identity and representation for Black students have been examined in terms of how students are and are not able to construct their individual and group identities and develop these within the current educational system. Problems of representation, whether with respect to the absence of role models or in the abstract production of knowledge, and issues of identity are closely tied to the process of disengagement, and as such require closer analysis. As students, parents, and educators reflect on questions of identity and issues of Eurocentrism within schools, they explore alternative visions for the delivery of education.

Many Black youths and parents made a simple connection between the problem of student disengagement and the lack of representation of Black role models in the schools. Students and parents wanted to see more Black and other minority teachers, guidance counsellors, and administrators in the school system. Many Black students and parents saw the Black teacher as an important role model, and students in particular spoke about the likelihood of this teacher having a social perspective with which they could identify. Parents saw a representation of Black teachers as essential in helping students connect and identify with the school. However, a few students and parents were quick to add that having Black teachers would not necessarily make a major difference unless it is accompanied by other fundamental changes in the school system. Although non-Black students and many teachers felt that a teacher's race should not be an issue in education, many nevertheless saw having teachers from different racial backgrounds as a good idea.

Black/African-Canadian parents and students wanted Black history and Black studies to be integrated fully into the schools' curriculum. Teachers also saw the importance of such studies. Black parents made the connection between learning about one's history and cultural heritage and the eventual academic well-being of students. Parents talked about the importance of rooting students' learning in an appropriate cultural context. Many stakeholders, particularly Black students, drop-outs, and parents, also approached the issue of a Black-focused school. This chapter will explore these discussions as they relate to the issue of knowledge production and its connection to student engagement.

Black Heritage / Black History

Most of the drop-outs interviewed did not have access to a Black Heritage Club when they were at school and noted its absence. Some believed that because they did not have access to this type of support group, they had more struggles than students have today. This seems to corroborate the participation-identification model (Finn 1989), which holds that the greater one's sense of belonging and participating, the greater the likelihood of remaining in school. The fact that drop-outs were denied such avenues for culturally based participation was seen to enhance their sense of alienation, which had significant impact on their decision to leave school.

Some non-Black students expressed that it was unfair that the school recognized a Black History Month but no other cultural or racial celebration. They felt that if the school was going to sponsor events for Black culture, then it should do so for all cultures. Melissa, a White Anglo-Saxon student, suggested that these celebrations indicated that the Black students had more 'power' in the school than someone like herself:

Why didn't we have a European history month? And if we did, I honestly think that the Black kids wouldn't have attended. But, we had to attend [Black History Month activities]. (File CG02: lines: 894–7)

This defensiveness was shared by other students. There was a tendency for non-Black students to view Black History Month as another example of the preferential treatment Black students are receiving. This is typical of the view that social justice is somehow tied to particular interests, and therefore not seen as contributing to the betterment of society as a whole. Yet when understood and implemented correctly, inclusive education, far from being divisive, would serve to broaden the scope of what constitutes the 'Canadian experience' for all students and allow them to feel connected to the curriculum and to each other.

Non-Black students did not mention that they considered the current history courses biased or unfair. The intention and purpose of Black history was not seen by them within the context of knowledge production and social relations. Many students reported that they did attend Black History Month activities and enjoyed them. Others said they did not attend because they did not think it would be interesting or useful and, furthermore, felt that these events were for Black students only. No non-Black students mentioned having been involved in the organization or presentation of any Black History Month celebrations. It seems that while the school is allowing Black students a forum for expression, it is not doing enough to promote the event or to encourage the involvement of the general student population. This suggests that the school may consider the celebration as a token gesture and that it is not seriously committed to the fundamental principle.

A number of teachers felt that Black History Month and African heritage organizations cause divisiveness in schools and allow Black students to express anger at non-Black teachers and students. Such organizations were seen to foster a separatism that is not healthy for the school itself. These teachers did not feel that positive messages about African heritage, or associating on the basis of race, are at all helpful or conducive to student well-being in general.

Black parents wanted to see more Black history taught in the classrooms. They appreciated the creation of Black History Month but felt that this information needed to be provided on a more regular basis within the curriculum. They felt that currently Black history serves only as a palliative rather than constituting meaningful change. Tania, a mother of three, emphasized the peripheral nature of Black History Month:

> Black History Month, to me, is better than nothing, but it's sort of like Caribana: you have one month and you tell students … a few things and the kids remember a few great guys and then it's forgotten. To me, that's not really incorporating Black history in the school. It's seen as a festive occasion. How seriously it's taken and how much respect it's getting, I really don't know. I'm not saying don't have Black History Month. It's nice that they would give us a whole month, you know. It's almost as if, well, you're important for this month … It's good to have, but long term, you know, I'm still concerned. (File P08: lines 1564–84)

Amma, a mother and community worker, furthered the argument by calling for a more globally oriented curriculum, but restated the important fact that African peoples must also be constituents of that world:

> I think it's necessary to have that sort of world vision, but definitely you have to be in that world … (File CW01: lines 819–22)

Fears of exclusion even within a globalized discourse stem from the fact that 'world vision' must necessarily be presented from a vantage other than Eurocentrism, in order for the authentic representation of non-White cultures to occur. It is therefore necessary to include knowledge from outside of the dominant historical paradigms, rather than continuing to colonize the knowledge and experience of those represented as social and cultural 'others.'

Black Teachers and Counsellors

When asked if it would make a difference if their teachers were Black, there were differences in the responses of males and females and those of Black students born in Canada and Black students born abroad. Overall, 66 per cent of female students stated that it would make a difference to them, as opposed to 54 per cent of male students. Of students born in Canada, 59 per cent stated that Black teachers would make a difference. This represented 68 per cent of the female respondents and 48 per cent of the male respondents. Of those students born outside Canada, 63 per cent thought that it would make a difference. This represented 64 per cent of the female students and 63 per cent of the male students.

Black teachers were seen by Black students as being able to provide students with positive role models, as well as advice, hope, encouragement, and a sense of the wide range of opportunities that exist for them. Patricia and Neil, both grade 12 students, commented how as role models, Black teachers enable Black students to believe that their success can be emulated:

> ... they could actually give the Black kids ... you know, 'Look. I made it. I know it's hard because you're Black. You know, when I was younger, it was even harder because there were more struggles. So stick with it.' You know, just give them a bit of encouragement. (File O28: lines 774–80)

> ... we're young, right, and for ones, like the older ones, then would like to see the younger brothers want to make it in life, not like leaving school and end up on the road or in jail or something like that. (File B16: lines 284–91)

Black teachers were also seen as able to provide a social perspective more congruent with that of Black students; one that emanates from similar experiences and struggles. Rhonda, a mature student completing her high-school education, commented:

> ... if I saw a Black teacher in a classroom, I'd be proud. It's, like, it's someone that I can look up to, you know. I could identify with this person. This person knows what I have been through or he's ... already paved the road for me and if he can do it then I can do it. (File W35: lines 688–98)

Black students found that they were better able to connect with teachers who have firsthand knowledge of the Black community and do not have to base their understanding on second-hand (and often biased) information. Stephanie, a grade 10 student, noted the importance of teachers having this experiential knowledge:

> Well, I know that they'd, you know, be there to help me and I will feel ... more comfortable. If I want to talk about something about Black, you know, that they will carry on the conversation ... [not like] the teachers who just go [by] what they read from the book and from the TV and everything ... (File W10: lines 1123–33)

Black teachers were understood as people to whom the students could relate, and vice versa. The students know that these teachers have likely encountered the same societal barriers and survived, a basis of respect for many students. Some students also mentioned that a Black teacher may even make them feel like they are a part of the school. This feeling of connectedness, a commonality of experience, is strongly linked to the students' sense of ease in the system. Their level of comfort can be elevated by this representation, with students finally 'seeing themselves' reflected in the school system. Samuel, a grade 12 student, was explicit on this issue:

> ... it was just like a sea of White faces. I was, like, 'Wow!' You don't really feel comfortable you know, but [with] ... a couple of Black faces in there, you feel closer to the staff kind of. (File O22: lines 520–5)

Students also suggested that they respond better to the teaching style of Black teachers than to that of White teachers. This relates to the fact that there are cultural differences in learning and cognitive styles which respond more effectively to alternative pedagogical practices than to those which exist within mainstream education. Black students are aware of these differences and feel that a Black teacher may be better able to provide learning strategies more consonant with their own learning styles and the ways they were taught at home.

Often, Black teachers were referred to in familial terms, revealing the affinity Black students felt towards them. As Kimberly, a grade 12 student, related:

> I feel like I've got to act a certain way. There's a standard act I've got to live up to ... [We've had] Jamaican supply teachers, and I feel like I've got to be 'proper' because it's like my mom there, so I've got to be proper and behave myself. I wouldn't think of acting any other way. (File O06: lines 459–68)

In terms of classroom procedure, Black students felt that White teachers let certain things 'go by' and thus tend to discipline less than Black teachers. As an example of culturally different communicative styles, some students noted that while White teachers 'suggest' things, Black teachers are more explicitly 'demanding.' Students seemed to appreciate and respect this directness, as Wendy and Tamara, both grade 10 advanced level students, noted:

> ... Black teachers, I find that they're a bit more strict. You can't really get away with some stuff that you did before. (File R02: lines 699–702)

> ... they're more, like, they're strict, and then they can be fun. But ... White teachers, they're just easy ... they don't, they don't reach me like the Black one's will reach you ... (File B12: lines 289–95)

When Black students spoke about encounters with Black teachers, anecdotes were filled with positive and memorable experiences. Indeed, the general absence of Black teachers in the school system elicits a certain amount of anger and sadness among Black students. Vanessa and Sandy, both grade 12 students, felt that having a Black teacher would help to mitigate the feelings of alienation they felt within predominantly White schools:

> ... all my courses, it's all White teachers. It's just, it would make a little difference if there's a Black teacher, even one of them through my day. Just one would make me feel more comfortable. (File O29: lines 583–8)

> When we moved around this neighbourhood, it was our first time going to a school with all White students and we were so outcast. It wasn't funny. And I'm telling you, looking back now, if I had a Black teacher who I could just go to and just sit down and even talk ... that ... would have made a difference. (File R06: lines 1271–86)

Other Black students stressed the need for minority teachers in general and for a wide variety of teaching staff. In their opinion, minority teachers of any group might be more likely to relate to their experiences than would White teachers.

Of the Black students who said that having Black teachers would make no difference to them, many qualified this statement by saying that race does not matter as long as the teacher is not racist. Others, like Noel in grade 10, stressed that teaching ability is the most important factor:

> ... if they want to help you, if they care about you, they want you to get a nice grade in the class, stuff like that. If they're prejudiced or whatever, I just switch to a different classroom. But, it doesn't matter if he's Black or White or Chinese or whatever, I don't care. (File W29: lines 488–503)

Interestingly, while some students expressed a desire to have Black teachers, they did not see as great a need for Black counsellors. Only 41 per cent of students believed that having Black counsellors would make a difference. While there was not a significant difference between male and female responses, there was between those students born in Canada and those born abroad. Of the former, 45 per cent believed that Black counsellors mattered, compared with 37 per cent of the latter. The majority of students may not feel Black counsellors are as important as Black teachers because of their lack of contact with the counsellors.

Those students who did see Black counsellors as important believed that they are more likely to understand Black students' personal experiences than are White counsellors. They felt that it would make a difference particularly when problems involving racism or family relations arose, as Cheryl and Beth, both grade 12 students, noted:

> I can relate to the Black counsellor more and maybe I can talk to her about things that I can't talk to my White counsellor about. Maybe because, what if I have a personal problem that I don't want the White counsellor to know about? ... but, like, maybe I'll feel better that the Black counsellor knows ... she can relate to you ... like you're on an even basis ... (File W11: lines 553–67)

> ... [when] there's a problem where there's, you know, something culturally based that they'd be able to understand more than someone who was White. I don't want to have to go into an office and first of all explain my culture to someone and then explain my problem. I want to be able to go in there and say, 'This is the problem. Can you help me with it?' (File O04: lines 1145–61)

Black counsellors are seen by students as being able to provide an environment in which their experiences are understood. Cheryl also highlights the racialized climate of schools and the fact that when she needs help with a personal problem, having to negotiate race becomes a barrier.

Drop-outs were more emphatic about their ability to relate better to Black teachers. While some Black students felt that the race of a teacher does not matter, drop-outs maintained that race was relevant, a major reason being that they felt Black teachers are not only more understanding, but also more demanding and 'strict' with Black students. This was important to drop-outs because they believed it showed that someone is watching out for them, that someone cares. Being strict, however, is distinguished by drop-outs from asserting power and authority for the sake of dominance. Again, in a focus-group meeting, a drop-out spoke of Black teachers in familial terms:

> If there was a lot of Black teachers now like my mother, like, I know nobody would be messing around. They wouldn't be joking around ... (File F05: lines 1511–29)

Unlike the Black students, drop-outs saw Black counsellors to be as important as Black teachers. This is likely because drop-outs have spent many more hours in counsellors' offices, specifically White counsellors' offices.

Of greatest importance to drop-outs was that the chances of helping a student who is in the process of disengaging are greatly increased when a counsellor has a comprehensive grasp of the situation. In their opinion, Black counsellors would have a deeper cultural understanding of the realities that Black students face, as stated at a focus-group meeting:

> ... if you have a counsellor come from your own country, religion and everything, it's good, because ... like, if it's a White counsellor and a Black kid, the White counsellor is going to try to put himself in the kid's place, but it's impossible; he's not Black. (File F05: lines 1695–1703)

The feeling that White counsellors would not be able to empathize with the reality of Black students was common to both students and drop-outs. The lack of Black counsellors was also said to be a deterrent for Black students voluntarily taking advantage of counselling services.

There was some difference in opinion among non-Black students regarding the importance of the race of a teacher or counsellor. In their view, personality and teaching or administrative ability were the more important factors. These same students did not feel that it would matter to Black students either if there are not many Black staff members in their schools. Others thought that it would be a good idea to have teachers and counsellors from different racial backgrounds. They added that for them it did not really matter, but for Black students and for students of other races it probably did.

Some non-Black students had not even noticed the absence of Black teachers in the schools. Although when questioned about the issue they were not opposed to the idea, in general, they were unaware of bias in schools. They accepted White staff as the norm and did not critically analyse this practice. Their failure to challenge this situation could partly be a result of the lack of educational tools to do so. This also relates to the social and cultural location which non-Black students occupy. It was difficult for non-Black students to understand the reality of Black students when they themselves have not had experiences of systemic discrimination and differential treatment on the basis of race.

Several teachers were unsure of the benefits of an increase in Black staff. Their uncertainty seemed to stem partly from a lack of critical analysis of the make-up of school personnel and a lack of clarity on the processes and objectives of employment equity initiatives. A number of teachers felt that equal opportunities are already being given to minorities and did not understand what was left to be discussed. Others, like Oscar, a science teacher who had worked in the school system for many years, indicated that while more minority teachers do need to be hired, they were concerned that racial background would overshadow actual teaching qualifications:

> ... people should be judged strictly on the basis of their ability... if you want to have a very good article on that I suggest you read the article ... 'Affirmative Action. A Worldwide Disaster' ... As a matter of fact it's written by a Black ... in that article he makes the point that affirmative action programs do not help those who need it. They help the most privileged members of those groups. So it helps most privileged Blacks, most privileged yellows, most privileged reds. The people who need it don't get it. (File T12: lines 606–31)

While Oscar suggests that affirmative action programs target only the most privileged minorities, he defeats the argument that these minority individuals are not qualified. Those who are privileged have the means to acquire the requisite skills needed in order to succeed in mainstream society. The subsequent effect, then, is the development of a 'community of support,' which they are able to provide to other members of their community by occupying the institutional spaces which oversee the distribution of rewards in society.

A pervasive idea among some teachers was that even if Black

teachers are apt role models, any teacher could effectively give encouragement to students. Teachers who expressed this view did not explore the reality of the situation, which reveals extensive racism in the schools and in society. Further, the view does not account for the unequal relations of power – that White teachers as role models, regardless of how encouraging they are, simply do not make the same impact as would Black role models.

Other teachers acknowledged that the presence of Black teachers may offer Black students strong role models. However, they did not think that this would necessarily make any difference in terms of teaching quality and, in turn, student academic achievement, as noted by Peter, an art teacher:

> I completely agree that it's legitimate [to have Black teachers]. That's why women are here. That's why Jewish people and Catholic people and so on, are teachers. Is it such a concern that the students aren't being served? I don't agree. I don't agree with that. (File T03: lines 1161–72)

This understanding of serving the students is restricted. Education encompasses more than just absorbing educational materials that are presented in a formal way. Students learn from teachers outside the classroom as well, be it through the advice they give, the personal memories they share, or simply the way they act.

A smaller group of teachers stated that the system could definitely benefit from the presence of more Black teachers. This group also identified the need for Black role models in the school, adding that the students would have much to gain from being taught by people who share their perspectives. Some of these teachers observed that several of their White colleagues refuse to acknowledge that racism even exists in the school. Undoubtedly, such denial creates problems for Black students and was cited by some teachers as reason enough to hire more minority teachers.

Parents were unanimous in expressing a desire for more Black teachers. They too believed that Black teachers would serve as role models for their children and would be more sensitive to Black students' needs. The presence of Black teachers would boost students' self-esteem and help them to feel more connected to the system. One mother, Jane, noted:

> ... children need to see themselves reflected among, not only their peers, but people that they can use as role models. In the most ideal of all circumstances it should not matter. Parents and teachers should be there mutually to support each other and the children. But, that's not the case. Therefore, I feel it is necessary to have teachers represent children: Black teachers, teachers that are Asian or whatever other group that is in a school ... [to] see that multiculturalism, of which Canadians are so proud, reflected in their lives. (File P12: lines 399–417)

While Black students, drop-outs, and parents are overwhelmingly supportive of an increased representation of Black teachers in the schools, non-Black students and teachers did not readily accept this as a valid issue. Understanding the importance of making the representation of Black teachers among school staff a reflection of the student population means accepting that issues of employment equity are directly related to educational equity. Schools are understood as having the potential either to reproduce the social relations of society or function as a site for social change. Therefore, working towards equitable representation within the schools clearly becomes a matter of addressing issues which go beyond the boundaries of the schools and which have broader implications in terms of the power relations within society.

Black-Focused Schools / African-Centred Schools

Discussions about the need for Black teachers usually led to some Black students expressing a desire for 'our' school. A few students said, 'We need a Black school.' Not all students were in favour of a 'Black school'; in fact, a good number of Black students were strongly opposed to the idea. There were ambiguities in students' articulations of what such a school would look like or should be. But there was a basic understanding that the 'Black school' would definitely be different from mainstream schools. A critical analysis of students' views on this subject reveals a yearning for a school with which they can identify, in terms of both the official and the hidden curriculum, including the school culture, classroom pedagogy, learning styles, and the make-up of the teaching and administrative staff.

Some Black students were strongly in favour of Black-focused/African-centred schools. They felt that they are not being adequately served by the current system and did not appear confident that the situation would change anytime during their high-school career. This sense of despondency over the current state of education overrides any concerns that Black-focused schools are a reversion to segregation, as expressed in a focus-group meeting:

> I don't think it matters about segregation, because as long as ... the children are being helped more, segregation has nothing to do with it ... the teachers will reach out and help the kids. And in a mainstream school like this, like, the kids have to go to the teachers, or else the teachers won't really help them. (File O10: lines 64–75)

Black-focused schools were also viewed as a valid response to the devaluation of Blacks in the mainstream system:

> ... here [in a mainstream school] some people, they think that you don't know anything about the situation and they treat you like you're nothing. (File W02: lines 388–403)

Some students wanted to go to a Black-focused school but feared the social repercussions, referring to the impact that racism has had on 'Black projects.' Not only do such projects tend to be devalued, but they are often not given adequate resources to ensure their success:

> ... when you look at the States, you know, now they have public schools and private schools ... Public schools are violent ... and the education level is not as good as the private ones ... and mainly those who attend public schools are Black students. (File W02: lines 167–79)

Other students were opposed to the idea of Black-focused schools.

Students in focus-group meetings who did not feel that Black-focused schools would benefit Black youth generally spoke about the consequences of voluntary segregation and of turning a blind eye to the multicultural nature of Canadian society:

> I don't think it's necessary ... It would just harbour segregation, you know. It's a multicultural society that we're living in. There's all kind of people here. Why should we have just a Black school? There shouldn't be just a White school either. (File O10: lines 24–34)

> I don't agree with segregating. I don't think it's right ... I just don't think we should have to separate to learn ... because if we segregate in schools, does that mean that when we get out in the real world we're going to segregate again? ... we'll still have to be with other groups, so there's no point in separating us. (File O8: lines 18–28)

Some students talked about the notion that segregation, however necessary, may continue in the wider society after the students have graduated. These students felt that such schools might not serve to combat systemic racism, particularly since they felt that graduates from a Black-focused school would not be accorded equal status with students from the mainstream schools:

> A Black school, to be realistic, in my opinion, would be a disaster ... because ... if you have a Black school, right away it's going to be classed as the worst school in Metro Toronto. I mean, you graduate from that school, they're probably not going to want you, to hire you or anything like that, once they think it's a Black school. (File D06: lines 202–20)

This suggests, of course, that, in order to eliminate racism, we need both educational and societal reform to occur:

> That means we have to have Black investors to hire those students ... we have good example from the United States. There's a Negro college which is funded by Black millionaires. But, after they graduate, I think they have [a program for students] to be hired by the

Black business owners. But right now ... the number of the Blacks who own some ... properties, it's not comparable with the population of the students. (File W02: lines 239–58)

Therefore without corresponding changes in society which would provide the equitable allocation of students in the labour market, Black students argue that corporate sponsors from the Black community would be necessary to hire Black graduates.

Conversely, drop-outs were virtually unanimous in their support for Black-focused schools. This response is not surprising, given that the mainstream system had failed to meet their needs. One drop-out, Michelle, was clear on this point:

I think a Black teacher might have the tendency to pay greater attention to Black children. And if that's going to be so, it's better we create schools for Black and White ... If segregation is so much a part of the system, do just that. Make it obvious, because in my eyes it is obvious. (File F12: lines 1247–55)

Those drop-outs who had attended an all-Black school, after having left the mainstream schools, reported feeling a greater sense of freedom and comfort:

... the school of only, like, all people of colour ... I went to a school like this and I feel free, like, you don't have no problem. It's like it's your own world ... (File F05: lines 2301–10)

These arguments in favour of Black-focused schools relate to factors which may also serve to promote student engagement by providing an atmosphere which is more culturally congruent and free from negative racial and cultural biases. Moreover, students relate to these schools as their 'own world,' having a true sense of belonging and therefore a vested interest in the school and their role in it. It is clear from the narratives that the absence of these factors in mainstream schools are very real deterrents for Black students continuing their education.

The majority of non-Black students interviewed were opposed to the idea of Black-focused schools. The primary reason cited was that it would be a type of segregation which they did not feel was right. They thought that everyone should try to get along and that this could best happen if everyone went to the same school. Others felt that, although it was true that the different racial and cultural groups in their schools currently separated themselves into groups, to divide them up completely would be worse, destroying any hope of students integrating. Black-focused schools were understood as only making the lines of separation between different racial groups more rigid, causing further problems. Some students also suggested that it might be difficult in the long run for Black students to get along with the rest of society once they had left school and were surrounded by people of various races.

Some non-Black students also opposed Black-focused schools because they feared that the Black students would feel superior to them. Moreover, others felt that Black resentment towards other racial groups would grow if Black students were separated from them and given special treatment. Some students were also afraid that it may encourage Black students to 'band together' against Whites, and that putting all Blacks in one school would be 'asking for trouble.' This is very indicative of the type of negative racial stereotypes which exist in relation to Blacks – wherever Blacks congregate, society is 'asking for trouble.'

Other non-Black students objected to Black-focused schools on the grounds of what they perceive to be preferential treatment of Blacks, as expressed clearly by Erica:

> [Black-focused schools are] stupid because ... like, they don't have a school only for Whites; they don't have a school only for Chinese people ... If [Black students] were to go to a different school, like an all-Black school, they'd probably be going, 'Yeah, we're better than you' like, you know ... I think it would just be bad. (File CG09: lines 333–5; 339–42)

Erica does not see the issue in terms of educational parity, but rather as a form of preferential treatment being accorded to Blacks. Yet such a view fails to interrogate the issue of differential treatment of Blacks in mainstream schools as a means to contextualize the argument for a separate system.

A number of teachers thought that Black-focused schools are not the solution. They believed that in order to have a healthy society people should not separate themselves on the basis of ethnicity or race. Everyone should feel welcome in a supportive climate, which they were convinced already exists in the schools. Yet this view is inconsistent with the realities expressed by Black students, who have reported feeling marginalized and alienated within the same school environment these teachers have referred to as 'welcoming and supportive.' Although the issue of divisiveness was raised in relation to Black-focused schools, this was not recognized as being a fact of life within mainstream schools, as much of the testimony of students and drop-outs has shown. Racial division was also witnessed in terms of the social interaction among Black and non-Black teachers within the schools chosen for observation in the study. Black and minority teachers were not found to use the staff common-rooms as much as White teachers, demonstrating that issues of social distancing are not confined only to students.

Some teachers did feel that the system needs to become more inclusive but believed that this transformation process has to occur from within. Anne, an ESL teacher, stated:

> If you're unhappy with something, I think you work within the system to change it. You don't opt out of the system. (File T18: lines 1468–71)

Other teachers saw how Black-focused schools might be advantageous but were torn between these benefits and the negative consequences of segregation.

Most Black parents and educators who were aware of a recent call by some community workers and educators for a 'Black-focused school' appeared to understand and sympathize with the spirit and motivation behind such advocacy, even though they may disagree and argue that it will be 'segregationist.' Black parents were not unanimous on the merits of such a school. A few even wondered if the idea of a Black-focused school could be subverted to feed into societal stereotypes of Black people.

Many parents believed that both they and their children need to have at least the choice of a Black-focused school. It was clear that parents had given much thought to the idea. Indeed, many of the parents were actively involved in groups that were working towards establishing a Black-focused school. They realized that such an initiative would be met with resistance within and outside their own community, but they stressed that choice was the key to it all. Parents, such as Betty, clearly saw the various benefits and advantages a Black-focused school would offer:

> I think Black-focused schools are a good idea. I think we have to be careful that they don't become ghettoized ... that people see it as less important than regular high school, that it doesn't become the Black school as opposed to a normal school. I think a Black-focused school ... builds self-esteem ... Black students feel themselves as the centre, which they usually don't feel within a regular school setting, and we see that. During the summer I sent my daughter to ... a school made up primarily of Black and Caribbean kids and, whether or not they perform well academically, which they usually do ... just the fact that what they learn in history class is about Black people, the examples they use in English class are Black examples of things ... (File P07: lines 692–720)

Therefore, while the issue of Black-focused schools remains controversial, both drop-outs and Black parents have provided important and valid reasons for their existence. In their view, these schools would provide what public schools are not, namely, a more culturally congruent environment, free from racial hostility, stereotypes, and low expectations. In addition, the centrality of African and African-Canadian history, culture, and experience focuses intellectual attention on the lived realities of Black students, rather than situating them on the margins of Euro-Canadian history and discourse.

That Black-focused schools are problematic for some teachers and non-Black students could be the result of a misunderstanding of the purpose of these schools and the social, economic, cultural, and political factors which give rise to the need for such alternatives.

These are not issues of preferential treatment, as some non-Black students felt. Preferential treatment can be said to be inherent within the mainstream educational system, with its privileging of the Anglo-Canadian experience and the creation of advantages for Anglo-Canadians above all other racial or ethnic minorities. Rather, the purpose here is to achieve greater parity for those students who do not find the mainstream school comfortable or hospitable, by carving out a parallel niche within the Canadian educational structure. This should not, however, be regarded as a panacea, merely an alternative to the dominant 'unicultural' school.

The struggle for antiracism education, however, does not end at this point. Public schools are at the forefront of social change and must be prepared to host the diverse needs, interests, and realities of students from all walks of life. Therefore, Black-focused schools must not be seen as an excuse not to reform mainstream schools or to dilute the movement towards greater cultural and educational democracy.

Chapter Eleven

Family, Community, and Society

To this point, much attention has been paid to the structures within schools which contribute to processes of disengagement for Black students. While schools play the most direct role in affecting the educational experiences of students, including those experiences which contribute to a process of disengagement, schools do not operate in isolation. Students are profoundly affected also by broader social conditions. Schools serve the families and communities that make up our society. As such, these stakeholders also have responsibilities and identifiable roles to play in the delivery of education.

In the last chapter, visions of alternative educational practices were articulated by Black students, drop-outs, and parents. We will now turn to issues of educational partnerships, specifically with family and community, and some of the visions for relationships that are hoped could contribute to successful educational experiences for Black students.

Parental Involvement in Education

Black youth and parents/guardians did not see the school as the only source of concern regarding school disengagement, nor did they see it as the only site for political action and social response. Students understood the importance of the family and, particularly, parental guidance in their schooling. Students also discussed why relationships in their homes may not permit them, sometimes, to seek or receive help with schoolwork from their parents. Some students simply did not want to bother already busy parents, or they felt their parents would not be able to help because they (parents/ relatives) did not reach the students' educational levels. Others would prefer not to share work with parents in case it gave rise to parental pressure for high academic excellence.

While students understood the structural realities of their parents' lives, they also wanted parents to take a more proactive role in their children's schooling. They did not want parents to wait until problems arose before responding or getting involved. Students felt that parents could help by listening more and by becoming 'sounding boards' to their children as the young people work through their problems.

Unfortunately, for some students there is actually no 'home' in the conventional sense of the word. They have been physically and emotionally abused by a parents/guardians/caregivers, or their families have actually disintegrated or been decimated by the harsh economic realities of today's society.

Black students saw home support as an integral part of their educational success. Almost all of the students interviewed said that parents should show an interest in their children's education, especially by giving them moral support and encouragement. The following three students, Roland, Candice, and Victoria, respectively, highlighted the basic issues addressed by most Black students:

I think they should support them and everything, and they should help them ... just be available for them. Make time for them, even if they have ... their work laid out at night or something, and their kid asks them for help, I think it should be their priority to make time available the next day for them ... (File W13: lines 837–47)

What the parents have to do is sit his or her daughter or son down and say, 'Listen, this is not the time to drop out of school. This is the time for you to hold your head up and look towards the future. You hold your head down, it won't reach anywhere. You understand?' (File W28: lines 359–65)

When I'm feeling down about myself [my parents] always seem to

sense it and always come and tell me, 'You can do it. You can do it'
... they're pushing me in some sense, but it doesn't feel like they're
pushing me ... So it's like they're always there. (File W33: lines 445–58)

Students also thought that family (parents, siblings, cousins) can
serve as a source of help for schoolwork. Most students reported
that if a parent helped them with their homework, it was usually
their mother. At times, however, while mothers were eager to help,
they did not have the necessary educational background, time, or
language skills. Abbey, a grade 11 student taking advanced and
general level courses, explained:

I live with my mom alone. And ... she dropped out of school when
she was, like, a teenager. So the type of work I'm doing, she doesn't
know how to do it ... I never ask her. I do my work on my own. (File
W37: lines 230–42)

Perhaps of greater importance to students is that their parents have
a stronger presence in the school, attending meetings and advocating on behalf of their children. Sam, a grade 12 student, highlighted
the need for parents to be vigilant:

They should come often to school and talk to the teacher and be more
part of their kid's life because I don't think ... parents have enough
control over their kids, you know. That's why they just do whatever
they want because they know they can get away with everything.
(File W26: lines 842–51)

Elizabeth, a university student, also stressed the need for parents to
be active:

... make more of a presence, they have to go [to] the PTA meetings
and ... set up their own little Black students board ... and discuss
things and, if you feel shy, go and talk to the teacher ... for you. But,
you should never say, 'Okay, we're intimidated,' and you're just
gonna leave it in the hands of the educators. You're selling out your
child like that ... (File R07: lines 2263–74)

It was obvious that students saw some danger when parents placed too much trust in the school. However, Donna, a grade 12 student, was sympathetic and realized that whatever it is within the school that renders some students 'powerless,' it can also affect their parents:

> ... I guess they trust the school system to take [care] of their children and they assume that they don't have to ... or maybe they feel powerless that there's anything they can do. (File O06: lines 691–7)

This sense of powerlessness which students attribute to their parents' role within schools is also a reflection of the subordination they themselves feel.

Unlike the Black students, drop-outs rarely described situations in which their parents gave them encouragement, shared advice on how to survive in school, or helped them with their assignments. They also tended to mention abusive home environments more often than did the other groups interviewed. The combined lack of support at home and at school creates a significant mountain of odds against a student's success.

Many drop-outs strongly expressed the belief that parents should serve as advocates for children. Indeed, as Mike noted, they feel that parents should be vigilant:

> [Parents] should take a demanding role in the school system. When ... the teacher's trying to put the kid in general, ask, 'What the hell are you talking about? No, my kid's in advanced' ... parents should take a demanding role and demand some history, Black history in there and demand some Black teachers. Demand it! (File F19: lines 2263–77)

A problem common to many drop-outs, however, is that their parents did not know how to deal with the system in order to advocate on their behalf. Furthermore, there are few structures in place to help parents better understand the system, so that they can be more effectively involved in their children's education. Jennifer, another drop-out, noted:

My parents, they were old fashioned. They didn't know how to fight the system. My mother did complain a lot about that teacher, but, on the other hand, a lot of situations went down and they didn't fight it and they just sort of let things slide. They were told this and that, that I couldn't do this and I couldn't that ... (File F03: lines 347–56)

Therefore, many Black parents may lack the 'cultural capital' necessary to negotiate successfully within the system.

Parents also figured prominently in the decisions of non-Black students not to leave school. Many students suggested that their parents would be upset if they left school early, and this deterred them from doing so.

Teachers listed parental involvement as an important and positive element in a student's academic success. However, many, like Hugh, acknowledged that currently there is not much parental participation in the system, particularly at the secondary level:

... parents, they seem to feel that they need to be interested when they're in elementary but when you get into secondary they forget about it. For the immigrant kids it seems to be even worse in terms of getting that kind of involvement. They like to view us as the experts, which is good for my ego, but it doesn't help me if I perceive that there's a problem ... or even the opposite ... a surfeit of strength in the kid. You want to take advantage of talking to the parents. (File T04: lines 168–81)

Teachers realized that parents come up against some barriers which hinder their participation. They also knew that many parents have neither the time nor the energy to participate in schools or to help their children do homework. For other parents, the system can be an alienating sea of bureaucracy. For this reason, some teachers believed that schools need to make more effort to reach out to parents in order to form a strong partnership. One teacher, Gayle, outlined some of the ways in which schools have to be more accommodating in order to effect this partnership:

I think what we need to do is try to bring parents in ... we also have

to be very flexible with parents ... flexibility in time. We can't operate on a 9:00 to 3:30 mould; we have to be able to give of ourselves in
the evening ... to work alongside the parents. I think that the school
system needs to find out the educational levels of parents and how
well they understand or not understand the school system and ...
have information that is written that is easy to read, easy to access
for parents so parents... can associate themselves with schools. I
think we need to work alongside not just with parents, but with the
broader community and get community agencies involved in school
issues. (File T02: lines 977–8, 983–92, 1023–34)

Parents saw clearly a role for themselves in the school system.
But, they also realized that it is very difficult for some parents to
participate in their child's education within the current system.
They too understood that in order to be most effective, both teachers
and parents are going to have to make a significant effort to understand one another, to cooperate and to support and encourage each
other's involvement. Anita, a mother and university student, described a recent parent/teacher meeting to highlight this issue:

The other day I was at a parent/teacher meeting and the teacher said
something ... he said, 'You know, the people who are here, it shows
that they're interested in their children' ... and I said, 'No, it's not
necessarily that you're interested in your children ... there are other
parents who cannot make it. There are some that work nights ...
[others] are probably sick. They can't make it. So, therefore, thank
the ones that are here and try to find out why the others didn't show
up.' (File P06: lines 808–22)

From the various vantage points, there was consensus that parental
involvement is important to students' success in school. As primary stakeholders in their children's educational future, parents
must be seen by themselves and by the school as an important
resource. Developing a positive relationship between families and
schools can contribute to a student's sense of support and encouragement.

Community Involvement in Education

Schools contribute to the production and reproduction of the phenomenon of 'dropping out' from the distinctive environments, cultures, and peoples that form constituent parts of schools. The social formation, with its segmentation of the labour force, and the consequent unequal distributions of rewards, penalties, valued goods and services, knowledge, etc., requires the existence of drop-outs in order for the economic system to function. There is an increased societal concern with drop-outs when they are 'on the streets,' but not when they are employed in low-paying jobs.

Society reproduces the social conditions which allow for the perpetuation of racism, sexism, poverty, hunger, and material deprivation. These conditions have extremely significant consequences for students' educational experiences (e.g., academic achievement). While schools can be part of the solution to these problems, society cannot expect schools alone to solve them.

Black students felt that their community could also play an active role in helping them succeed in school. For example, they felt that community members could help in setting up a homework club by donating space and tutors. These clubs would give students a place to go after school where they could be with peers and work with adults on their homework. As well, people in the community could be guest speakers in schools and act as role models to students. Students, like Sandy and Rhonda below, suggested that communities could also sponsor Black-focused schools in their neighbourhoods and set up a summer jobs program for Black students:

Just be simple role models. Come in and talk for free ... and say, 'Hey, this is how business is going and what not, and you can do this.' (File R06: lines 2993–3000)

Set up their own school! Set up their own school and educate their own children. I mean, the Jewish do it. A whole bunch of people do it. But, when Blacks do it, they really, you know, they have a label for it or a name for it, they don't accept it or they don't support it. (File W35: lines 918–28)

Rhonda's suggestion also highlights the way in which Black projects are measured negatively against those of other groups, and how legitimacy is therefore differentially accorded.

Students, like Thomas in grade 12, further suggested that those community members in powerful positions should advocate on their behalf:

> ... their voice has to be heard by government or ... the board of education. They have to pose plans and suggestions to keep Black kids in school, to make school more appealing to Black students. (File O02: lines 1540–7)

It was often difficult for students to conceive of what role the government, in particular, played in education. This may be because students were unable to conceptualize the possibilities related to the role of government. However, it may also be because students rarely see Black people in any positions of power in government and thus do not consider it a realistic or sympathetic source of help. Students did, however, offer some suggestions as to how government could be involved in education. Common student responses were to give people more jobs, improve and diversify the teaching staff, eliminate racism, and listen to the Black community and implement its ideas. Victoria, a mature student, and Elizabeth, a university student, were able to express their expectations for the role of government:

> The government ... should listen to what the Black community says and do the stuff that they're telling them to do instead of just, 'Yeah, yeah, yeah,' and not doing anything about it ... Blacks ... are just dropping out and saying, 'Forget it! The government isn't doing anything and there's no jobs out there anyways for us to go to even if we graduate.' (File W33: lines 812–24)

I see that the government is pulling a lot of funding from different

programs [but] that they realize there's a problem with racism …
there should be more forums [on antiracism] where all high-school
students attend … to promote tolerance within our community. They
should be putting more funds in … (File R07: lines 2431–9)

The reality is that such funding is, of course, limited because of the
current political and economic climate. Yet the Draconian cuts in
educational spending are not only myopic but run counter to the
very real needs which exist within society. In the long run, by
undercutting programs which can help ameliorate the problems
related to student disengagement, the government creates a potential drain on social welfare services if drop-outs do not have the
requisite skills to compete in an already declining labour market.
Therefore, initiatives designed to help keep students in school
and improve their life chances should be evaluated with this in
mind.

Black parents know that they have roles and responsibilities in
the education of their children. A few parents are critical of their
peers who they claim renege on their responsibilities, or are falling
into the trap of the materialism and consumerism of contemporary society. Parents point out that regular parental visits to schools
can be helpful to the child and to the school. However, they question conventional social definitions of the 'family' and a 'parent.'
They argue that conventional definitions have tended to favour
and accord powerful voices to certain groups in society. It is these
parental voices that are often privileged and highlighted in current debates about school reforms. Parents believe schools have
not reached deeply enough into the resources of the local communities to assist parents in overcoming some of the structural
barriers and constraints to meaningful partnerships. They call for
a more meaningful partnership, based on a respect of the knowledge, ideas, rights, and responsibilities of all stakeholders in the
educational system.

Parents are concerned about the nature and structure of the communication lines between the school and the home. They point
out that while the school is not always forthcoming, it is quick to
lay blame on parents. This gap in communication is critical in that

students facing problems cannot be quickly identified and assisted before they fade out from the system.

In conclusion, many of the youth feel that neither society nor the school listens to them, and it makes them wonder if people actually care. This sentiment is expressed in their frustrations about being asked repeatedly to 'speak out' for the sake of academic research. In their minds, much research has brought no fundamental change to their lives, and yet they have been speaking about the problems 'for years.' And yet, some students are able to express creative ideas about how the community and broader society can take responsibility. Some teachers share these concerns and recognize the need for the school to participate in building positive partnerships with families and the community. However, Black parents continue to decry what they perceive as the lack of action to address their expressed concerns about the schooling process in Canada. While parents believe there are good intentions out there, some wonder if good intentions alone are enough.

Chapter Twelve

Visions of Educational and Social Change

It is important when examining the relations of oppression and injustice within society and the structures which produce and reproduce these relations, that the ways in which subjects act and have agency are also highlighted. As we develop our understanding of the relations between oppression and agency, we are able to see glimpses of possibilities for social change. In the study, students, drop-outs, parents, and teachers were asked about how they understood student input within schools, the social limits faced by students, concerns which face youth, the future of Black youth in the school system, and possibilities for change. This chapter will explore their narrative responses to these issues, focusing particularly on how these issues articulate with the problem of student disengagement and how students, drop-outs, and parents envision change.

Student Input

Most Black students did not elaborate on their roles and responsibilities in school. Apart from going to class and doing homework, little else was mentioned. This limited interpretation of their input is consistent with their general opinion that there is not much they can do to change the system. This feeling is heightened in a system that neither encourages student activism nor tolerates any behaviour that agitates the status quo. Douglas, an OAC student, gave a graphic example of the kind of incident which serves to wear down a student's willingness to try to effect change:

> I tried to deal with … my physics teacher … Some kid did something, like, that lit off a match or something like that … and [the teacher] collected all the Black people … and he let all the White people go because he said, 'I know it's your kind of dude that does this kind of thing and we're not leaving until we find out who it is.' And he let all the White people go. Nothing was done about that … He had no clue [as to who did it], but he said, 'Your type of people who does this kind of thing.' I was told [about this incident] by one of the students and I told him to complain [but] he didn't want to. (File O02: lines 1153–86)

Douglas addresses the issue of the inequality of voice which subverts the equitable treatment of Black students. Even in the face of such blatant acts of discrimination, some Black students do not see the value in pursuing equity – perhaps seeing a challenge to the structures of the school as an exercise in futility.

In some cases, students talked about demanding certain standards of behaviour in the classroom and challenging the racial and cultural biases which find their way into classroom discourse. Susan, another OAC level student, mentioned providing a system of checks and balances on the behaviour of the teacher:

> I was the only Black student in [this class] … I would sit in the back in the corner. But [the teacher] knows he can't say nothing about Black people because I'll start arguing … I could see that the way that I acted was having an influence because whenever he said something, he'd go, 'I don't mean it that way … I don't mean Black people are this' … so, I think in a way you do [have input in school]. (File B19: lines 746–60)

Whereas the student in Douglas's example did not take up the issue of racism within the structures available to register a complaint, Susan did act within these structures and was able to measure the difference she was making. In fact, as students became more proactive in their school environment, their perseverance also became stronger. Victoria, a mature student, explained:

> I try and get good grades ... I try to be there for other students if they need my help. I try and help the ESL students a lot. I'm also on the Black Heritage Club. And I went to a camp for a race relations thing, to help them do policy and ... I'm going to be doing stuff so that other students know about the policy, their rights in schools. And I'm going to be doing stuff for the grade nines for next semester ... so they'll learn about racism and how it started. And we're trying to do a policy on homophobia and sexism in the school ... (File W33: lines 569–85)

Victoria's involvement may be an example of how the logic of the participation-identification model (Finn 1989) operates. While this model cannot be seen as a wholly adequate means to explicate the diverse experiences of minority students, it may be germane to situations such as the one described. The fact that Victoria's participation and identification with the school occurred within the context of African heritage and antiracism activities is important. In order for participation and identification with the school to occur – a process which can serve to prevent disengagement – these activities must be in accordance with the needs and interests of students. Clearly, then, schools with multicultural and antiracism initiatives have the best opportunity for helping to 're-engage' minority students.

Drop-outs were well aware of their lack of input into the system when they were there. This conscious attempt not to get involved was likely a result of too many overwhelming barriers or a desire not to submit to a destructive system. In order to protect themselves, they 'preferred' to disengage from the system as a whole.

Drop-outs also tended to be more cynical as to what their input would ultimately do. In their past experience, their voices were rarely heard. More than any other group, they conveyed the idea that little change would come from outside the Black community. While they sometimes acknowledged that schooling was better now than it was when they were in the system, this positive feeling did not lead them to believe that things were going to change for the better. The idea that anything could be changed seemed somewhat far-fetched to the drop-outs. They questioned the value of the study in terms of who was likely to listen to their narratives and, even if they were heard, if anything would really be done. One drop-out, Marshall, was clear in this regard:

> I know [Black youth] have been saying some of these things about the school system for a while now and no one has listened to us. I am not sure it is because no one seems to care. Why do you think people will take seriously what we say to you now? Maybe I'm a sceptic ... What I want to know is, what do we get for speaking out? What would come out of your work? Some more silence and denial? (File F07: lines 5–17)

Social Limits, Concerns, and the Future

Black students were asked explicitly if they felt they could be whatever they wanted to be in this society. The question was intended to probe their perceptions of systemic barriers in Canada. Overall, students were closely divided in their responses: 54 per cent believed that they could be or do anything they wanted. Interestingly, female students had a more positive outlook, with 63 per cent of them responding in the affirmative, compared with only 43 per cent of the males. Differences also emerged in light of students' place of birth. Canadian-born males expressed the least amount of optimism, with only 36 per cent feeling optimistic, compared with 65 per cent of Canadian-born females. Among students born abroad, 50 per cent of males and 60 per cent of females felt positive about their opportunities in society.

Some students related the social limits placed on them to their financial status and how the lack of money restricted their access to further education and to power in society. Geoff, a grade 10 student, commented:

> Say I wanted to be a lawyer, right, I could not afford to go to law school. Right? If I wanted to be a doctor, I could not do that because

I could not afford to go to medical school. Right? (File O24: lines 1096–106)

Moreover, some Black students tended to perceive a person's position of power or powerlessness as more or less static, which is perhaps why half of the Black students were pessimistic about their ability to succeed. Devon, an OAC level student, related power and social mobility to class issues:

Once you have the money, you have the power. And for poor people, they don't really have that much power. They don't have that much status. They're not respected in the community the same way as a rich person is respected. So that is something that will keep them down. (File O26: lines 936–43)

Racism was another factor that was seen as a constraint to Black youths' aspirations. Real and psychological barriers interconnect to lower Black youths' job prospects, chances for success, and economic advancement. This was related by Beth, an advanced level grade 12 student, as a part of the legacy of slavery and domination:

I think a lot of that comes from history … the White male is the one that was dominant … and, I think a lot of that stems back from slavery and the kind of the way that Blacks were just completely dehumanized and desensitized. The slavery, the way we were treated and everything, it's made the Black male especially take on this attitude that he can't get anywhere or he's not supposed to … 'success' is just not a word in his vocabulary … It's not only Black males, it's females also. But it has affected the male in that way because [he] used to be such a dominant force in his culture…and now he's been reduced to, you know, getting a job at McDonald's, or whatever, and not being able to support his family. (File O04: lines 1938–64)

Racial and social hierarchies which privilege Whites were seen by Blacks students as precluding the mobility of Blacks into positions of overriding power and authority. Many students, such as

Henry, quoted below, were acutely aware of how such glass ceilings operate to maintain their subordination in society:

> If you're a Black ... although you can make it good, there's only so far you can go. Like, a White kid can say, realistically, 'I want to be Prime Minister.' There's no way a Black kid can say that ... [Canada] can't even handle a Black premier or a Black mayor much less a Black prime minister. And there's no Black people even in the runnings ... If you're going to be anything as a Black person here you have to set up your own shit. You can't expect to make it in White people's stuff ... White people don't like to give Black people nothing. (File R04: lines 733–56)

Black students also talked about the inherent problems of the Canadian identity, specifically in terms of a hierarchy; that is, the superior status of White Canadians vis-à-vis their non-White counterparts. They spoke of the need to have their status as Canadians socially validated. Amy, a grade 11 student born in the Caribbean, spoke of her personal experience in dealing with the question of identity:

> To be identified as a Canadian now that I'm a Canadian. I'm not Trinidadian. I'm not in Trinidad ... I have a culture, yes, but I'm in a country that I identify as my home and I want to feel an equal right to where I'm at and whatever I proceed to do. (File W19: lines 1407–16)

The sense of affinity students of all walks of life have to Canada cannot be disputed. Evidence to this effect was noted during visits to participating schools in the study. When the national anthem was played over the intercom, it was seen as a very solemn occasion. Students, irrespective of their race or ethnicity, stood still for the duration of the anthem out of respect and as a means to affirm their identity as Canadians.

Violence was another element of concern for Black students. While females particularly feared rape, Black males mostly feared police brutality. Black students grow up in a society in which they do not feel safe or free. They go to school in an environment in which they have similar feelings of oppression. Neither situation stimulates learning and positive self-development. Moreover, students are angered and frustrated by the school's unwillingness to deal with these issues, and by how the negative stereotypes of Black youth go largely unchallenged. When asked about her greatest worries, Elizabeth, a university student, responded:

Well, number one the police. The police and these shootings, and just the idea of racism in the police force. And I think that school should be addressing that as well. I see people do studies and say that there's no racism on the police force, but I have a feeling that there is ... Young Black kids, I kind of worry about them because they're very antagonistic now towards the police and that might get them in trouble ... I think that their attitudes towards young Black children, it's disgusting the way that they view them. They ... see a baseball cap turned backwards and maybe some baggy jeans and they automatically pinpoint that person ... they might not arrest them or harass them but they have their eye open ... (File R07: lines 2707–46)

The reality of being from neighbourhoods where drugs and violence are commonplace also compromises a student's ability to deal emotionally with the demands of schooling. Jeewan, a grade 12 student, described this reality:

... right around [where I live] there's a lot of drug dealers. You can step out of your house and you could get shot, right. You come to school and the people in this school have guns on them ... you piss off the person they could pull out a gun and shoot you. And then you have to worry about your marks in school, [and] if you're going to get into any trouble today. (File W32: lines 1726–38)

Despite these concerns, many students have ambitions involving college, university, and a professional career. Others simply said that they wanted to be rich and/or successful, and could not identify a specific goal. Generally, though, students had positive images for their personal futures, such as this declaration by Irene, a grade 9 student:

I want to be somebody great. I want to be, like, a great speaker or something. I don't know, that's what I want, that's what I feel like doing. (File D14: lines 718–31)

These high aspirations are reflected in the students' optimism for the overall future of Black youth (70 per cent were hopeful). Their enthusiasm, however, varied by gender and place of birth. Interestingly, 80 per cent of males, those who encounter the most overt racism in society, felt optimistic, in contrast to only 64 per cent of females. Among Canadian-born students, 92 per cent of males and 65 per cent of females were hopeful. Among students born abroad, 73 per cent of males and 64 per cent of females were hopeful for the overall future of Black youth in Canadian society. These responses differ significantly from those offered by students regarding their individual futures. This difference suggests a bifurcation in their perceptions of the future, one which perhaps places greater confidence in the Black community as a whole than in individual potentials.

This optimism, however, did not carry over to their concerns about the school system, which, to them, is an obvious source of their oppression. Aisha, a young woman in grade 12, expressed concern for bringing her children into the educational system as it is:

... the future of my children ... I have a fear of having sons, okay, because ... even if you become a stable family, there's still some way they can, you know, grasp you ... a study showed [that] it was grade 3 or something ...that [Black boys] started to show the decline ... I even see [it with] my two little brothers ... It just scares me too much to see it. (File O09: lines 1040–63)

Devon made a direct connection between the need for the school to change before any change in the students could be considered:

... if the school system doesn't change, the students won't change. (File O26: lines 1053–62)

Drop-outs identified the same social limits as did Black students. They took their analysis further, however, and discussed how the school and economic systems interconnect. They explained that 'success' is defined in terms of money and power, and that part of their disengagement from school was related to decreased expectations of their earning power as graduates, especially given the academic levels into which they had been streamed. Drop-outs felt that they were given the message that economically they were not going 'to make it' and that school was not going to give them the skills necessary to improve the situation.

Of all the interview groups, drop-outs consistently were able to see life within a larger context. They linked their concerns about society to a group identity, specifically, in terms of Black experience. They also philosophized about the Black community's experiences vis à vis racism, stereotyping, and police targeting. Their goals, however, were much more on an immediate and personal level. Unlike students, who always mentioned the distant goals of a career, drop-outs were much more focused on meeting the goals of everyday life (e.g., finding a job, raising a child). Their visions of the future, however, expanded beyond the immediacy of their goals. Drop-outs expressed hope for the future, not in terms of themselves, but rather in terms of the Black youth population and of their own children. Drop-outs had faith that, because today's Black generation is more aware of racism, the youth may have a more developed sense of group strength and identity. They hoped this solidarity would help the youth overcome the barriers that they would surely encounter throughout their lives.

In their contribution to the empowerment of the Black population, drop-outs are working at the grass-roots level, strengthening the self-confidence of their children, advocating on their behalf in the schools, constantly conveying high expectations and strong support, and encouraging good work habits. This raises their hope that their children will not experience the disengagement from school and the marginalization in society that they themselves experienced.

Although the non-Black students were not specifically questioned on whether they felt that society limited them in any way, none of them voluntarily brought up any perceived social limits. They did, however, have concerns about society and their future. These concerns ranged from broad issues such as the state of the environment to more personal issues such as their education and job prospects. Nevertheless, students appeared optimistic about their general welfare in the future and had a fairly clear idea of how their lives would evolve. Most planned on continuing their education beyond high school and pursuing a career. They expressed goals that were well defined – a contrast to the vague responses of Black students. This specificity could be because non-Black students do not perceive as many barriers, and thus have the confidence to pursue their aspirations in a direct manner. Black students, although optimistic, were perhaps better aware of the struggles ahead and, in turn, more hesitant.

The concerns expressed by parents about the future often reflected those of their children. Again, these worries stem primarily from economic concerns conditioned by the current political and economic climate. One mother, Anita, who was in the process of upgrading her own education, was succinct:

I'm worried about the future because I don't know what the future holds ... Is Canada going to become worse? Is there a place in society for our children? Are there going to be jobs for our children? I mean, I'm going to school right now. Is there going to be a job for me? ... and you find out that the government's cutting this, cutting that. University's getting more expensive. Will your children be able to get postsecondary education if you're not from middle-class background? Yes, I'm worried about it. (File P06: lines 2370–98)

However, Elizabeth, a university student, expressed optimism for the future in terms of her hopes for a strengthening of communal bonds and self-esteem through greater access to Afrocentric knowledge:

I'm hopeful simply because I see a resurgence within the Black community of some sort of a Black pride, a coming of an identity, more accessible information about Black people ... Hopefully, within the high-school system there will be more accessible information about other cultures and more glorification of the Black past rather than the slave history that we've all been taught. And, if more people in my age range become a little bit more conscious of what they're doing ... and be more encouraging of their race and be more proud of what they are, hopefully the next generation of young Black people ... will not have to ... plough through the barriers that we had to, and have better self-esteem and better self-value ... from day one, understanding about their past – Africa ... the good things about Africa, not necessarily the bad things, and ... better self-images ... And, hopefully, that will be an end to this long, long history of Black people, just the discouragement of Black people ... (File R07: lines 2971–3012)

The Role of the School and Reflections on Change

Students, drop-outs, teachers, and parents were asked what role the school had in preventing students from dropping out. Black students observed that the school seems 'not to notice' or, indeed, care when students start to disengage or fade out of the system. Susan, an OAC level student, implied that with respect to some students there was a willingness on the part of the school to see them leave:

> If they said you're out because you missed this many days, they should try and deal with it before that, instead of saying, 'Well, you did this. Get out' ... I've missed a lot of classes sometimes and teachers talk to me, but I think if you want to drop out, it's no big deal. Of course, if you're some kind of brain or something, I think they're going to ... they want you ... But, if you're Black and they see you've got problems or something ... 'Okay, he's missed a certain amount of days, let's just get rid of him.' (File B19: lines 96–112)

Here, Susan addresses the sense of invisibility Black students experience in what they feel is an unresponsive school system which enables many of them to fall through the cracks. Ultimately it seems to them that there is less impetus to rescue 'at risk' students who are Black:

> ... half the Black guys that I know that used to come here are out there on the streets right now. They all got kicked out somehow or

another. The principal is nice, but it's just that some of them he just kicked out. They screw up once and they just don't give them another chance, just kick them out like that. (File W05: lines 783–92)

Students perceived the system as a little too eager to kick them out. Expulsion, it has already been noted, is often a culmination of disengagement for students who already feel they are being pushed out of a system which does not want, and does not understand, their difficulties. Such conscious or unconscious school practices, combined with negative attitudes and poor teaching styles on the part of teachers, led students to formulate negative opinions of the educational system. Kyle, a grade 12 student, gave an example of such attitudes:

Come on, when you're in class he has statements like, 'I don't care if you don't do the work, I'm still getting paid.' What kind of statement is that? (File B01: lines 591–8)

Consequently, students recommended that there had to be a more sensitive and diverse staff in the schools:

I'd change some of the teachers ... Some of them give you negative vibes, like, say things that are racist, but they don't know that they offend you. I would change that. (File W34: lines 773–86)

Okay, make teachers make the students feel like ... they're somebody. Like, make them feel like they have a chance in life ... give them that feeling of, you know, reaching those stars. (File W14: lines 783–90)

They have to have more Black teachers ... because mostly they'll understand more than any White teacher will understand, saying, 'Okay, this is where you're coming from,' and things like that. (File B03: lines 468–73)

This recommendation for diversity holds true for the formal curriculum as well. As discussed in chapter 8, it was felt that the curriculum is Eurocentric and excludes the contributions and achievements of non-Whites. Black students talked about a need to rethink and challenge a curriculum that is limited in its scope and representation of history. Aisha, a grade 12 advanced student, suggested:

I would change all the textbooks in not only history [but also] in other subjects like science an math ... when you look through the science textbook and it's like all these White people invented everything, and even one science teacher said, 'Every civilization has contributed to science except African.' He actually said that! (File O09: lines 840–69)

The restructuring of education along these lines, it was felt, would provide Black students with the motivation to remain in school. Victoria made a clear connection:

Well, I have this friend that dropped out because they're not learning what they want to learn. And, a lot of it comes down to the fact that they want to learn about their history and they're not getting it. They're getting only that Blacks were slaves and that's not what they want to hear. They want to be able to identify with their roots
    if the school could show it that way, then ... a lot of Blacks would feel a lot better and probably stay in school. And ... don't make them feel like they're stupid either ... (File W33: lines 791–806)

In terms of the roles of various school agents in the educational and personal life of students, it is interesting to note that Black students in general had very little interaction with the guidance department. Few of them could even identify the role of a guidance counsellor. There was no indication in student responses that counsellors facilitate a process of joint decision-making. Of the few students who had had contact with a counsellor, only a couple recounted positive experiences. More often, students encountered a heavy top-down lecture (e.g., student responsibility to attend class). Others, like Victoria and Rana, talked about experiences that were neither comfortable nor helpful:

I went to find out about a course and he's just, like, 'Not right now.'

And, I had an appointment! … So I came back a couple of times and, like, 'No, no, no. You can't take it' and that was the end of the conversation. But, why can't I take it? They made me feel like I wasn't smart enough to take the course … (File W33: lines 514–22)

Yeah, they just kind of shove you off … just, you know, throw a class in there [and say], 'Okay, go back in now.' (File O30: lines 776–80)

Consequently, this negative image of the counsellor begins to circulate in the student population. Moreover, it creates a sense of mistrust and a lack of respect among students towards counsellors. Black students rarely considered counsellors as a source of help when they needed career advice or when they were experiencing personal problems. The result is that schools are fragmented – all parts of the system are not working together, and this is creating dysfunctional educational institutions.

Students advocated a better system of tracking to help students 'at risk' re-engage in the system. Kirk, a grade 12 student, like others, also made the point that such positive support may not be well received if the agents of the school are unable to share the social and cultural vantage points of the student:

I think they should have, like … a social worker … that goes to their house … like, if they see [that students] are not going to school … and, not bring them but, like, stay on them, stay on them … Of course, [their race] would matter. Why would I want some White talking to me, like, 'You could do it!' It's like get outta my face … But … you don't also want the Black person who seems to have it all … [they] don't even know where I'm coming from … (File O01: lines 1797–1818)

Similar to their view of counsellors, students also saw principals in a mostly negative light. Principals were seen more as icons of authority and discipline than as people who were on the side of students as a source of support. Those students who had tried to elicit help from their principal mainly encountered resistance. This fosters an 'us' and 'them' sentiment which can result in an antagonistic institution of education that is far from student-friendly. However, when principals do visibly support their students, there is a great opportunity to build a caring and positive learning environment. Racquel, a grade 11 student, identified strongly with her principal:

> The principal's like a father to me, like a second father. Sometimes I have no home, I'm hungry. He finds me some place to stay. He tells me ... he doesn't want me to be hanging around the streets at midnight, drinking and all that stuff ... (File A01: lines 1558–67)

In this instance, the school and, in particular, the principal became a surrogate family for Racquel, who lacked such support structures at home. Success for many students therefore is contingent upon the ability of school agents to adapt to the changing needs of society.

From their experience, drop-outs had learned that the role of the school is to perpetuate social inequality. To move towards a school system that actually engenders a progressive learning atmosphere, they recommended that the school provide race relations training for school staff, hire more Black teachers and counsellors, and include Black history and other Black experiences in the overall curriculum. In addition, they suggested that the school initiate a tracking system targeted towards people who seem to be disengaging from the school. In this way, the school would be aware of who needs help and thereby be able to deploy efficiently its resources to find ways to intervene and reverse the disengagement process.

Non-Black students basically saw the role of the school as an institution in which they can get an education which will eventually lead to a good job. They felt that the school was fulfilling this function in a somewhat adequate manner. However, they did suggest that improvements could be made by hiring teachers who have better teaching styles and attitudes and who are more sensitive to the needs of students. These students further suggested that changes need to occur within the student population itself. For example, they cited the need for better school spirit in order to improve community relations within the school. This, they advised, could come from a change in student attitude and effort.

Teachers responded in a variety of ways to the question of what role the school should play in addressing the issue of dropping out. A few teachers took very reactionary positions. Following individualized notions of achievement, they found that the fundamental duty of schools is to 'kick out' those students who do not want to be there. As Hugh, a history teacher, felt, students who 'choose' not to succeed only hold back others:

> We've got a great deal we can do within the school setting and that's what we have to decide to do ... no matter what colour, race or anything the kids are ... we are living in a society of choice, and ... what we have to do is provide a quality education for the kids who chose to be here. We can't just say to society, 'Give us all of your kids and we will turn them out to be brilliant and adjusted,' ... I mean, we have to say to the kids, those very small minority of kids, who have no business being here, 'Get out.' (File T04: lines 1043–67)

Although schools cannot be expected to solve all social problems, some teachers failed to see the interconnected relationship of the school and society. No one system works in isolation. Perhaps the lack of insight on this matter stems from a general reluctance to accept the responsibility of helping students for whom the system is not working. Instead, some teachers tended to blame individual students for their lack of motivation, thereby denying any need to change the system.

Some teachers, like Barbara, identified the logic behind teachers and schools maintaining an ethnocentric world-view as the foundation of a working system:

> ... it's ... a means of maintaining the same old thing ... a means of ensuring that a Eurocentric curriculum exists at the centre, because that's known and it has been proven and, see, it's worked so well before. Like, why fix it if it's not broken? (File T21: lines 1116–36)

However, this logic fails to interrogate for whom the system is working and how this correlates with the structures of power which privilege certain forms of knowledge and subordinate others. Oscar, a teacher of many years, was explicitly critical of attempts to rupture the status quo:

> Very often I think that what's happening today is … that the objective of some educators in power is to create a curriculum which is designed to produce a politically correct automaton. It's designed to brainwash students to think a certain way. (File T12: lines 334–62)

Other teachers also seemed resentful of having to accommodate the needs of a diverse student body and, in fact, questioned whether immigrant students should expect to be accommodated. Andrew, a history teacher, observed:

> [Some teachers] just want to [teach]: 'This is Canada, and it's English and French. And if you come from Afghanistan or you come from Uganda, this is Canada. You learn our way. We don't have to learn your way back [home]. We don't even know your way.' (File T01: lines 243–9)

Barbara also commented on the views of certain colleagues:

> They say, 'We live in Canada. We teach Canadian history,' or 'We should teach them the Canadian way.' I'm still having difficulties defining what the 'Canadian way' is, and I am a born Canadian! (File T21: lines 1116–36)

This attitude further highlights the need to renegotiate the Canadian identity, so that it is inclusive and representative of all members of society.

In a less explicit resistance to inclusive practices, other teachers felt that schools should focus on the '3 R's' rather than delving into social issues. Still, this fails to understand that discussing social issues is an integral part of student development and creates a valuable awareness of human rights and social inequities. This group of teachers felt that the school was fulfilling its role as a provider of education. For this reason, they felt that no changes are necessary within the system. They added, however, that the quality of education could improve if the students themselves just tried a little harder.

More progressive teachers stressed that the role of the school is to promote learning for *all* students, and that many changes need to occur in order for this to happen. Their recommendations called for teachers from more diverse backgrounds, even though in some cases it would jeopardize their own job security, as Catherine, an art teacher, noted:

> ... if you're into affirmative action, and I mean if you're White and you're dominant, you don't want to give up a penny of your position. Well, no, I feel there should be a complete overhaul, and I could be one of the first to go, you know, I mean I know that ... and it's hard, it's very, very hard to realize that if I were in a competition with someone else and then affirmative action was in place and it was not around gender then, then I'm going to lose out, and that's tough. Yeah. (File T33: lines 233–47)

As well, changes in teaching styles, curricula, and learning environments were recommended by some teachers. They also suggested an increase in peer counselling, community and parental involvement, and resources (e.g., money and staff). One teacher, Joyce, emphasized the vigilance required and the importance of parent-teacher linkages:

> ... and just be very vigilant about what is happening with the kids in school because you know, by and large I still think Black kids get the short end of the stick. Particularly though, I think Black kids on a whole, I mean as a generalized statement, but they do not like to deal with the guidance department, and I can understand why. They'll come and tell me, you know, Miss, you know, I couldn't get this course, they're telling me to take this instead of computers. So you go down there and you tell them, you know ... they'll sign up for general level classes because it's easy, and I'll say I'm not signing it until you change that *G* to an *A*, you know, and you have to be watching out for them. And I think parents need to become a little more astute about what the kids are doing in school. And you know, when

they find a teacher who is working with the kids, to really link up with the teacher. You know, in high school those parent-teacher links get very strained and kids will literally sabotage communication. But in this day and age, I think with so many issues being so pertinent that it's really the responsibility of Black parents to be very well informed and as much as their time and personal commitments will allow to be involved in the school somehow. Even if it's just attending the regular parent-teacher nights and, you know, making yourself seen, you know, just being there. (File T27: lines 1365–1405)

These teachers also saw a need to develop a more effective method of tracking students who begin to disengage from the system and to find more ways to connect students to their school (e.g., antiracism education, Black heritage clubs). Finally, they suggested that schools should actively consult with students who have dropped out, so that the schools can gain valuable insight into what it is they can do to strengthen the system and eventually render the word 'drop-out' obsolete.

Parents had a variety of ideas of what the role of the school should entail. Not surprisingly, many of these ideas have as their basis the formation of a strong partnership between parents and school staff, as one mother, Wilma, noted:

I see a gap between parents, teachers, principals, directors, and other sources that are very important to the welfare of the child. There should be communication between them so that the child knows exactly what is happening in the system and ... is able to grasp what is there, [and that] the teacher knows the child and the child knows the teacher, and [that] when a problem arises, the child knows who to turn to ... and why ... there should be someone specifically paid to ... find resources, [to go] door-to-door to invite parents to come out... to let the parents see that the child is learning or what help that parent should be able to give to that child. So, educating the system, educating the parents and other goodwill fares for the benefit of the child ... And until we get to that type of way of doing this, we will never be able to have the system that we can be very proud of. (File P13: lines 944–56, 960–76)

Parent associations were seen as one way to facilitate such a co-operative relationship between parents and the school. Nadia, a Pakistani-Canadian mother who had dropped out of the Ontario school system and has since gone on to graduate studies, commented:

> If they have parent/teacher associations ... it would be a good forum to discuss issues of race or other types of problems that students are facing. Because if the school recognizes these problems and can bring them up in this type of forum where you have parents, it would be beneficial because maybe the students can't ... talk to parents about it; it might be the first time they're even hearing about it. So, I think the responsibility of the school is not just to educate the students [but also] parents and [the] larger community ... (File F01: lines 1207–8, 1211–25)

Parents understood themselves to be a valuable resource for schools, as active participants in the system and as stakeholders in their children's education. The school culture, however, must be accessible to parental involvement and must have mechanisms in place to reach out to parents, particularly minority parents, who may have cultural and linguistic barriers isolating them from the school system. Alliances between schools, parents, and the community can provide an important resource in negotiating the complex issues which face students today.

Several themes emerge from these reflections on experiences, realities, and the ways in which they are negotiated in various sites. The issue of student input produced accounts of withdrawal and engagement. Students equipped with encouragement and a strong sense of identity and purpose sought out ways in which to participate in the school system with an eye to change. Other students, already disaffected by the system, regarded engagement within the existing structures as futile. Inherent in both responses is a sense of resistance to the inequities faced by students – however they may differ in terms of resulting visions. Students interpreted realistically the constraints they face in terms of social limitations and structures, and the implications these have for their futures. Similarly, they identified broad and systemic issues which cause them concern in their everyday lives, issues which eluded many of their educators. Nevertheless, students were able to hold fast to positive aspirations for the future of Black youth in the school system. These notions were constructed on positive images about the future of Black identity within Canadian society and schools, an identity which draws its strength from community cooperation, solidarity, and participation.

Chapter Thirteen

The Missing Link

Our intellectual and political objective is to move beyond a deterministic and causal, as well as classist and structuralist, explanation for 'school drop-outs.' In doing so, we join many critical educators in challenging the fairly insular and isolationist conceptions of schools as playgrounds unto themselves, apolitical and unaffected by the larger fabric of society. Schools reflect the inequalities and inequities of society. A critical perspective on Black youth disengagement from school examines the 'inside/outside' split as a method for understanding 'dropping out.' A critical approach to understanding 'dropping out' must focus on the structures and forms of students' resistance, life histories, and educational choices. Such a perspective allows us to see schools as actual sites, and students and teachers as actual subjects. It also permits us to examine conflict, struggle, active subject participation, and the possibilities of educational transformation (see Sheth and Dei 1995).

Conventional theoretical analysis and social interpretations of 'dropping out' have a tendency to overdetermine class at the price of absenting race and social difference. But if the notion of resistance offers alternative interpretations, then it is important to view resistance in terms of social difference. Weiler draws our intention to 'the ways in which both individuals [and social groups] assert their own experience and contest and resist the ideological and material forces imposed upon them' (1988, 11). We must understand resistance as embodied; that is, as raced, gendered, and classed.

There are tensions, contradictions, and paradoxes embedded in the process of schooling and education in North America. For example, the educational system is caught in a double bind. On the one hand, the system is intent on resolving the problem of dropping out. Yet, on the other hand, the educational system is incapable of making the necessary changes without dismantling the very structures that allow schools to function.

The question we face, then, is twofold: in which societal and institutional contexts do disengagement from school and dropping out occur; and, specifically, how are they framed by the dynamics of race and the politics of social difference? In attempting to answer these questions, we began with the premise that students are the experts in their own lives, at the same time knowing that, as researchers, the onus and responsibility for identifying the meanings they attach to their lives, and placing this knowledge within a sociological context, was ours.

Creating textual accounts of the reality of others involves the transformation of subjective realities into an objectified discourse. According to Smith, 'claims for the admission of accounts to membership in a textual reality depend upon establishing the proper relations between the original that it claims to represent and the account that has been produced' (1990, 73). Ethnography, then, must accept the self-defined truths of its subjects in order to validate its claim to represent who they 'really' are. It also involves acknowledging the relationship of power which the researcher holds over the subjects, who must surrender their lived experiences for the former to label, define, and legitimate in accordance with her or his own academic concerns and political intentions.

And so it becomes a very serious business. The integrity of an ethnography relies on our ability as researchers to relay the uncompromised truths of others, without appropriating their voices or inferring our own biases. It involves derailing many of our *a priori* assumptions before they become our intellectual guides into the empirical reality we are there to document. Therefore, the task of reconceptualizing 'drop-out' necessitates a methodologically and intellectually inductive process – a process which, in this case, maintained a correspondence between the transformative political and social goals of those affected by the dynamics of school disengagement and our own goals as researchers attempting to bring a sociological understanding to their dilemma.

A valid account of the drop-out issue must be grounded and contextualized within the lives of those who have been labelled, defined, and stigmatized by the process. It must be a culturally specific model of understanding the various causes associated with dropping out, without essentializing them, and it must take into account the racialized, classed, gendered, and sexualized identities which locate individuals within the hierarchical framework of a given social order.

There are those who make a rational and pragmatic choice to leave school, while others are compelled to do so. The analytical distinction, then, between drop-outs and push-outs can be argued to hinge on the issue of whether such decisions are made by conscious deliberation and amount to a pragmatic solution to a given personal situation such as pregnancy or the desire to work, or whether they represent the absence of choice for individuals who feel forced out because of negative social and institutional conditions which are perceived as endemic to the situation of schooling in a racialized, patriarchal, and capitalist society.

It can be said that the social construction of a 'drop-out' is the product of the same 'ideological conditioning' which sustains the logic of capitalist social formations. When we speak of the 'conventional wisdom' concerning drop-outs, it is an understanding informed by the hegemony of capitalist culture; that is to say, it is a rationale for the perceived failure of certain individuals which is sustained through the ideological dimensions of the Protestant work ethic and referenced by a meritocratic world-view. Locating individuals as the sole architects of their success or failure in a world of equal opportunities individualizes and at the same time depoliticizes 'drop-out.' This diverts responsibility away from the structures of schooling and relocates it exclusively within the domain of individuals and their primary group relationships.

In applying a critical antiracist framework, this study has reversed this logic by interrogating the structures of schooling and society which produce the dynamics of disengagement. Other stud-

ies have also attempted to discern the social and structural correlates of 'drop-out.' The findings are often consistent in terms of isolating as correlates to dropping out such factors as placement in
non-academic streams, coming from single-parent households or
from economically disadvantaged backgrounds, a desire for adult
jobs, or being pregnant (see Davies 1994; Morris, Pawlovich, and
McCall 1991; LeCompte and Dworkin 1991; Sullivan 1988; Lawton
et al. 1988). However, there is also the consistent lack of a cohesive
theory to analytically structure the association among these key
variables. As Davies points out, while drop-out variables such as
socio-economic status, streaming, gender, and student behaviour
and attitude appear to be correlated, it remains unclear how socio-
economic patterns emerge and which cultural processes accompany them (1994, 332).

As pointed out in the introductory chapter, notoriously absent
from these studies is the issue of race and how race intersects with
social difference. We can argue that it is the amalgamation of all of
one's social identities and labels which locates them within a given
social context. One cannot, therefore, view class, for example, in
isolation from race and gender. The narratives of Black students
illustrate the centrality of race in their lives and the salience of
race in their school experiences. Since race can be described as the
central organizing principle for understanding the experiences of
Black students, it is impossible to examine student disengagement without examining how race and cultural disparities inform
educational practice and structure the social milieux of schools.

Similarly, various theoretical paradigms concerned with the dilemma of 'dropping out' fail to take into account the issue of race.
Certain theories point to issues of deviance, whereby students
who fail to support institutional norms and values and rules of
the school are labelled as deviants and are denied the privileges
and rewards garnered by those who conform. Deviance, then, is
classed in terms of oppositional behaviours, and therefore students
who determine that the 'sanctions against rule violations are less
punishing than the costs of rule conformity' are likely to engage
in behaviour which supports these conceptions (LeCompte and
Dworkin 1991, 174–5; see also Tanner, Krahn, and Hartnagel 1995).

Similarly, control theory stresses that youth in disadvantaged positions (e.g., trapped in non-academic streams or with lower grades) suffer from status deprivation and limited opportunities, which in effect weakens their stakes in social conformity (West 1979; Davies 1994).

The issue of non-conformity as violating certain sanctions embedded within the structure and ethos of schooling has particular relevance for Black students. As the narratives have shown, some Black students react negatively to the institutional power structures of the school and the rationality of dominance. They employ behavioural tactics that constitute part of a 'culture of resistance' which is anti-school (see Solomon 1992). It is not coincidental that many of the students who fade out of school also exhibit what the school system sees as 'problem behaviours' (i.e., truancy, acts of delinquency, or even disruptive behaviour). These students perceive the school system as more interested in maintaining arbitrary forms of authority and discipline than in providing education. In such contexts, students are less cooperative with teachers who are disrespectful to them and seem uninterested in their welfare.

As the following discussion will show, understanding the racialization of 'drop-out' involves an eclectic theoretical approach. Since the existing conventional theories on dropping out do not take into account the issue of race, they must be viewed as partial, yet at the same time determined in an attempt to be totalizing. In isolation, these paradigms cannot be extrapolated to the situation of Black and minority students, although many themes have a certain resonance with the situations about which Black students have spoken. Nevertheless, they still fall short of encompassing the situation of race and status differentiation which separates the realities of minority students from those of their dominant group counterparts. In order to fill the theoretical void, we will attempt to provide the 'missing link'; a theoretical dimension which will not only aid in linking certain variables but will provide the missing analytical framework linking the dynamic of race to some of the existing theoretical perspectives on dropping out.

Some of the theories we will address, in light of our own findings, deal with very specific yet interrelated dimensions associated with dropping out. As discussed in the introduction, reproduction theories as well as Bowles and Gintis's (1976) correspondence principle, relate to a societal and structural level of analysis often used to contextualize dropping out. The structural strain model (LeCompte and Dworkin 1991) examines the interplay between society and educational institutions and the resulting impact on drop-outs, while theories of cultural difference and the theory of castelike minorities (Ogbu 1978) focus on minority status and the dynamics of classroom interaction. Control theory and theories of deviance, as discussed in the introduction, deal with social and psychological issues which help produce disaffected youth. Finally, the theory of resistance in education, as articulated by Giroux (1983a), provides an ideological dimension which may account for why students from subordinated groups express oppositional behaviours and attitudes. As well, resistance theory has conceptual links to all of the dimensions associated with the process of disengagement.

While each of these theories has currency at a specific level of discourse related to dropping out, there is a lack of analytical cohesion which would account for the process of disengagement as being a multidimensional phenomenon. The attempt here will be to link analytically some of the aetiological aspects of dropping out, as revealed in this study, with a multidimensional theoretical scheme which integrates the existing theoretical approaches outlined and adds the missing element of race to the equation.

While drop-out theories necessarily evolve from an aetiological framework, it is impossible to fit together the various causal elements to create a singular notion of dropping out without essentializing the conditions which lead to it. Drop-outs, then, cannot be classified as a homogenous category, nor can the process be reduced to a singular cause. Similarly, any theory relating to dropping out should never attempt to contain the totality of experience represented by the diverse categories of drop-outs, but rather should attempt to contextualize common scenarios by providing a perspective which deciphers the aetiology of disengagement.

In order to accept the validity of the existing theories we have mentioned, we must question why the causes they propose have a disproportionate effect on Black students. That is to say, since

Black students have disproportionately higher rates of disengagement from school (Brown et al. 1992; Brown 1993; Cheng 1995; Daenzer 1995), the salience of the social, structural, ideological, and psychological correlates said to be associated with dropping out must also be more predominant in their case. It is also necessary, therefore, to account for intra-group differences with respect to the impact of these factors. So, while the factors articulated in these theories are determined to have a disproportionate effect on Black students (as evidenced by the higher number of Black students who drop out), why are some Black students who share the same situations not similarly affected? Put differently, why do some Black students stay in school and/or act out, but not drop out? Later in the discussion, we will return to this question more directly.

It is by problematizing the existing frameworks for understanding student disengagement that we can begin to construct a theory more specifically related to the experience of Black students, yet one that does not necessarily preclude the effects postulated by theoretical predecessors. Integrating the dynamics of disengagement with the specificity of race and making connections with other forms of social difference produces a different dimension to other non-discursive frameworks. This attaches new meanings to the ideological, structural, social, and psychological realms which relate to the process of disengagement and define the lived experiences of Black students.

Examining the narratives of the Black students and drop-outs in this study has elicited the emergence of several analytical themes. While the narratives allow us to speak with certainty of how alienation, exclusion, invisibility, cultural incongruence, and marginalized resistance inform the educational experiences of Black students, what is missing is a conceptual framework which links these emergent themes. This linkage may be possible to develop by exploring how the differential evaluation and treatment of Blacks in schools and society are implicated in the process of racializing 'drop-out.'

Ideological Discourses

Speaking of the differential evaluation of Blacks in schools and society hints at an ideological context. This ideology, as previously stated, is informed by a political investment in the notion of meritocracy, which legitimates social inequality by contextualizing it as the natural outcome of equal opportunity for equal reward, thereby revealing the inherent and unequal qualities of individuals and groups in their attempt at acquiring the means for material success in society. This is a sociologically misinformed idea which nonetheless has maintained currency in our liberal democratic society. It supports the inequity of a capitalist system which promotes racism through the creation of a non-White underclass. Power and privilege are ultimately concentrated in hands that are male and White. The predominance of Eurocentric norms and conventions also attest to the normativity of Whiteness and the Otherness of colour. The narratives in this study have shown that this is not merely cynicism, but a lived experience in which one becomes essentialized through the negative construction of difference.

Althusser (1971) refers to education as being part of the 'ideological state apparatus.' It is a vehicle for the values and norms of the dominant society and a primary agent of socialization. Althusser, along with Bowles and Gintis (1976), asserts that the function of schooling in a capitalist society is to provide the ideological conditions necessary in order to reproduce the social relations of production. While Althusser stresses the role of ideology in structuring the unconsciousness of the working class to accept its position of subordination within a capitalist system, Bowles and Gintis bring this understanding to the level of classroom discourse, where the social dynamics are perceived to mirror the hierarchical structure of dominant norms and values, and eventually provide the appropriate channels into the workforce. Therefore, the combination of ideological conditioning and the belief in a structural correspondence between education, social relations, and the needs of capital are used as a means to account for the location of individuals within a social and economic hierarchy.

However, as we pointed out earlier, there are certain conceptual deficiencies in theories of social reproduction. Along with an overemphasis on the socio-economic imperatives of schools, they ignore the issue of student agency and resistance (Davies 1994). Reproduction theories appear to be grounded in structural-functional visions of social order which are ahistorical and have limited impetus towards social change. The notion that social systems maintain stasis by reproducing the ideological and social conditions which sustain the dynamics of social order, assumes that all elements in society will have a vested interest in maintaining that system or at least will be ideologically conditioned to believe that they do. This theoretically precludes the social and ideological basis of resistance.

The fact is that ideology may inform, but does not construct, consciousness. As Giroux has argued, reproduction theorists fail to account for the complex ways and diverse sites through which working-class subjectivities are developed, and thus present a 'homogeneous image of working-class life fashioned solely by the logic of domination' (1983a, 85). Domination is a powerful and tempting concept in the attempt to construct a theory of dropping out based on the experiences of Black students, but we would be equally as reductive if we did not discuss the dialectical aspects of ideology, the social construction of meanings and subjectivities, and the dynamics of resistance.

Before we discard the conceptual basis of reproduction theories, we need to establish that there is an ideological basis or, more precisely, a justification for the social inequalities embedded within the framework of capitalist societies which has a certain effect upon maintaining the status quo. Yet these ideological constructions cannot be seen as static, but rather as existing in a complex association with social, economic, and political structures of power in society.

In what we propose as a differential evaluation/treatment model of disengagement among Black students, we can glean this element of ideological conditioning as being responsible for the negative conceptions and stereotypes of Blacks in society. Meritocracy in a racialized society means that if there are a disproportionate number of Blacks who occupy lower positions within the social and economic hierarchy, then this occurs as a result of their intrinsic lack of the skills required to achieve material success. The emphasis, then, is not upon the structural domination of White society, but on the perceived inferiority of Black people. The inequality of social outcomes is therefore seen as being the result of the lack of work ethic or 'laziness,' rather than of systemic barriers constructed along racial lines.

Stereotypes maintain currency through hegemonic discourses and common-sense notions which become naturalized when they suit particular political purposes. Negative racial stereotypes have a historical legacy of permeating the collective consciousness of various societies. These stereotypes can be traced to colonialist discourses and produce a certain frame of reference through which Blacks are evaluated. While there is not a universal acceptance of these stereotypes, the narratives in this study have shown that they can be decisive in the ways in which they inform social and educational practices.

Social-Structural Realities

When Black students speak of differential evaluation and differential treatment within schools, it is manifested through specific attitudes, behaviours, and practices on the part of teachers, guidance counsellors, and administrators. The narratives of drop-outs were all linked by this common experience. The incidence of differential evaluation and treatment permeated various facets of social interaction and discourse as related by the drop-outs as well as being evidenced within the formal and 'hidden curriculum.'

Drop-outs have referred to specific experiences in which differential evaluation and treatment act as a corollary to explicit racist attitudes. They report in the narratives being demeaned and belittled by totalizing and derogatory remarks such as 'You guys aren't very intelligent are you?' Black students also reported being frustrated by the fact that they were reprimanded for behaviours otherwise accepted from White students. Some teachers also attested to observing the preferential treatment of White students, and stated that they saw some teachers act with greater tolerance with respect to White students' behaviour and any issues it might raise. Situations like these were described as contributing to feelings of subordination among Black students.

The behaviour of teachers was commonly seen by drop-outs as favouring White students. One example given was that some teachers would engage in informal conversations or 'chatting' with White students, but would ignore Black students. Drop-outs also reported feeling excluded within the participation structures of the classroom, where they felt disregarded in their attempts at gaining recognition. The feelings of alienation and invisibility which resulted from this sort of treatment were seen as precursors to the process of fading out of school.

The narratives were clear and consistent about Black students feeling they were constantly being evaluated through a climate of prejudgments and preconceptions which were fuelled by racial stereotypes. Notions such as those expressed by one drop-out who felt that the guidance counsellor saw her as coming from 'another pathological Black family' not only generalize a negative understanding of the Black community, but are also strong deterrents for Black students in discussing their problems with teachers or guidance counsellors, who, they feel, would evaluate them on the grounds of such misconceptions.

Encountering constant discouragement was typical of the drop-out narratives and was seen as endemic in their perceptions of an unresponsive school system. Much of this was attributed to the lower expectations teachers held for Black students. One of the teachers interviewed, who had expressed an understanding of systemic racism in the school system, sadly admitted that she was surprised when she saw Black students achieve. The 'progressive' minority of teachers felt that lower expectations were conveyed to Black students in subtle and unconscious ways by teachers, as part of the 'hidden curriculum.' These teachers reluctantly cited behaviours on the part of colleagues which they felt exemplified their lower expectations. Such behaviours included Black students not being encouraged to go into math and sciences, and being placed in lower streams. Observations within the schools participating in this study confirmed that few Black students could be found in either science or math classes. One student's comment sums up the struggle that many Black students face in dealing with racialized notions of inferiority: '... as a Black student you are usually trying to prove to all teachers that just because of my skin colour, doesn't mean that I can't succeed ...'

Low expectations of Black students can therefore be seen as being inscribed within the daily facets of school life. These were conveyed through channels of the hidden curriculum, which 'encompasses all the ideological stances of the schooling process that "silently" structure and reproduce hegemonic assumptions and practices' (Giroux 1983a, 71). The hidden curriculum can also be seen, then, as a vehicle for the cultural hegemony of the dominant society which maintains legitimacy by reproducing a silent discourse based on the negative construction of Otherness. It also becomes part of the nexus where differential evaluations of Blacks become constructed as modes of differential treatment.

Much of the hidden curriculum is realized through the subtle behaviours and attitudes of teachers and guidance counsellors that have been revealed through the narratives. For most dropouts, the subtle messages of inferiority they felt they were receiving had very real consequences in their lives. They led to feelings of despondency and an eventual sense of fatalism regarding their educational future:

> Sometimes too, because the school system has low expectations of Black students, you say to yourself, 'Why bother?"

Bickel and Papagiannis have stated that 'dropping out is sometimes better understood as a rational response to social circumstances than as an individual-level manifestation of bad judgement or psychopathology' (1988, 128). This is a mandate for suspending frames of reference which pathologize the drop-out process as well as drop-outs themselves. As the narratives in this study have shown, while drop-outs may give up on school, this does not necessarily imply that they have given up on themselves. Drop-outs have articulated clearly a critical understanding of the social, cultural, and political dynamics of schooling and were able to ascertain their location within these structures.

Dropping out within this context becomes a measure of self-preservation, as weighed against the reality of economic disadvantage, which students and drop-outs were all too aware was a consequence of dropping out. Under these circumstances, therefore, leaving school can be a personally empowering moment, by liberating the individual from a seemingly irrelevant and socially and culturally stifling environment:

> When I left school, I left a situation that was very negative and I put myself into a situation where I was able to get some power, get some control over my life ...

Colour-coded streaming was also regarded as a process which was based on low expectations of Black students, and was recognized as limiting their ability to transcend their socio-economic and class backgrounds. Being streamed in school was understood by drop-outs as a process which led to being streamed in society. Streaming, in effect, can be seen as contributing to the reproduction of extant social-class inequities, particularly as they occur along racial and ethnic lines. Being denied access to social mobility led to a profound sense of disempowerment and, as the preceding quote illustrates, a sense of not having control over educative experiences. Similarly, constant messages of one's inadequacy, as expressed in other narratives, made school a lower priority than getting some sense of power and control in the world.

Yet at the same time, the lack of educational credentials consigns drop-outs to almost certain subordination in the labour force. This catch-22 situation illustrates Willis's (1977) point that leaving school as a form of cultural resistance has the effect of reproducing the stratification of social class. Class was also experienced and identified as a basis for differential treatment within schools. One student made the following comment:

> I think they could achieve the same thing, but the poor student would have to work harder to get the same treatment.

The emphasis, then, was not on the issue of there being a lower potential or lack of cultural capital among lower-class students, but rather, as in this student's acknowledgment, on how lower-class students were treated differentially within schools.

Other areas of structural contention within schooling are reflected in LeCompte and Dworkin's (1991) structural strain model. This theory holds that alienation occurs for both students and teachers when they perceive their efforts and participation in education to be purposeless. Disengagement occurs when there is perceived to be a lack of fit between schools and society; that is, when school is seen as irrelevant in maintaining a correspondence with the structural conditions of society. This theory, then, argues for a connection between the structural strain on institutions and the behaviour and attitudes of their employees and clients.

The lack of relevance of schooling in relation to work is commonly cited as a reason for student disengagement (Davies 1994; Willis 1977). LeCompte and Dworkin argue that societal changes can precipitate a perceived lack of correspondence between school and work. Yet for Black students, as we have seen, practices of differential treatment such as placement in non-academic streams automatically seal their fate in the workforce and help construct the basis of their subordination. Therefore, alienation and regarding the pursuit of education as purposeless are conditioned more by these factors than the influence of social and structural strain on educational institutions themselves.

At another level, studies on cultural differences in learning (see Ramirez and Castenada 1974; Cox and Ramirez 1981; Au and Kawakami 1994; King 1994) reveal the hidden codes and structures of everyday classroom interaction which subordinate certain groups on the basis of their social and cultural differences, while they exalt the abilities of others who conform to the dominant norms and conventions of learning. Therefore, success is only deemed possible if students can be taught mainstream cultural capital and correspondingly appropriate ways of behaving in school: in other words, if they can be taught to conform to the codes and rules of the 'culture of power' (Delpit 1988). This was summed up by one Black student whose advice on passing a test was 'just think White.'

Some of the teachers interviewed in this study recognized the mono-cultural nature of school culture, values, and practices and saw the differential effect that this had on students from outside these social boundaries:

> I think we have a very middle-class White environment. I think that's the majority of the teachers, the majority of the focus of the curriculum. I think in terms of values altogether, it's middle-class and White. I think, in terms of, for instance, what is acceptable noise level in a room or in a hall or in a cafeteria, that's a middle-class White perception. So I think there's a discrepancy for kids who aren't part of that. I mean I think there's a cultural discrepancy ...

At the level of classroom discourse, theories of cultural difference argue that a lack of correspondence between home and school culture can result in minority students resisting the rules and institutional modes of conduct within schools. Schooling, as much as anything else, is a culturally mediated experience. Conflict and dissonance occur when the 'culture of power' becomes the basis of standardizing school policies, practices, curriculum, and assessment procedures, and simultaneously produces a culture of subordination among those disenfranchised by the status quo.

The issues of cultural dissonance and incongruity, which emerge from these theories, were also expressed by the students and drop-outs in this study, and in some cases were explicitly linked to the process of disengagement. Students and drop-outs felt that their experiences were not validated in an essentially Eurocentric curriculum. They also cited barriers they encountered in trying to organize Black clubs within their schools. The devaluation of Black culture within mainstream education did not go unnoticed by these students. In fact, it served to challenge their sense of identity, which they felt was being threatened by the need to conform to the 'acceptable' standards of the dominant society.

The introduction of Black History Month in some schools was seen as more of a palliative than as constituting meaningful inclusion. While students enjoyed participating in Black History Month, it was still regarded as compartmentalizing and marginalizing the

Black experience. The marginalization of Black students and their experiences is also the product of the differential evaluation of Black culture. Students related explicit comments made by teachers which devalued their culture and denied the contributions of African civilizations to the development of world culture.

Black students and drop-outs reported being alienated by the Eurocentrism of school culture and curriculum. Inclusion and ethno-cultural equity in education, therefore, rely on challenging the pre-eminence of Eurocentric discourses and require the validation of non-Western epistemologies. This is part of the process of validating the students themselves and the knowledge and experience of those who do not come from mainstream backgrounds. Ethnocentrism, therefore, represents both a retreat from difference and the point at which difference is excluded.

Racialized Subjectivities and Resistance

We begin this discussion with a note on the concept of 'race.' Contrary to Miles and Torres (1996), among many others, we see the concept of race as having analytical and conceptual significance. Despite the lack of scientific validity, race is significant for its social effects. Race is a social-relational category defined by socially selected (real or imagined) physical characteristics (see also Wilson 1973, 6). The relevance of *race* for understanding youth schooling experiences lies in its socio-historical construction as relations of power among individuals and groups. Race is significant for understanding school racism and, particularly, the continuing practice of racializing students for differential and unequal treatment. Race identity emerges from a construction of race difference which accords privilege and punishment differently to students.

In Euro-American contexts, questions of racial identity have come to the fore of the progressive politics of educational and social change in part because race still remains a powerful and 'fundamental principle of social organization and identity formation' (Omi and Winant 1993, 5). As Anthias and Yuval-Davis (1992, 50) put it, in a racialized society, to be without racial identity is 'to be in danger of having no identity' at all. Therefore, we cannot deny the influence of race on social relations and practice. The ascriptive and value-driven category of race (like ethnicity, class, gender, and sexuality), which constructs an individual's identity and social meaning and practice, plays an essential role in determining one's status, aspirations, desires, and potential in life.

Based on the discussions of cultural difference theories, and more specifically the differential evaluation of Black culture within schools and society, we must now examine how the construction of meanings and subjectivities are affected within this context and lay the social psychological groundwork for the disengagement of Black students. As Giroux (1983a, 1983b) has argued, there are multiple sites and complex processes through which subjectivities are constructed. Schools as agents of socialization are an important, yet not exclusive, site where the production and politics of identity are negotiated.

There is no standard formula through which racialized subjectivities are constructed, yet we can probably best understand this as an historical process which articulates with both gender and social-class location. Who we are, vis-à-vis those we assign to the category of 'Other,' is fundamental in locating us as part of a specific group or social category, and is grounded in the historical and cultural development of that group. What Hall referred to as 'seeing the self as it is inscribed within the gaze of the Other' (1991, 48) typifies the relational aspect of identity construction and implies a sense of self-evaluation that is based on external evaluation or, put more abstractly, the internalization of the self as Other. This prefaces an important understanding of the point at which marginality ceases to be an acceptable factor for self-definition among Black students.

The fact that subjectivities are constructed within the framework of the asymmetrical relations of power in society means that the social boundaries between 'Us' and 'Them' are not level playing fields. This does not mean, however, that Blacks and minorities should be perceived through victim-centred stereotypes, but that the constructions of Self and Other occur within a specific social and temporal reality which is based on binary relationships of power and social prestige. Racialized subjectivities organized within this oppositional dynamic are framed by cultural politics, and may therefore result in modes of social, cultural, and political resistance.

Ogbu (1978) proposes a theory of the resistance of 'castelike minorities.' He does not necessarily argue that this is a factor in student disengagement, but the discussions that follow will further illustrate this correlation. For the most part, Ogbu argues that in racially organized systems of social stratification, oppressed racial groups or 'castelike minorities' develop a sense of distrust and cynicism with respect to the educational system's ability to provide social mobility. This results in the development of oppositional attitudes and an oppositional culture which frame minority students' relationships with school agents. There is, therefore, a corresponding lack of compliance among these students with the structures and agents of the school. According to Ogbu, this is a social structural problem which finds expression within the classroom. By showing how the politics of social difference affects the dynamics of a multiracial and multi-ethnic classroom, Ogbu has constructed an important basis for understanding the issues of power and authority and the need for student agency which has significant implications in understanding the dynamics of disengagement among Black students.

Giroux has critiqued the homogeneous manner in which resistance theories have traditionally been applied. Theoretically weak handling of the nature of resistance, according to Giroux, does a disservice to understanding resistance as a construct:

> What must be urged is that the concept of resistance not be allowed to become a category indiscriminately hung over every expression of 'oppositional behaviour' ... it must be an analytical construct that contains a moment of critique and a potential sensitivity to its own interests, i.e., an interest in radical consciousness raising and collective critical action. (Giroux 1983a, 110)

Therefore, it is the issue of intentionality which separates resistance from other forms of oppositional behaviour. Following Giroux's definition, then, the validity of Ogbu's theory of the resistance of 'castelike minorities' hinges on whether it is empirically bound to the knowledge that these specific actions were consciously guided by serious political intent.

Similarly, Davies (1994), in a study on the issue of resistance and rebellion among high-school drop-outs, has also claimed difficulty in ascertaining whether certain behaviours qualify as resistance; that is, determining the nature of the intentions embedded within specific actions or behaviours. He argues that 'concrete evidence for the claim that drop-outs engage in a critique of schooling remains elusive' (1994, 345). However, the framework of his research, being a secondary analysis of quantitative data on dropping out, compromised the certainty with which he could speak on the issue of resistance among drop-outs.

In examining the narratives of the drop-outs in this study, however, we feel able to speak of marginalized resistance as an explicit factor in student disengagement. Students and drop-outs have expressed their feelings of subordination as the result of the differential evaluation and treatment they have received within both schools and society. They have discussed engaging in oppositional behaviour such as truancy, arguing with teachers, and ultimately dropping out as their response to being Black in a predominantly White school system. Their resistance, then, is to a system which is out of sync with their reality and their needs, devalues their culture, and proves stifling to their sense of identity:

> ... the system destroys their inner strength and character ... the school system has tried over the years to deny us our self-worth ... This ... is a big issue with some people when they say the kids lack self-esteem or what have you. It may be true for a few but we have to ask 'Why?' It is the school that makes them lack that self-esteem.

Black students, therefore, must weigh the practical benefits of schooling against the personal costs they feel would be incurred by remaining in school, namely loss of cultural and self-esteem. Black students have also reported resisting the assimilative forces within schools. As one student put it, 'My philosophy of life is ... don't hang around in places and among people who are only interested in remaking you.'

Throughout the narratives, we have heard the voices of resistance: resistance to the social, cultural, and academic subordination that they, as Black students, face within schools. For most dropouts, this has been the product of a lifetime of differential treatment and disenfranchisement within the school system. Such experiences may relate to what Giroux (1983a) calls the 'hidden logic of resistance,' which must be interpreted through the historical and cultural mediations which shape it. Black students are products of their personal, as well as their collective, cultural histories. It is these experiences and this knowledge that they bring with them to their educative experiences and to their interactions with others.

By redefining resistance and including race as a factor, a theoretical void has been filled. Giroux himself has commented on traditional approaches to resistance as containing 'no theoretical room for exploring forms of resistance that are race- and gender-specific' (1983a, 105). Davies has also critiqued the overemphasis on class in resistance theory. He argues that critical educational theorists such as Giroux, Apple, Willis, and McLaren presume that 'primordial working-class culture' is a catalyst for opposition to school authority and, as a result, that 'resistance theorists overgeneralize the experience of a small number of disaffected youth to the bulk of working-class students' (1994, 335). Davies argues that such ascription casts doubt on the salience of class in the 'subjective perceptions of Canadians.'

There can be no doubt, however, of the salience of race in the experiences of the Black students we interviewed, and how it framed their struggles and modes of resistance. Within class-based paradigms of resistance, issues of race and gender become erased by a totalizing discourse which gives primacy to the issue of social class and marginalizes other forms of social difference which, in certain instances, have greater relevance to the nature of student resistance.

For Blacks living in predominantly non-Black societies, race can be said to have primary significance in the construction of individual and collective social identities, which then create a specific vantage point for resistance and the development of an oppositional culture. In a racially stratified society, racial group membership is used to assign to people their social, economic, political, and other valued roles (Ogbu 1978). Class, or socio-economic status, is therefore a corollary to racial identity, and directly affected by it. Similarly, to view gender outside of the context of race would isolate racial subordination from patriarchal domination and provide only a partial account of the multiplicity of oppression faced by Black women. Therefore, it is necessary to examine how racialized, classed, and gendered identities are articulated and how they are used to construct a culture of resistance.

Fordham has discussed the development of a collective identity among African Americans as being based on the anthropological concept of 'fictive kinship.' This refers to a system of common association which is not simply based on skin colour or common ancestry, but rather implies the particular world-view of those who are considered to be, and are socially constructed as, 'Black.' This system of identification, as a brotherhood or sisterhood of Blacks, symbolizes their 'sense of peoplehood in opposition to White Americans' social identity' (1988, 56). This is the point at which identity finds its reference within social difference, and is mediated by its historical and political ties to it. Solomon (1992) argues that an oppositional social identity for Blacks has its roots in slavery and the perceptions of White superiority and Black inferiority which served to justify the subordination of Blacks. Formation of a collective social identity, then, coalesced around the differential evaluation of Black culture and the disenfranchisement of Blacks from social, economic, and political life. According to Solomon, this has become a powerful response strategy to the institutional subordination Blacks are still facing.

Conscious articulations of a collective social identity have clearly emerged from the narratives in this study. Of the Black students interviewed, 88 per cent felt a commonality of consciousness and experience with other Black students, which was expressed through statements such as 'We're Black, we understand each other' or 'We have the same experiences.' These statements express common ties to oppression in a White-dominated society which is experienced to a greater or lesser degree by all sectors of the Black community. Group identity and solidarity are established and strengthened through participation in Black heritage clubs and in social interaction with other Black students. No only did students report that such participation provides a source of strength and effectual support, but they also felt they would be evaluated in a more positive light among their Black peers.

Ogbu (1993) has referred to some Blacks within the North American context as 'involuntary minorities' whose presence in society was brought about by force, that is, through slavery. He argues that this experience relegates Blacks to a position of lasting subordination in society based on their perceived inferiority, and that the manner of their incorporation has limited the exercise of self-determination. The attempt to extricate themselves from this disadvantaged position has created a historically informed counter-culture among Black students which has had decisive and negative effects upon their academic lives (Ogbu 1978; Weis 1985).

Ogbu (1982a, 1982b) argues that primary socialization within the home and community preconditions Black students to resist the dominant cultural institutions, which they perceive as racially biased. Therefore, the ideological preconditions for cultural resistance exist prior to entering school. The ideological basis for resistance among Black students, as we have discussed, is informed by historical injustice and oppression, resulting in continuing economic, social, political, and cultural subordination. The school, in effect, has a role to play in bringing about the status differentiation of Blacks within each of these spheres, and therefore is rejected for its complicity with the reproductive process of social class formation. Yet, at the same time, the school inspires some optimism as a tool for social transformation.

The reproductive element of schooling must be understood as part of a dialectical process linked to resistance. The seeds of cultural resistance germinate within the social, economic, political, and ideological processes associated with reproduction. This does not represent a simple binary analytical formula, but a process which is continually acted out as an expression of counter-culture. These latent forms of resistance become manifest within institutional settings that serve the purpose of perpetuating social inequality through practices such as colour-coded streaming, which continue to relegate Black students to inferior status. In this sense, schools can no longer be viewed as apolitical. The body of evidence shows that they represent sites of contestation and struggle among differentially empowered social groups engaged in a battle of social reproduction and marginalized resistance (see Freire 1973; Bourdieu and Passeron 1977; Apple 1979; Giroux 1983b). These elements emerge as competing and contradictory paradigms in terms of how the issue of agency becomes implicated. In reproduction theory, students are erased by social, cultural, economic, and political processes, yet resistance theory reasserts this lost agency through political consciousness and transformative struggle.

We cannot assume, however, that social differences can be united in oppression; that is, that socio-economic subjugation or class-based subordination creates a common front which cuts across racial lines. In fact, McCarthy and Apple (1988) have argued that social-class forms of resistance often lead to divisive cultural politics rather than solidarity with racial minorities, who are often regarded derisively and negatively stereotyped. According to Solomon, in such instances, 'class and racial cultures reproduce antagonisms within institutional settings. They compete with each other rather than build solidarity against authority structures in educational, economic and political systems' (1992, 102). Therefore, racial divisions along class lines can lead to conflict rather than cooperation, and impede the basis for concerted social action.

The Question

Having examined the historical, economic, and ideological basis for Black resistance, the question still remains as to why all Black students do not engage in oppositional cultural behaviours or are similarly guided by racially motivated imperatives for social change. In confronting this question, we must accept the fact that theoretical paradigms have limited powers of explanation with regard to specific social phenomena. Attempts at totalizing these explanations become partial representations of certain realities where unaccounted-for variations can often negate the original premise. To avoid such a pitfall, it is necessary for us to examine also the conditions which preclude Black students from dropping out of school.

As discussed in the introduction, dropping out of school can be interpreted as a specific mode of resistance tied to the differential evaluation and differential treatment of Blacks in schools and society. But many of these drop-outs are, in fact, 'push-outs,' having been motivated to leave school prematurely by the structures of schooling which institutionalize racial inequality. It becomes all the more necessary, therefore, to determine why other Black students, who exist within the same social, cultural, and economic contexts, are not similarly inclined. In other words, it becomes necessary to understand what factors mitigate against dropping out.

One explanation is put forth by Fordham (1988), who argues that 'racelessness' is a factor in Black students' school success. The desire for success in mainstream society, argues Fordham, causes members of subordinate groups to distance themselves from their racial or ethnic group affiliations. The practice of becoming 'raceless,' therefore, emerges as a strategy to elude the negative stigma associated with being Black, and enhance the potential for social and economic mobility. However, this theory fails to interrogate the fact that 'racelessness' is a quality traditionally ascribed to the social category of being White, and that transcending race and the negative connotations attached to it is a luxury that has not been afforded to Blacks despite the efforts and social mobility of some. Furthermore, we should not accept uncritically the view that attempting to abrogate one's identity is simply part of the cost of academic or economic advancement in a hierarchically organized and racialized society. To do so validates the hegemony of dominant cultures which seek to subjugate all forms of social difference. Nevertheless, taking all this into account, the need to negate Black identity for some students follows Ogbu and Matute-Bianchi's (1986) argument that Black cultural styles, language forms, and identity symbols, which students bring with them to school, are differentially evaluated within the normative standards of Eurocentric schools and therefore do not contribute to their academic success.

The process of 'disidentifying' with the Black community involves adopting the attitudes, behaviours, and characteristics of the dominant society. Delpit refers to this as conforming to the rules for participating in the 'culture of power.' These rules specifically govern 'linguistic forms, communicative strategies and presentations of self; that is, ways of talking, ways of writing, ways of dressing and ways of interacting' (1988, 283). This behaviour, however, often leads to intra-cultural conflict and dissonance for those who see keeping social distance from their peers as the means for success in the dominant society. Many of the narratives dealt with the issue of students who tried to 'act White,' thereby alienating themselves from their peers:

> They were imitating Whites and having some White person be their head, have them led on a string ... on the one hand they'd be cursing the White thing, but the next minute you see them buddy-buddy up with them, taking on their culture, dressing in the clothes they dress in ...

Another student spoke candidly of moments when they felt that identifying with the Black community meant having to contend with the negative stereotypes associated with being Black:

> ... I'll tell you where I was at that moment I didn't want to be associated with Black people, with anything that has to do with Africa, because well, like I said before, what I hear was all negative things ... I didn't want to be associated with.

Other students felt less comfortable with having to compromise their identity in order to be accepted by the White mainstream:

> ... I want to be myself and show everybody who I am, but you can't, you can't be yourself too much, you have to hide some of your Blackness when you're around White people, because then you become like an alien to them.

These narratives speak to the various ways Black students negotiate their identities in relationship to either their group norms or the external standards imposed by the dominant society. Either route leads to a certain form of alienation and exclusion.

Those who conform to the cultural styles of the dominant society have been referred to as 'mainstreamers' (Pryce 1978) and have made a conscious choice to distance themselves from Black culture and society in order to better their chances for academic and economic success. According to Solomon (1992), this is driven by an 'achievement ideology,' or a belief in the folk theory of education as being the major determinant in social success or failure. The rewards, then, are perceived as justifying the costs expended in order to achieve them. So, while the 'double-culture syndrome' may create conflict and ambivalence in students, Fordham's (1988) study found that the long-term socio-economic benefits were substantial.

Therefore, compliance counteracts resistance when the promise of future gains provides the necessary impetus for social conformity. Culturally sanctioned behaviours, then, must replace the oppositional strategies of those unwilling to conform. D'Amato summarizes that 'where the situational rewards for compliance and sanctions for resistance are sufficiently compelling, the implications of school performances may be said to provide children with a situational rationale for limiting group opposition and resistance to school and for justifying participation in school processes' (1993, 191). Yet the rationale may not necessarily have to be situationally specific in order to achieve compliance. Following the arguments presented, compliance and conformity with the standards imposed by the dominant culture may stem from a certain understanding that one's own culture is perceived as a deficit and therefore must somehow be de-emphasized in order to achieve status and success. This, however, can lead to negative self-perceptions which hinder both academic and personal growth.

There may be greater impetus for engaging in cultural dissociation among Black students with higher socio-economic backgrounds. Increased financial resources provide greater means for acquiring fluency and proficiency within the 'culture of power.' Having the ability to gain access to the socially privileged form of cultural capital provides greater gains in acceptance and avoids being trapped within traditional Black stereotypes. Also, successful role models within one's family and corresponding sets of expectations for achievement may provide students with achievement-oriented standards that are defined by their family's social location.

The debilitating effects of poverty on social and academic achievement must also be taken into account when discussing the effect of social class on educational outcomes. Economically disadvantaged Black students must confront both economic and racial oppression in their daily lives. Many leave school in order to help provide for their families. Those who remain must contend not only with social and financial pressures, but also, without the requisite brand of cultural capital, they become subject to lower teacher expectations and the reproductive effects of school practices such as streaming. There may also be less impetus for these students to attempt to negate their identity as a means for economic advancement, and therefore racial identity may form the basis for solidarity and resistance.

The danger in adhering uncritically to the cultural difference theory, however, is that it runs the risk of becoming a totalizing response to why racial and ethnic minority students have differential patterns of achievement. It cannot reasonably be argued that all Black students who are committed to remaining in school give up their identities. It is necessary, then, to look at those who cannot be contained within such a framework and provide other reasons for their perseverance.

While all Black students are to some degree affected by differential evaluation and differential treatment within various social and institutional settings, this does not always lead to opting out of the system completely. One explanation for this may be located within the family. While the image of the 'pathological Black family' has been a convenient scapegoat for Black students' difficulties at school, we found many Black parents strongly committed to helping their children succeed. Some parents were former drop-outs themselves and spoke with profound understanding about both the problems of Black students' disengagement and possible solutions. The structural significance of school, then, or its implications for future success in society, along with meeting family expectations and maintaining approval and acceptance within the family, may, for some students, provide the impetus and support for staying in school (see D'Amato 1993).

We cannot overemphasize family and peer support as extremely relevant factors in understanding why some students only act out but not drop out. While students expressed frustration with the school system, they pointed to parental considerations as key to their decision to stay at school. Some students joked that 'my parents would kill me if I dropped out.' Other students argued that they persevere because of their parents and that they do not want to end up in the same economic position as their parents. A few students saw their parents as sounding-boards who provided encouragement and support to help them deal with the alienating and exclusionary tendencies of schools. Similarly, there are students who stay in school in order not to lose their friends. These students do not drop out because of peer encouragement to 'hang in.' It seems to us, then, that family and peer support are part of the reasons not all Black students drop out of school. This assertion is a far cry from pathologizing and blaming Black parents and families for the problems of youth education. It speaks of the distinction that ought to be made in terms of asking parents to take responsibility and blaming these parents for school problems. We can speak of parental responsibility in youth education at the same time as we ask schools to examine critically the structures of schooling that cause students to disengage and eventually drop out of school.

The knowledge of family and community support as important factors for youth staying in school suggests the need to find ways to integrate families and communities into schools. This means exploring more effective ways to transform the current organizational life, culture, and environment of schools so as to give a more direct and effective role for parental and community knowledge. This call for transformation translates into searching for alternative forms of schooling in Euro-American contexts which break down the rigid power barriers between home, school, and community.

The redefinition of the role of family and community in schooling provides a case for Black-focused/African-centred schools, which were an option favoured by many of the Black students and drop-outs interviewed. Whereas Black History Month and African heritage programs have the effect of compartmentalizing Afrocentric knowledge within the Euro-centred focus of public education, Black-focused schools provide an immersion in African-centred studies. For many Black students, these schools represent a safe and culturally congruent environment where they can acquire knowledge and perspectives more consonant with their experience as African Canadians. Such schools also provide a decisive role for parents and the local community in terms of becoming part of the decision-making processes that guide what goes on in them (see Dei 1995c). For critics, this represents a return to segregation, yet this system is not based on a desire to discriminate, but rather to provide an alternative to mainstream education, which has the demonstrated effect of producing a disproportionate amount of Black students who drop out.

The forms of student resistance are diverse and may in fact mitigate against student disengagement. As discussed in the introduction, increased student participation within school structures, such as establishing clubs or participating in student councils, when done as a means to effect institutional and social change, can be seen as the nexus between resistance and accommodation. While trying to effect change through the very structures being challenged runs the risk of systemic co-optation, it nevertheless provides a channel for Black students to engage in cultural practices and find a forum for their concerns. Finn's (1989) 'participation-identification' model holds that students who are engaged within school activities feel less marginalized and alienated and therefore are more likely to stay in school. Many of the drop-outs in this study did not have access to Black heritage clubs and felt that where these programs exist, Black students would have greater chance for effectual support, and consequently less struggle negotiating the system.

In terms of gender, there are also significant differences with regard to the nature of resistance and the implications for school disengagement. The feminization of resistance, or gender-based accounts, such as that put forward by McRobbie (1981), argue that gender traditionalism, characterized by female school rejectors' adopting motherhood, symbolically scorns the middle-class image of the female student (on related concerns, see also Gaskell and McLaren 1987; Gaskell, McLaren, and Novogrodsky 1989; Acker 1995). However, it can be said that such theories allow the socio-logical imagination to overshadow the simple logic behind specific actions. While pregnancy is a common reason for premature leaving among female drop-outs, becoming pregnant is most often not a planned or deliberate action among high-school girls. Therefore, attaching class-based political intentions to their predicament overextends the paradigm of resistance, to say the least. Pregnancy does, however, ignite certain sentiments with respect to gender politics. Our interviews showed that female students felt that pregnant teens were stereotyped as 'whores,' while males escaped taking any responsibility for their actions.

Gender bias in channelling students was also identified as an important issue, where Black males where channelled into sports and females were discouraged from math and sciences or opting for male-dominated career choices. Davies (1994), however, argues that gender traditionalism, in fact, distinguishes and dichoto-mizes male and female responses to school. It is, therefore, not a retreat from traditionalism, but rather the embrace of culturally sanctioned and gender-stereotyped modes of behaviour which accounts for the more disruptive behaviour of males and their preference for work over school, versus the desire for domestic traditionalism among females who drop out. Davies cites the work of Lynn Davies (1984) and Holland and Eisenhart (1990), who argue that these gender roles are used by less successful youth in order to mould alternative identities other than that of a failing student.

This sort of argument redirects the emphasis for failure back to the student without interrogating any other potential sites of conflict which might account for why these students are not succeeding in the first place. It also fails to connect the issue of race to gender differences. In our study we found that, while Black females felt that racism was the most significant inter-cultural problem, sex-ism was recognized as being a greater problem within the Black community. This understanding outlines the multiplicity of their oppression and the varied sites of resistance. Black males, however, experienced heavier surveillance by authority figures in the school and the broader society than females, which may account for a greater lack of compliance with authority structures. Black males were also identified as being subject to more negative stereotypes and more likely to be labelled as 'troublemakers.' This is an issue of racially defined gender bias out of which patterns of resistance emerge. Where this occurs, these actions have the reproductive effect of reinforcing the validity of negative stereotypes which are often attached uniformly to all sectors of the Black community.

As this discussion closes, we must restate the need to distinguish pragmatic reasons for dropping out of school from those related to the structural conditions of schooling in a racialized capitalist society. There is an important distinction to be made between those students who make pragmatic decisions to drop out of school because of matters of circumstance and those who are pushed out by the specific social, cultural, and organizational practices of schooling which contribute to the reproduction of the racial, economic, and gender-based system of social stratification. Differential evaluation and differential treatment based on any of the above-mentioned 'isms' influence corresponding actions which either lead to forms of resistance such as dropping out of school (which has the paradoxical effect of reproducing social inequality) or compliance, which symbolizes an acceptance of the status quo to the extent that it garners social and economic benefit.

There is a need to understand the process whereby 'acting out' culminates in dropping out. As students exhibit what the school system sees as 'problem behaviours' (i.e., truancy, acts of delinquency, or even disruptive behaviour), some educators further ignore or stigmatize these students. An educator's perceived lack of interest in students sends a powerful message to the youth that schools can do without them. It is not surprising, then, that most drop-outs often remark on what they view as the absence of a caring adult who could have affected their decision to leave school prematurely. When students 'act out,' it is important that the behaviour should be contextualized and understood within a potential process of disengagement.

The interrogation of the processes of dropping out suggests that students whose values, norms, and social objectives do not conform to the conventional school ethos develop alternative means to survive and learn. Often schools are not attractive to these students, who may argue that education does not necessarily buy a better lifestyle situation. Since the state has made it compulsory for youth to attend school there is added pressure on the youth. Within the formal school context, students become increasingly aware of the impossibility of this situation. The cultural knowledge from both home and the street with which students enter the school competes with the dominant ideologies that define students as inferior. As Sheth and Dei (1995) argue, it is this tension between what students experience themselves to be and who they (students) are taught they are that produces a line of 'deviation.'

Even students who are taught to 'value' education develop a contradictory consciousness. It is no coincidence that so many drop-outs often ask, 'Why do I know many Black educated professionals who have no jobs?' or 'I am only fifteen and I own my own business, had I stayed in school would I have earned this kind of money?' These questions reflect drop-outs' experiences of school. These questions point to the real dilemmas of power relations and schooling. Michele Fine also discovered in her study of a particular urban school in the United States that 'in uncovering layers of systemic, widespread school failure, the question was no longer why a student would drop out. It was more compelling to consider why so many stayed in school ...' (1991, 7).

The discussion in this chapter has been an attempt to develop a theoretical understanding of how 'dropping out' is a socially and structurally constructed phenomenon which engages the politics of social difference with the dynamics of schooling. It has been a lesson in how ideological and political forces are redefined within institutional settings and serve to reinforce a social order based on racialized and class-based hierarchies. And finally, it has been an attempt to link theory to, and develop it from, the lived experiences of Black students and drop-outs who have framed our understanding of the dialectical relationship among all these factors and the formidable challenges they pose to the issue of student agency.

Conclusion

What I want to know is, what do we get for speaking out? What would come out of your work? Some more silence and denial?

Many of the voices we have heard throughout this study speak for themselves in ways with which we can only claim to have empathy. Unfortunately, the questions this student has left us with still remain unanswered. Critical ethnography carries many lofty goals related to social change and transformation, yet, in truth, it is a call for action which has no guaranteed effect. So it is not surprising that this student should be cynical about where all of this was going to lead.

Sociology is a practice which combines politics, ideology, and desire in an attempt to understand the lived realities of others. Anne Game (1991) interrogates the issue of regarding sociology as providing a 'mirror to the real'; that is, the idea that sociology, anthropology, and the social sciences are capable of revealing the real lives of people through their methods (i.e., ethnography, surveys, and interviews). Yet, in concluding that this practice provides a 'mirror to the real' is a somewhat misleading metaphor. It implies that sociology passively reflects reality, in no way altering how it will be perceived. This not only de-emphasizes the role of the sociological imagination in apprehending 'social facts,' but it also depoliticizes the practice of ethnography and its representations of the Other.

What we write and speak about as 'text' does not always (if ever) provide a mirror of real-life situations. Rather, it represents a complex narrative that speaks about how the researcher and her/his subjects are socially and politically located, situated, and positioned (see Walcott 1995). Positionality influences interpretations. An awareness of these ideas moves sociology and the social sciences away from structures that objectify people/subjects of study to methodological and discursive approaches that see people as creators of their own lives and world, and as resistors of established social orders.

Nevertheless, social research is governed by specific political intentions and ideological perspectives which often precede the research process. Grounded approaches to social research are often as much grounded in the political biases of the researchers as they are within the lived realities of the subject. The nature of sociological inquiry, then, can never be characterized as neutral in its claim to represent the 'authenticity' of experience. Even when sincere attempts have been made to allow the subjects' voices and concerns to guide the research project, as we have attempted to do, abstracting this knowledge and placing it within a sociological context divorces the subjects from defining the theoretical shape their experiences will ultimately take. We can claim, however, to have the same political goals in mind as those about whom we speak in this study – that is, to understand the dynamics of Black students' disengagement from school and hopefully to provide a focus for educational and social change dedicated to improving schooling for all racial and ethnic minority students.

While effecting social change requires collective action, we have learned in this study that the caring and responsive actions of a single individual – a teacher, guidance counsellor, or parent – can often make the difference to a student who is fading out of school. We have seen that the educational experiences of Black drop-outs have been characterized by a series of moments when they were evaluated and treated differentially on the basis of their race. These were often the defining moments of their academic careers, and the cumulative pressure of these moments forced many students to leave school prematurely. Many of these students felt trapped within an unresponsive school system which did not take into account their needs and interests. These students were falling through the cracks of an educational system which had, in effect, denied and disowned their reality as a means to protect the integrity of its practices.

We cannot overstate the need to re-examine the effects of schooling from the perspective of racial and minority students. Education should provide avenues for personal and academic growth as well as the potential for economic and social mobility. Where this is being denied to specific groups in society, we can no longer avoid looking at the cause, even though we may fear being implicated. As social researchers, it is our job to delineate the causes of social inequality and propose solutions regardless of who or what is implicated. And so, as Jewel Smith writes, '... it would be exceedingly misguided for a researcher to overlook, or de-emphasize, the destructive and ubiquitous presence of race ... Rather than an emphasis on race, what is truly excessive, it seems, is the amount of time spent avoiding a "direct hit" on the issue' (1995, 5). Therefore, to do any less than providing this 'direct hit' on the issue of race in understanding the dilemma of drop-outs would make us accomplices in the complacency which is created through silence and denial.

Appendix 1

Survey Questions for Black/African-Canadian Students

Note: You may choose not to answer any of the following questions.

1. Name _____
2. Gender _____ male/female _____
3. Age or Date of Birth _____
4. Were you born in Canada? _____ Yes/No _____
5. If not born in Canada, where? _____
6. When did you come to Canada? _____
7. What languages do you speak other than English? _____
   _____
8. Which school do you attend? _____
   What grade are you in? _____
9. Are you in the general/basic/advanced level program?_____
10. How long have you been going to your present school? _____
11. If you have brothers or sisters attending school, what grades are they
    in? _____ (brothers) _____ (sisters)
12. What work do your parents do? _____
13. Do you live at home with both of your parents? _____ Yes/No
14. Do your parents help with your schoolwork/assignments?
    _____ Yes/No
15. Do you have any input in decision-making at your school?
    _____ Yes/No
16. Has the school done enough to make attending school a worth-
    while experience for you? _____ Yes/No
17. Does the school discuss with students the consequences of dropping
    out? _____ Yes/No
18. Do you know anyone who has dropped out of school? _____ Yes/No
19. Have you ever considered leaving school? _____ Yes/No
20. Would you say that you are treated fairly at school by the authorities?
    _____ Yes/No

Interview Guide for
Black/African-Canadian Students

For an in-depth, open interview, we probed students' responses to some of the following pilot-tested questions:

1. When you hear the phrase 'school drop-out,' what does it mean to you?
2. Can you think of any reasons why people drop out of school?
3. Have you contemplated dropping out of school? If yes, why?
4. Did you discuss your intentions with someone?
5. Why did you decide to stick around and stay?
6. What do you like the most about going to school?
7. What do you dislike about your school (if anything)?
8. Who is your favourite teacher and why?
9. Whom do you discuss any problems you have at school with?
10. Do you think your experiences at school would be different if you were male/female?
11. Do you think your experiences at school would be different if you came from a wealthy/poor family?
12. Do you think your experiences at school would be different if you were White?
13. Please describe the ways you are able to express who you are while at school.
14. What school activities are you involved in?
15. Who are your best friends at school?
16. Whom do you look up to in society and why?
17. What are your future aspirations in life?
18. How do you hope to accomplish these goals?
19. Do you think that you can still accomplish these goals if you were to drop out of school?
20. What do you think about those who drop out of school?

21. Tell me about what your school has been doing to encourage you and other students to stay in school.
22. In what ways could school be made more interesting for students, so that they will be more likely to finish rather than dropping out?
23. What do you know about the roles and responsibilities of your school's guidance consellors?
24. How often do you see a guidance counsellor?
25. How often do you see the school principal?
26. What are your roles and responsibilities as a student in your school?
27. How do you contribute to the decisions that affect your life at school?
28. Tell me about your most pleasant experience at school.
29. Tell me about the most unpleasant experience at school.
30. To what do you attribute some of the bad experiences you have recounted to me?
31. If you were given a magic wand to change something at your school, what would that be?
32. How do your parent(s) help with your schoolwork/assignments?
33. What do you think parents can do to prevent students from dropping out of school?
34. Do you see any role for the business community in helping students stay in school?
35. What do you want to see the government do about the drop-out problem in the schools?
36. As a Black youth living in Toronto, what four things worry you the most?
37. How hopeful are you that these concerns/worries will be resolved?

Appendix 3

Interview Guide for Focus-Group Interviews with Black/African-Canadian Youth

1. What are your views about the Black male(s)/female(s) at your school?
2. What are your views about the Black male/female in today's society?
3. Describe any Black male/female interrelations that you are aware of at school.
4. Describe any Black male/female intrarelations at school you are aware of (i.e., social relations with others of same gender).
5. Do you think your experiences at school would be different if you were male/female?
6. What is your understanding of sexism in the school?
7. What are your views about an all-Black male/female school?
8. What are your views about a Black-focused school?
9. Whom do you discuss any problems you have at school with?
10. Describe the ways you are able to express who you are while at school.
11. What school activities are you involved in?
12. Who are your best friends at school?
13. Whom do you look up to in society and why?
14. What are your future aspirations in life?
15. How do you hope to accomplish these goals?
16. As a Black male/female in today's society, what are your greatest concerns or worries?
17. In what ways could school be made more interesting for students, so that they will be more likely to finish rather than dropping out?

Appendix 4

Survey Questions for Non-Black Students

Note: You may choose not to answer any of the following questions.

1. Name _____
2. Gender _____ male/female
3. Age or Date of Birth _____
4. Were you born in Canada? _____ Yes/No
5. If not born in Canada, where? _____
6. When did you come to Canada? _____
7. What languages do you speak other than English? _____
   _____
8. Which school do you attend? _____
   What grade are you in? _____
9. Are you in the general/basic/advanced level program?
   _____
10. How long have you been going to your present school?
    _____
11. If you have brothers or sisters attending school, what grades are
    they in? _____(brothers) _____(sisters)
12. What work do your parents do? _____
13. Do you live at home with both of your parents? _____ Yes/No
14. Do your parents help with your schoolwork/assignments? _____
    Yes/No
15. Do you have any input in decision-making at your school?
    _____ Yes/No
16. Has the school done enough to make attending school a worthwhile
    experience for you? _____ Yes/No
17. Does the school discuss with students the consequences of dropping
    out? _____ Yes/No
18. Do you know anyone who has dropped out of school?
    _____ Yes/No

19. Have you ever considered leaving school? _____ Yes/No
20. Would you say that you are treated fairly at school by the authorities? _____ Yes/No

Appendix 5

Interview Guide for Non-Black Students

For an in-depth, open interview, we probed students' responses to some of the following pilot-tested questions:

1. When you hear the phrase 'school drop-out,' what does it mean to you?
2. Can you think of any reasons why people drop out of school?
3. What do you like the most about going to school?
4. What do you dislike about your school (if anything)?
5. Who is your favourite teacher and why?
6. Whom do you discuss any problems you have at school with?
7. Do you think your experiences at school would be different if you were male/female?
8. Do you think your experiences at school would be different if you came from a wealthy/poor family?
9. Do you think your experiences at school would be different if you were Black/African-Canadian?
10. Do your parents help with your schoolwork and how?
11. Please describe the ways you are able to express your own personal and cultural identity while at school.
12. What school activities are you involved in?
13. Who are your best friends at school? (Probe racial/ethnic/gender background.)
14. Whom do you look up to in society and why?
15. What are your future aspirations in life?
16. How do you hope to accomplish these goals?
17. Do you think that you can still accomplish these goals if you were to drop out of school?
18. What do you think about those who drop out of school?
19. As a youth in today's society, what are your greatest concerns or worries?

20. Tell me about what your school has been doing to encourage you and other students to stay in school.
21. In what ways could school be made more interesting for students, so that they will be more likely to finish rather than dropping out?
22. If you had a magic wand to change something about the school system, what would that be and why?

Other Issues for Further Investigation

1. Students' views about discipline in the schools
2. Students' accounts of racial incidents at school
3. Students' accounts of sexism in the school
4. Whom students associate with at school and why?
5. Students' responses to Black/African-Canadian students' observation that 'they are always put under a microscope'
6. School's/students' expectations of the Black/African-Canadian student
7. Students' views regarding the importance of Black teachers in the schools
8. Students' views about Black/African History Month
9. Students' views about Black-focused schools

Appendix 6

Interview Guide for Teachers and School Administrators

For an in-depth, open interview, we probed teachers' and school administrators' responses to such questions as the following:

1. How does the teacher view dropping out from school, and what reasons can s/he assign for why some students drop out?
2. How would the teacher describe his/her philosophy of teaching?
3. In the teacher's view, how do such factors as race/ethnicity, gender, and class influence schooling and education?
4. In the teacher's view, what pedagogical styles facilitate learning for Black children, in particular?
5. What does the teacher see as his/her greatest challenge in teaching Black/African-Canadian students?
6. What are the special contributions that Black children bring to the classroom?
7. What are some of the lived experiences of the teacher that have significantly impacted on his/her educational and teaching career?
8. How would the teacher describe a typical day at school?
9. What specifically should be done to keep students in school?
10. What changes would the teacher want effected in the school to improve upon Black students' learning, and their sense of connectedness and belonging in the school?
11. What measures have been taken to encourage students to stay in school?
12. What is the teacher's view regarding the suggestion by some parents and community leaders that the introduction of antiracist, and specifically Afrocentric, education would assist in dealing with Black students' alienation and vulnerability in the schools?
13. What are the teacher's views about the call for Black-focused schools?
14. What are the teacher's views about Black/African History Month?

15. What are the teacher's views about streaming/destreaming?
16. What are the teacher's views about standardized testing?
17. What are the teacher's general views about the current school system?
18. Is the teacher happy with his/her current job?
19. What reforms are needed to improve upon the current school system?

Observation Guide for Schools

A. School

1. A day in the life of the student (e.g., time of reporting to and leaving the school premises; activities during class sessions; nature and conduct of recreational activities)
2. The nature and conduct of student-peer interactions
3. The nature and conduct of student-teacher interactions
4. The scheduling of school activities
5. Work roles, division of labour, gender roles
6. Content of teacher and student workloads
7. Ethos and culture of the school, including the observance/practice of rules and regulations, school norms and values

B. Classroom

1. Classroom seating arrangements
2. Subject matter discussed
3. Students' note-taking and attention to the teacher
4. What questions students ask and in what manner
5. Time classes begin and end
6. Amount of classroom discussion
7. Terms of reference between teacher/student and among students

Survey Questions for Black Parents/Guardians and Community Workers

Note: You may choose not to answer any of the following questions.

1. Name _____
2. Gender _____ male/female _____
3. Age or Date of Birth _____
4. Were you born in Canada? _____ Yes/No _____
5. If not born in Canada, where? _____
6. When did you come to Canada? _____
7. What languages do you speak other than English? _____
   _____
8. Which school did you attend? _____
   and what grade level was reached? _____
9. Do you have children attending high school? _____ Yes/No
10. Do the children live at home with you? _____ Yes/No
11. Do you help with their schoolwork/assignments? _____ Yes/No
12. Do you have any input in decision-making at your children's school?
    _____ Yes/No
13. Has the school done enough to make attending school a worthwhile experience for your child? _____ Yes/No
14. Do you know any child who has dropped out of school?
    _____ Yes/No
15. Would you say that your child is treated fairly at school by the authorities? _____ Yes/No

Appendix 9

Interview Guide for Parents/Guardians and Community Workers

For an in-depth, open interview, we probed parents'/guardians' and community workers' responses to some of the following pilot-tested questions:

1. When you hear the phrase 'school drop-out,' what does it mean to you?
2. Can you think of any reasons why students drop out of school?
3. What do you think of those students who drop out of school?
4. Do you discuss your child's school problems, and if so with whom?
5. Do you think that a child's experiences at school would be different if s/he was male/female?
6. Do you think your child's experiences at school would be different if s/he was White?
7. Do you think your child's experiences at school would be different if you were wealthy/poor?
8. What school activities are you involved in as a parent?
9. How often do you go to your child's school, and for what?
10. How often do you talk to your child's teachers?
11. What do you think teachers can do to facilitate learning for Black children, in particular?
12. As a Black parent, what do you think are the special contributions that Black children bring to the classroom?
13. What are some of the daily experiences you go through that you think significantly impact on your child's schooling?
14. How would you describe a typical day for you?
15. What do you think are your child's aspirations in life?
16. What is your greatest concern/worry for the Black youth in today's society?
17. In what ways could school be made more interesting for students, so that they will be more likely to finish rather than drop out?

18. If you had a magic wand to change something about the school system, what would that be and why?
19. What can be done about the current public school system to improve upon Black students' sense of connectedness and belonging in the school?
20. What measures have you taken as a parent to encourage your children to stay in school?
21. What reforms are needed to improve upon the current school system?

Other Issues for Further Investigation

1. Parents' responses to racism in society and particular racial incidents in the school and how they affect the child
2. Parents' views about sexism in society and in the school
3. Parents' response to the perception of some Black/African-Canadian students that they are always put under a microscope at school
4. Parents' views regarding the importance of having Black teachers in the schools
5. Parents' views about the call for Black-focused schools
6. Parents' views about Black/African History Month
7. Parents' views about streaming/destreaming
8. Parents' views about standardized testing

References

Acker, S. 1995. *Gendered Education*. Toronto: Ontario Institute for Studies in Education Press.

Alladin, I., ed. 1995. *Racism in Canadian Schools*. Toronto: Harcourt Brace Canada.

Allison, D., and J. Paquette. 1991. *Reform and Relevance in Schooling: Dropouts, Destreaming and the Common Curriculum*. Toronto: Ontario Institute for Studies in Education Press.

Althusser, L. 1971. 'Ideology and Ideological State Apparatuses.' In *Lenin and Philosophy and Other Essays*. Trans. Ben Brewster. New York: Monthly Review Press.

Amos, Y., and P. Parmar. 1987. 'Resistance and Responses: The Experiences of Black Girls in Britain.' In *Gender and the Politics of Schooling*. Ed. M. Arnot and G. Weiner. London: Hutchinson. 211–22.

Anthias, F., and Nira Yuval-Davis. 1992. *Racialized Boundaries: Race, Nation, Gender, Colour and Class and the Anti-Racist Struggle*. New York: Routledge.

Appel, R. 1988. 'The Language Education of Immigrant Workers' Children in The Netherlands.' In *Minority Education: From Shame to Struggle*. Ed. T. Skutnabb-Kangas and J. Cummins. Clevedon, Avon: Multilingual Matters.

Apple, M. 1979. *Ideology and the Curriculum*. London: Routledge and Kegan Paul.

– 1986. *Teachers and Texts: A Political Economy of Class and Gender Relations in Education*. New York: Routledge and Kegan Paul.

– 1989. 'American Realities: Poverty, Economy and Education.' In *Dropouts from School*. Ed. Lois Weis et al. New York: State University of New York Press. 205–23.

– 1993. *Official Knowledge: Democratic Education in a Conservative Age*. New York: Routledge.

Apple, M., and L. Weis. 1983. 'Ideology and Practice in Schooling: A Political and Conceptual Introduction.' In *Ideology and Practice in Schooling*. Philadelphia: Temple University Press.

Asante, M. 1990. 'The Afrocentric Idea in Education.' *Journal of Negro Education* 60(2): 170–80.

Association of Universities and Colleges of Canada. 1991. 'The High School Dropout Rate.' *University Affairs*, August: 5.

Au, K.H., and A.J. Kawakami. 1994. 'Cultural Congruence in Instruction.' In *Teaching Diverse Populations: Formulating a Knowledge Base.* Ed. E.R. Hollins, J.E. King, and W.C. Hayman. New York: State University of New York Press.

Bhyat, Alice. 1993. 'Bias in the Curriculum: A Comparative Look at Two Boards of Education.' Unpublished major research paper, Department of Sociology in Education, Ontario Institute for Studies in Education.

Bickel, R., and G. Papagiannis. 1988. 'Post-High School Prospects and District-Level Dropouts.' *Youth and Society* 20(2): 123–47.

Black, K. 1988. 'A Response to "Ontario Study of the Relevance of Education and the Issue of Dropouts."' *Ontario Education*, May/June: 9–12.

Black Educators Working Group (BEWG). 1993. *Submission to the Ontario Royal Commission on Learning.* Toronto.

Board of Education, Toronto. 1988. *Education of Black Students in Toronto: Final Report of the Consultative Committee.* Toronto: Toronto Board of Education.

Bourdieu, P., and J.C. Passeron. 1977. *Reproduction in Education, Society and Culture.* Trans. Richard Nice. Beverly Hills, CA: Sage Publications.

Bowles, S., and H. Gintis. 1976. *Schooling in Capitalist America.* New York: Basic Books.

Brathwaite, K. 1989. 'The Black Student and the School: A Canadian Dilemma.' In *African Continuities / L'Héritage Africain.* Ed. S. Chilingu and S. Niang. Toronto: Terebi. 195–216.

Brathwaite, K., and C. James, eds. 1996. *Educating African-Canadians.* Toronto: James Lorimer & Co.

Brown, R.S. 1993. *A Follow-Up of the Grade 9 Cohort of 1987 Every Secondary Student Survey Participants.* Toronto: Toronto Board of Education, Research Services (report no. 207).

Brown, R.S., M. Cheng, M. Yau, and S. Ziegler. 1992. *The 1991 Every Secondary Student Survey: Initial Findings.* Toronto: Toronto Board of Education, Research Services (report no. 200).

Burgess, Robert G., ed. 1985. *Issues in Educational Research: Qualitative Methods.* Philadelphia: Falmer Press.

Cadieux, P.H. 1991. 'The Stay-In-School Initiative: A Call to Action.' In *Equation. The Newsletter of the Stay-In-School Initiative.* Ottawa: Ministry of State for Youth.

Calvert, J., and L. Kuehn. 1993. 'Pandora's Box: Corporate Power, Free Trade and Canadian Education' *Our Schools/Our Selves*, July/August.

Canadian Alliance of Black Educators (CABE). 1992. *Sharing the Challenge I, II, III.: A Focus on Black High School Students*. Toronto.

Carby, H. 1986. 'Schooling for Babylon' In *The Empire Strikes Back*. Ed. P. Gilroy, Centre for Contemporary Cultural Studies. London: Hutchison. 183–211.

Centre for Educational Research and Innovation (CERI). 1987a. *Immigrants' Children at School*. Paris: OECD.

– 1987b. *CERI Project No. 6: Education and Cultural and Linguistic Pluralism*. Paris: OECD.

Cheng, M. 1995. 'Black Youth and Schooling in the Canadian Context: A Focus on Ontario.' Unpublished paper, Department of Sociology, Ontario Institute for Studies in Education.

Cheng, M., G. Tsuji, M. Yau, and S. Ziegler. 1989. *The Every Secondary Student Survey, Fall 1987*. Toronto: Toronto Board of Education.

Cheng, M., M. Yau, and S. Ziegler. 1993. *The 1991 Every Secondary Student Survey, Part II: Detailed Profiles of Toronto's Secondary School Students*. Toronto: Toronto Board of Education Research Services (report no. 204).

Claudfield, D. 1993. 'The NDP Agenda and the Corporate Agenda in Ontario' *Our Schools / Our Selves* 5(1): 8–26.

Cohen, E.G. 1992. 'Teaching in the Heterogenous Classroom.' In *Beyond Multicultural Education: International Perspectives*. Ed. K.A. Moodley. Calgary: Detselig.

– 1994. 'Restructuring the Classroom: Conditions for Productive Small Groups.' *Review of Educational Research* 64(1): 1–35.

Comer, J.P. 1988. 'Educating Poor Minority Children.' *Scientific American* 259(5): 42–8.

Conference Board of Canada. 1991. *Profiles in Partnerships: Business-Education Partnerships That Enhance Student Retention*. Ottawa: Conference Board of Canada.

Cookson, P.W., ed. 1992. *The Choice Controversy*. Newbury Park, CA: Corwin Press.

Cox, B.G., and M. Ramirez. 1981. 'Cognitive Styles: Implications for Multiethnic Education.' In *Education in the 80's: Multicultural Education*. Ed. J. Banks. National Education Association of the U.S.A.

Crawford, J. 1993. '"Schools Just Don't Care Enough," Drop-outs Say.' *Toronto Star*, 1 June: A8.

Cummins, J. 1984. *Bilingualism and Special Education: Issues in Assessment and Pedagogy*. Clevedon, England: Multilingual Matters.

– 1986. 'Empowering Minority Students: A Framework for Intervention.' *Harvard Educational Review* 56: 18–36.

– 1989a. 'Education and Visible Minority Youth.' In *Visible Minority Youth Project*. Toronto: Ontario Ministry of Citizenship.

- 1989b. *Empowering Minority Students*. Sacramento: California Association for Bilingual Education.

Curtis, B., D.W. Livingstone, and H. Smaller. 1992. *Stacking the Deck: The Streaming of Working Class Kids in Ontario Schools*. Toronto: Our Schools / Our Selves.

Daenzer, P. 1995. *Black Highschool Dropout in Four Ontario Urban Centres*. A report prepared for the Canadian Alliance of Black Educators (CABE), Toronto.

Daenzer, P., and G.J.S. Dei. 1994. *Issues of School Completion/Dropout: A Focus on Black Youth in Ontario Schools and Other Relevant Studies*. Background paper submitted to the Ontario Royal Commission on Learning, Toronto.

D'Amato, J. 1993. 'Resistance and Compliance in Minority Classrooms.' In *Minority Education: Anthropological Perspectives*. Ed. E. Jacob and C. Jordan. Norwood, NJ: Ablex Publishing.

Davies, L. 1984. *Pupil Power: Deviance and Gender in School*. London: Falmer Press.

- 1989. 'Ethnography and Status: Focusing on Gender in Educational Research.' In *Field Methods in the Study of Education*. Ed. R. Burgess. London: Falmer Press. 79–96.

Davies, S. 1994. 'In Search of Resistance and Rebellion among Highschool Dropouts.' *Canadian Journal of Sociology* 19(3): 331–50.

Dehli, K. 1994. *Parent Activism and School Reform in Toronto*. Toronto: Ontario Institute for Studies in Education.

Dei, G.J.S. 1993. *The Examination of High Dropout Rates among Black Students in Ontario Public Schools*. Preliminary report submitted to the Ontario Ministry of Education and Training.

- 1994. *Learning or Leaving? The Dropout Dilemma among Black Students in Ontario Public Schools*. Second report submitted to the Ontario Ministry of Education.

- 1995a. 'Black/African-Canadian Students' Perspectives on School Racism.' In *Racism in Canadian Schools*. Ed. I. Alladin. Toronto: Harcourt Brace. 41–65.

- 1995b. 'The Emperor Is Wearing Clothes: Exploring the Connections between Anti-Racist Education and Afrocentricity.' *International Journal of Comparative Race and Ethnic Studies* 2(1): 86–101.

- 1995c. 'Examining the Case for African-Centred Schools in Ontario.' *McGill Journal of Education* 30(2): 179–98.

- 1996. *Anti-Racism Education: Theory and Practice*. Halifax: Fernwood Publishing.

- 1997. 'Race and the Production of Identity in the Schooling Experiences of African-Canadian Youth.' *Discourse* 18(1): in press.

Dei, G.J.S., and S. Razack. 1995. *Inclusive Schooling: An Inventory of Contemporary Practices Designed to Meet the Challenge of a Diverse Student Body*. Report submitted to the Ontario Ministry of Education and Training.

Delpit, L.D. 1988. 'The Silenced Dialogue: Power and Pedagogy in Educating Other People's Children.' *Harvard Educational Review* 58(3): 280–98.

Desnoyers, J., and J. Pauker. 1988. *School Attendance and Non-Attendance in Canada and the United States: Survey of Methods and Programs to Increase School Attendance, Decrease Absenteeism and Deal with Drop-out.* Toronto: Ontario Ministry of Education.

D'Oyley, Vincent. 1994. *Black Innovations in Canadian Education.* Toronto: Umbrella Press.

Eisenhart, M.A., and M.E. Graue. 1993. 'Constructing Cultural Differences and Educational Achievement in Schools.' In *Minority Education: Anthropological Perspectives.* Ed. E. Jacob and C. Jordan. Norwood, NJ: Ablex Publishing.

Eisner, R.B. 1991. *The Enlightened Eye: Qualitative Inquiry and the Enhancement of Educational Practice.* New York: Macmillan.

Employment and Immigration Canada. 1990. *Youth: A National Stay-in-School Initiative.* Ottawa: Minister of Supply and Services.

Erickson, F. 1993. 'Transformation and School Success: The Politics and Culture of Educational Achievement.' In *Minority Education: Anthropological Perspectives.* Ed. E. Jacob and C. Jordan. Norwood, NJ: Ablex Publishing.

Erickson, F., and G. Mohatt. 1982. 'Cultural Organization of Participant Structures in Two Classrooms of Indian Students.' In *Doing the Ethnography of Schooling.* Ed. G. Spindler. Toronto: Holt, Rinehart and Winston.

Ernst, G., E. Statzner, and H. Trueba. 1994. 'Alternative Visions of Schooling: Success Stories in Minority Settings.' *Anthropology and Education Quarterly* 25(3) [special issue]: 202–393.

Fagan, J., and E. Pabon. 1990. 'Contributions of Delinquency and Substance Use to School Dropout among Inner City Youths.' *Youth and Society* 21(3): 306–54.

Feuerstein, R. 1979. *The Dynamic Assessment of Retarded Performers: The Learning Potential Assessment Device, Theory, Instruments and Techniques.* Baltimore: University Park Press.

Fine, M. 1991. *Framing Dropouts: Notes on the Politics of an Urban Public High School.* New York: State University of New York Press.

– 1993. '[Ap]parent Involvement: Reflections on Parents, Power and Urban Schools.' *Teachers College Record* 94(4): 682–710.

Finn, C.E., Jr. 1987. 'The High School Dropout Puzzle.' *Public Interest* 87: 3–22.

Finn, J.D. 1989. 'Withdrawing from School.' *Review of Educational Research* 59(2): 117–42.

Ford, D.Y., and J. John Harris III. 1994. 'Promoting Achievement among Gifted Black Students: The Efficacy of New Definitions and Identification Practices.' *Urban Education* 29(2): 202–29.

Fordham, F., and J.U. Ogbu. 1986. 'Black Students' School Success: Coping with the Burden of "Acting White."' *Urban Review* 18(3): 176–206.

Fordham, S. 1988. 'Racelessness as a Factor in Black Students School Success: Pragmatic Strategy or Pyrrhic Victory?' *Harvard Educational Review* 58(1): 54–84.

Freire, P. 1973. *The Pedagogy of the Oppressed*. Trans. Myra Bergman Ramos. New York: Seabury Press.

Fuller, Mary. l980. 'Black Girls in a London Comprehensive School.' In *Schooling for Women's Work*. Ed. R. Deem. London: Routledge and Kegan Paul.

Game, A. 1991. *On Doing the Social: Toward a Deconstructive Sociology*. Toronto: University of Toronto Press.

Garibaldi, A.M. 1992. 'Educating and Motivating African American Males to Succeed.' *Journal of Negro Education* 61(1): 4–11.

Gaskell, J., and D. Kelly, eds. 1996. *Debating Dropouts*. New York: Teachers College Press.

Gaskell, J., and A. McLaren, eds. 1987. *Women and Education: A Canadian Perspective*. Calgary: Detselig.

Gaskell, J., A. McLaren, and M. Novogrodsky. 1989. *Claiming an Education: Feminism in Canadian Schools*. Toronto: Our Schools / Our Selves.

Gibson, M.A. 1987. 'The School Performance of Immigrant Minorities: A Comparative View.' *Anthropology and Education Quarterly* 18(4): 262–75.

Giroux, H. 1981. 'Hegemony, Resistance and the Paradox of Educational Reform.' *Interchange* 12(2/3): 3–26.

– 1983a. *A Theory of Resistance in Education: A Pedagogy for the Opposition*. South Hadley, MA: Bergin and Harvey.

– 1983b. 'Theories of Reproduction and Resistance in the New Sociology of Education.' *Harvard Educational Review* 53: 257–93.

Glesne, C., and A. Peshkin. 1992. *Becoming Qualitative Researchers: An Introduction*. White Plains, NY: Longman.

Goodlad, J.I. 1984. *A Place Called School*. New York: McGraw-Hill.

Hall, S. 1991. 'The Local and the Global: Globalization and Ethnicity.' In *Culture, Globalization and the World System*. Ed. A. King. New York: State University of New York Press.

Hargreaves, A., and L. Earl. 1990. *Rites of Passage: A Review of Selected Research about Schooling in the Transition Years*. Toronto: Ontario Ministry of Education.

Hargreaves, A., K. Leithwood, et al. 1993. *Years of Transition, Times for Change*. Toronto: Ontario Ministry of Education.

Hartnagel, T.F., and H. Krahn. 1989. 'High School Dropouts, Labour Market Success and Criminal Behaviour.' *Youth and Society* 20(4): 416–44.

Henry, A. 1992. 'Taking Back Control: Toward an Afrocentric Womanist Standpoint on the Education of Black Children.' Ph.D. diss., Department of Curriculum, Ontario Institute for Studies in Education.

Henry, A. 1994. 'The Empty Shelf and Other Curricular Challenges of Teaching for Children of African Descent: Implications for Teacher Practice.' *Urban Education* 29(3): 298–319.

Hitchcock G., and D. Hughes. 1995. *Research and the Teacher: Qualitative Introduction to School-based Research*, 2nd ed. London: Routledge.

Holland, D.C., and M.A. Eisenhart. 1990. *Educated in Romance*. Chicago: University of Chicago Press.

Jacob, E., and C. Jordan, eds. 1993. *Minority Education: Anthropological Perspectives*. Norwood, NJ: Ablex Publishing.

James, C.E. 1990. *Making It*. Oakville: Mosaic Press.

Jaynes, G.D., and R.M. Williams, eds. 1989. *A Common Destiny: Blacks in American Society*. Washington, D.C.: National Academy Press.

Kalbach, W., R. Verma, M. George, and S.Y. Dai. 1993. 'Population Projections of Visible Minority Groups, Canada, Provinces and Regions, 1991–2016.' Unpublished paper prepared for the Interdepartmental Working Group on Employment Equity Data.

Karenga, M. 1988. 'Black Studies and the Problematic Paradigm.' *Journal of Black Studies* 18(4): 395–414.

Karp, E. 1988. *The Dropout Phenomenon in Ontario Secondary Schools: A Report to the Ontario Study of the Relevance of Education and the Issue of Dropout. Student Retention and Transition Series*. Toronto: Ontario Ministry of Education.

King, A.J.C., W.K. Warren, C. Michalski, and M.J. Peart. 1988. *Improving Student Retention in Ontario Secondary Schools*. Toronto: Ontario Ministry of Education.

King, J.E. 1994. 'The Purpose of Schooling for African-American Children: Including Cultural Knowledge.' In *Teaching Diverse Populations: Formulating a Knowledge Base*. Ed. E.R. Hollins, J.E. King, and W.C. Hayman. New York: State University of New York Press.

Kozol, J. 1991. *Savage Inequalities: Children in American Schools*. New York: Crown Publishers.

Lawton, S.B. 1992. 'Dropping Out: A Literature Review, 1988–1992.' Unpublished paper, Ontario Institute for Studies in Education.

– 1994. 'Dropping Out: A Literature Review, 1988–1994.' Unpublished paper, Ontario Institute for Studies in Education.

Lawton, S.B., K. Leithwood, E. Batcher, E. Donaldson, and R. Stewart. 1988. *Student Retention and Transition in Ontario High Schools*. Toronto: Ontario Ministry of Education.

LeCompte, M.D., and A.G. Dworkin. 1991. *Giving Up on School: Student Dropouts and Teacher Burnouts*. Newbury Park, CA: Corwin Press.

Lee, E. 1985. *Letters to Marcia*. Toronto: Cross Cultural Communication.
– 1994. 'Anti-Racist Education: Panacea or Palliative.' *Orbit* 25(2): 22–4.
Lewis, S. 1992. Letter to the Premier. Toronto.
Little, D. 1992. 'The Meaning of Yonge Street: What Do the Kids Say.' *Our Schools / Our Selves* 4(1): 16–23.
Mackay, R., and L. Myles. 1989. *Native Student Dropouts in Ontario Schools*. Toronto: Ontario Ministry of Education.
– 1995. 'A Major Challenge for the Education System: Aboriginal Retention and Dropout.' In *First Nations Education in Canada: The Circle Unfolds*. Ed. M. Battiste and J. Barman. Vancouver: University of British Columbia Press. 157–78.
Manski, C.F. 1989. 'Schooling as Experimentation: A Reappraisal of the Post-secondary Dropout Phenomenon.' *Economics of Education Review* 8(4): 305–12.
Matsuda, M.J., C.R. Lawrence III, R. Delgado, and K.W. Crenshaw. 1993. *Words That Wound: Critical Race Theory, Assaultive Speech, and the First Amendment*. London: Westview Press.
McCarthy, C. 1990. *Race and Curriculum: Social Inequality and the Theory and Politics of Difference in Contemporary Research on Schooling*. Basingstoke: Falmer Press.
McCarthy, C., and M. Apple. 1988. 'Race, Class and Gender in American Educational Research: Toward a Non-Synchronous Parallelist Position.' In *Class, Race and Gender in American Education*. Ed. L. Weis. New York: State University of New York Press.
McRobbie, A. 1981. 'Settling Accounts with Sub-Cultures: A Feminist Critique.' In *Culture, Ideology and Social Process*. Ed. T. Bennett, G. Martin, C. Mercer, and J. Woolacott. London: The Open University.
Miles, R., and R. Torres. 1996. 'Does Race Matter? Transatlantic Perspectives on Racism after Race Relations.' In *Re-Situating Identities: The Politics of Race, Ethnicity and Culture*. Ed. V. Amit-Talai and C. Knowles. Peterborough, Ont.: Broadview Press. 24–46.
Ministry of Citizenship, Ontario. 1989. *Visible Minority Youth Project: Child, Youth and Family Project*. Toronto: Ontario Ministry of Citizenship, Research Centre.
– 1994. *Change Your Future Program. Report, Results and Analyses of 1993–1994 Students' Questionnaires*. Toronto: Ontario Ministry of Citizenship.
Ministry of Education, Ontario (MEO). 1992. *Changing Perspectives: A Resource Guide for Race and Ethnocultural Equity*. Toronto: Ontario Ministry of Education.
Ministry of Education and Training, Ontario (MET). 1993a. *The Common Curriculum, Grades 1–9*. Working document (version for parents and the general public). Toronto: Ontario Ministry of Education and Training.

- 1993b. *Antiracism and Ethnocultural Equity in School Boards: Guidelines for Policy Development and Implementation*. Toronto: Ontario Ministry of Education and Training.
- 1993c. *Violence-Free Schools*. Toronto: Ontario Ministry of Education and Training.

Ministry of Education, Quebec. 1991. *L'école ... facile d'en sortir mais difficile d'y revenir*. Quebec City: Quebec Ministry of Education.

Morris, S., W. Pawlovich, and D. McCall. 1991. *Evaluating the Effectiveness of School Dropout Prevention Strategies: Some Suggestions for Future Research*. Toronto: Canadian Education Association.

Mukherjee, Alok, and Barb Thomas. n.d. 'A Glossary of Terms.' Toronto: Toronto Board of Education.

Natriello, G., E.L. McDill, and A. Pallas. 1985. 'School Reform and Potential Dropouts.' *Educational Leadership* 43: 10–14.

Ogbu, J.U. 1978. *Minority Education and Caste*. New York: Academic Press.
- 1982a. 'Cultural Discontinuities and Schooling.' *Anthropology and Education Quarterly* 13(4): 290–307.
- 1982b. 'Equalization of Educational Opportunity and Racial/Ethnic Inequality.' In *Comparative Education*. Ed. P.G. Allbach, R.F. Arnove, and G.P. Kelly. New York: Macmillan.
- 1993. 'Differences in Cultural Frame of Reference.' *International Journal of Behavioural Development* 16(3): 483–505.

Ogbu, J.U., and M.E. Matute-Bianchi. 1986. 'Understanding Sociocultural Factors: Knowledge, Identity and School Adjustment.' In *Sociocultural Factors and Minority Student Achievement*. Sacramento: California State Department of Education.

Oliver, W. 1986. 'Black Males and Social Problems: Prevention through Afrocentric Socialization.' *Journal of Black Studies* 20(1): 15–39.

Omi, Michael, and Howard Winant. 1993. 'On the Theoretical Concept of Race.' In *Race, Identity, and Representation in Education*. Ed. Cameron McCarthy and Warren Crichlow. New York: Routledge. 3–10.

Penny, J., and L. Bond. 1991. 'Use of Ethnicity as a Predictor of Achievement: A Reply to Klingele and Warrick.' *Journal of Educational Research* 84(3): 133–4.

Philip, M.N. 1989. 'The Absence of Writing or How I Almost Became a Spy.' In *She Tries Her Tongue: Her Silence Softly Breaks*. Ed. M.N. Philip. Charlottetown, P.E.I.: Ragweed Press.

Pollard, D.S. 1989. 'Against the Odds: A Profile of Academic Achievers from the Urban Underclass.' *Journal of Negro Education* 58: 297–308.

Pryce, K. 1978. *Endless Pressure*. Harmondsworth: Penguin.

Quirouette, P., O. Saint-Denis, and N. Hout. 1989. *Dropouts in French Language Schools: Research Brief*. Toronto: Ontario Ministry of Education.

– 1990. *Identifying Probable School Leavers in Ontario High Schools*. Toronto: Ontario Ministry of Education.

Radwanski, G. 1987. *Ontario Study of the Relevance of Education, and the Issue of Dropouts*. Toronto: Ontario Ministry of Education.

Ramirez, M., and A. Castenada. 1974. *Cultural Democracy and Bicognitive Development and Education*. New York: Academic Press.

Rattansi, A. 1992. 'Changing the Subject? Racism, Culture and Education.' In *Race, Culture and Difference*. Ed. J. Donald and A. Rattansi. London: The Open University.

Riddell, Sheila. 1989. 'Exploiting the Exploited? The Ethics of Feminist Educational Research.' In *The Ethics of Educational Research*. Ed. R. Burgess. London: Falmer Press. 77–99.

Royal Commission on Learning (RCOL). 1994. *For the Love of Learning*. Toronto: Ontario Ministry of Education.

Seddon, T. 1990. 'Social Justice in Hard Times: From "Equality of Opportunity" to "Fairness and Efficiency."' *Discourse* 11(1): 21–42.

Share [Toronto Black community newspaper]. 1991. Editorial, 15 October 1991.

Sheth, A., and G.J.S. Dei. 1995. 'Deviations: A Conceptual Framework for Creating and Eradicating the "Dropout" Problem.' Unpublished paper, Department of Sociology, Ontario Institute for Studies in Education.

Sium, B. 1987. 'Streaming in Education and Beyond: Black Students Talk.' *Orbit* 18(1): 20–1.

Smith, D. 1990. *The Conceptual Practices of Power*. Toronto: University of Toronto Press.

Smith, J. 1995. 'In Search of Ogbu.' Unpublished paper, University of Wisconsin-Madison.

Solomon, P. 1992. *Black Resistance in High School: Forging a Separatist Culture*. New York: State University of New York Press.

Stage, F.K. 1989. 'Motivation, Academic and Social Integration, and the Early Dropout' in *American Educational Research Journal* 26(3): 385–402.

Statistics Canada. 1991. *School Leavers Survey*. Ottawa: Education, Culture and Tourism Division, Statistics Canada.

– 1993. *Ethnic Origin: 1991 Census Update*. Ottawa: Statistics Canada.

'Stay in School Supplement.' 1991. *Social Development Overview* [Canadian Council on Social Development] 1: 7–14.

Sullivan, Michael. 1988. *A Comparative Analysis of Dropouts and Non-Dropouts in Ontario Secondary Schools*. Toronto: Ontario Ministry of Education.

Tanner, J., H. Krahn, and T.F. Hartnagel. 1995. *Fractured Transitions from School to Work: Revisting the Dropout Problem*. Toronto: Oxford University Press.

Townsend, M. 1988. 'Dumping: An Unfair Trade Practice – Except When It Comes to Schools.' *Ontario Education*, May/June: 13–15.

Troyna, B., and B. Carrington. 1989. 'Whose Side Are We On? Ethical Dilemmas in Research on Race and Education.' In *The Ethics of Educational Research*. Ed. R. Burgess. London: Falmer Press. 205–23.

Trueba, H., G. Spindler, and L. Spindler, eds. 1989. *What Do Anthropologists Have to Say about Dropouts?* Basingstoke: Falmer Press.

Verma, G.S. 1987. 'The Swann Report and Ethnic Achievement: What Next?' In *Race and Culture in Education: Issues Arising from the Swann Report*. Ed. T.S. Chivers. Windsor: NFER-Nelson.

– 1989. *Education for All: A Landmark in Pluralism*. London: Falmer Press.

Vincent, C. 1992a. '"Three Pakistan Songs": Parental Choice and Multiracial Schools.' *Multicultural Teaching to Combat Racism in School and Community* 11(1): 7–10.

– 1992b. 'Tolerating Intolerance? Parental Choice and Race Relations – the Cleveland Case.' *Journal of Education Policy* 7(5): 429–43.

Walcott, R. 1995. 'Postmodernism Sociology: Music Education and the Pedagogy of Rap.' In *The Sociology of Music Education: Conference Proceedings*. Ed. S. Paul, H. Froehlich, R. Rideout, and G. Heller. University of Oklahoma.

Waterhouse, P. 1990. *Qualitative Research on School Leavers: Summary Final Report*. Ottawa: Employment and Immigration Canada, and Statistics Canada.

Watson, C. 1977. *Focus on Dropouts*. Toronto: Ontario Ministry of Education.

Weiler, K. 1988. *Women Teaching for Change: Gender, Class and Power*. Boston: Bergin and Garvey.

Weis, L. 1985. *Between Two Worlds: Black Students in an Urban Community College*. Boston: Routledge and Kegan Paul.

Weis, L., E. Farrar, and H.G. Petrie, eds. 1989. *Dropouts from School*. New York: State University of New York Press.

West. W.G. 1979. 'Adolescent Autonomy, Education and Pupil Deviance.' In *Schools, Pupils and Deviance*. Ed. L. Barton and R. Meighan. Nafferton: Nafferton Books.

Willis, P. 1977. *Learning to Labour*. Farnborough: Saxon House.

– 1983. 'Cultural Production and Theories of Reproduction' In *Race, Class and Education*. Ed. L. Barton and S. Walker. London: Croom Helm.

Wilson, William. 1973. *Power, Racism and Privilege*. New York: Free Press.

Woods, P. 1992. 'Empowerment through Choice? Towards an Understanding of Parental Choice and School Responsiveness.' *Educational Management and Administration* 20(4): 204–11.

Working Group. 1992. *Towards a New Beginning: The Report and Action Plan of the*

Four Level Government / African Canadian Community Working Group. Toronto: The Working Group, funded by the Department of the Secretary of State.

Wright, E.N. 1985. *The Retention and Credit Accumulation of Students in Secondary School: A Follow-Up from the 1980 Grade Nine Student Survey.* Toronto: Toronto Board of Education.

Wright, O.M., and N. Allingham. 1994. 'The Policy and Practice of Anti-Racist Education.' *Orbit* 25(2): 4–6.

Yau, M., M. Cheng, and S. Ziegler. 1993. *The 1991 Every Secondary Student Survey Part III: Program Level and Student Achievement.* Toronto: Toronto Board of Education, Research Services (report no. 205).

Youth Affairs Branch of Employment and Immigration. 1990. *Tackling the Dropout Problem.* Ottawa: Ministry of Employment and Immigration.

Ziegler, S. 1989. *Dropout Prevention* [*Scope* 4(3)].

Author Index

Subject Index